South East England and Channel Islands Sea Kayaking

Derek Hairon,
Andy Levick, Mark Rainsley, Mark Gawler, Annie
Davis, Guy Smith, John Brett and Kurt Finch

PESDA PRESS
WWW.PESDAPRESS.COM

First published in Great Britain 2015 by Pesda Press
Tan y Coed Canol, Ceunant
Caernarfon, Gwynedd
LL55 4RN
Wales

ISBN: 978-1-906095-50-5

Maps by Bute Cartographic.

Introduction

Though geographically close, the two areas covered in this guide are as different in character as it is possible to conceive.

The South East of England has a varied landscape of chalk cliffs, pebble beaches, vast expanses of sand, mudflats and river estuaries. At one extreme is the tidal Thames which runs through the densely populated city of London, and at the other is the deserted North Norfolk coast. It is true that some parts of this region are more attractive to sea kayakers than others, but we have been selective. All of the routes in the guide are worthwhile and many of them are real gems.

The Channel Islands consist of a small number of large islands and a vast number of islets and reefs. Here we are talking pink granite, white sandy beaches and very strong tidal streams. They are closer to France than to England (a mere 12km between Les Écréhous reef and mainland France) and are in fact what remains of the Duchy of Normandy. The French eventually recovered mainland Normandy but the Islands retained their independence and their links with the UK. Most Channel Islanders speak English as their mother tongue, but you will see French and Norman French place names everywhere. Many of the routes here are very committing but there are also a good number of gentler paddles.

Enjoy …

Contents

Contents

How to Use the Guide

To use the guide you will need an up-to-date tide timetable for the relevant area, the appropriate Ordnance Survey maps and the knowledge to use them. The Channel Islands section differs slightly to cope with the need for different maps and nautical charts. These are detailed in the chapter The Channel Islands.

Each of the trip chapters is set out into six sections:

Tidal & Route Information – This is designed as a quick reference for all the 'must know' information on which to plan the trip.

Introduction – This is designed to give the reader a brief overview of what to expect from the trip and whet the appetite.

Description – This provides further detail and information on the trip including the coastline, launching/landing points, the wildlife and environment, historical information and places of interest to visit.

Tides & Weather – Offering further tidal information and how best to plan the trip which takes the tides, weather and local knowledge into consideration.

Map of Route – This provides a visual outline of the route's start/finish points, landing places, points of interest and tidal information.

Additional Information – This section provides further information (including Admiralty Charts and other useful maps) that will complement the trip, or be of interest if in the local area.

Using the Tidal & Route Information

Each route begins with an overview of pertinent details beginning with the following information: grade of difficulty, trip name, route symbols, and trip number.

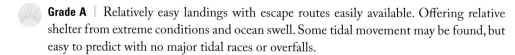 **Grade A** | Relatively easy landings with escape routes easily available. Offering relative shelter from extreme conditions and ocean swell. Some tidal movement may be found, but easy to predict with no major tidal races or overfalls.

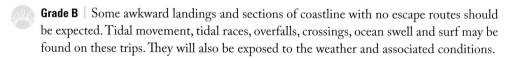 **Grade B** | Some awkward landings and sections of coastline with no escape routes should be expected. Tidal movement, tidal races, overfalls, crossings, ocean swell and surf may be found on these trips. They will also be exposed to the weather and associated conditions.

Grade C | These trips will have difficult landings and will have no escape routes for long sections of the trip. Fast tidal movement, tidal races, overfalls, extended crossings, ocean swell and surf will be found on all these trips. They will be very exposed to the weather and conditions, therefore require detailed planning and paddlers to be competent in rough water conditions. With this considered, the journey may require good conditions for the trip to be viable.

ROUTE SYMBOLS

Distance	Total distance for the trip.
OS Sheet	Number of Ordnance Survey 1:50,000 Landranger map required.
Tidal Port	The port for which tide timetables will be required to work out the tidal streams.
Start	△ map symbol, name and six-figure grid reference of starting point.
Finish	◎ map symbol, name and six-figure grid reference of finishing point.
HW/LW	The high and/or low water time difference between local ports nearest to the trip and the tidal port.
Tidal Times	Location or area of tidal stream movement, the direction to which the tidal stream flows and the time it starts flowing in relation to the tidal port high water.
Max Rate Sp	The areas in which the tidal streams are fastest and the maximum speed in knots attained on the average spring tide.
Coastguard	Name of the relevant Coastguard Station.

MAP SYMBOLS

△ △	start & alternative start	◎	areas of counter-currents / eddies
◎ ◎	finish & alternative finish	~~~	areas of rough water / overfalls
○	waypoint	🗼 ✦	lighthouse & light
⤷	possible escape	◆ lifeboat	lifeboat station
⚓	portage	NCI	Coastwatch lookout (NCI)
– – ➔ – – ➔	described route	🚤 🚢	ferry, passenger & car
· ◆ · · · ◆	alternative route	⛺	campsite
⟶	tidal stream direction	🦆	bird reserve
–0520 HW	time relative to Tidal Port HW	▪	town / buildings
7kn Sp	Max Rate at Springs	Prohibited Zone	prohibited area
∿➔	major counter-current	✲	Site of Special Scientific Interest

About the Authors

Channel Islands – Derek Hairon

Derek Hairon is a BCU Level 5 sea kayak coach and has paddled throughout the Channel Islands for over 42 years. In 1978 he completed the first circumnavigation of Ireland by kayak and has subsequently undertaken expeditions to Alaska, Nova Scotia, Faeroe Islands, Aland Islands, Brittany, whitewater rivers in Nepal, and most of the classic UK sea kayaking destinations. Recognising the growth of sit-on-top kayaking he wrote the guide *Sit-on-Top Kayak*. He owns Jersey Kayak Adventures and runs a range of sea kayak introductory and advanced courses plus guided coastal sea kayak tours.

South East England

The impetus for this section of the guide was originally provided by Chris Wheeler, whose enthusiasm and commitment to kayaking knew no bounds. On his untimely death on the River Dart others stepped into the breach, and the South East England section was a combined effort involving seven different contributors. They are (in order of the number of routes contributed):

Andy Levick, Mark Rainsley, Mark Gawler, Annie Davis, Guy Smith, John Brett and Kurt Finch.

To see who contributed a particular route please refer to the contents on page 4.

Environmental Considerations

RESPECT THE INTERESTS OF OTHER PEOPLE

Acting with courtesy, consideration and awareness is essential. If you are exercising access rights, make sure that you respect the privacy, safety and livelihood of those living and working in the outdoors, and the needs of other people enjoying the outdoors. Even jet skiers.

CARE FOR THE ENVIRONMENT

Sea kayakers are privileged to access remote places that others cannot. Many of these places have sensitive plant, animal and bird life. Be aware of, and respect, landing restrictions around nature reserves. Look after the places you visit, enjoy the land and leave it as you found it. Natural England (www.naturalengland.org.uk) has created magic.defra.gov.uk, a source of incredibly detailed maps outlining protected habitats and sites (does not cover the Channel Islands). The Marine Conservation Society (www.mcsuk.org) offers advice on how to act appropriately around marine wildlife.

WILD CAMPING

This guide provides information on many commercial campsites. Although most are pleasant places, if you value solitude and silence treat anything with 'holiday park' in the title with caution. The authors of this guide camp 'wild' whenever a commercial site is unavailable, and have almost always been able to find an appropriate spot, with a little thought. Wild camping provides a special experience and forms an integral part of sea kayaking. There is no legally enshrined right to camp on the English coast, and areas in the south east and the Channel Islands that obviously lend themselves to wild camping for sea kayakers are limited. Large groups hoping to put up numerous tents are probably in the wrong region; think discretion and low profile. If you decide to include a wild camp in your journey plans, choose a location away from dwellings and roads. Arrive late and do not pitch your tent until dusk. You should take down your tent early the following morning. *"Leave nothing but footprints and take nothing but photographs."*

Sea kayaking is inherently a potentially dangerous sport. The sea is one of the most committing and unforgiving environments. Conditions on the sea can change quickly and dramatically. When planning to venture out on any of the trips described in this book, ensure that your knowledge, experience, ability and judgement are appropriate to the seriousness of the trip. The authors recommend acquiring appropriate training and advice from experienced and qualified individuals.

The information in this book has been thoroughly researched; however the authors and publisher can take no responsibility, if tidal times differ or if the information supplied is not sufficient to negotiate the conditions experienced on the day. The outdoors cannot be made risk-free and you should plan and act with care at all times, for your own safety and that of others. The decision on whether to go out sea kayaking or not, and any consequences arising from that decision, remain yours and yours alone.

© Beachy Head Lighthouse | Tony Sandry

South East England

An introduction

Outlined in this book are many, but by no means all, of the sea paddling adventures that the south-east offers. It's common for UK sea paddlers to drive north or west when pursuing their sport. Hopefully, the information and ideas presented here will encourage more folk to rethink and to explore this under-appreciated region. The paddling is of markedly different character to that found on Britain's Atlantic shores, but make no mistake; it is often outstanding. Give the south-east a try ... you will get to experience a huge variety of beautiful, exciting and unique environments.

The intriguing creeks and harbours around the Solent in Hampshire were first described in Pesda Press's *South West Sea Kayaking* guidebook. Heading east up the English Channel into the Dover Strait, the Sussex and Kent coasts are marked by shingle and the ubiquitous groynes ... but also by startling chalk cliffs and a number of very powerful tidal rivers which allow paddlers to venture deep into the South Downs.

The Kent and Essex shores of the Thames estuary are a vast area of tidal flats, with various creeks and inlets inviting exploration; far more indeed than are described here. Within London itself, the Tideway is an unforgettable adventure, an absolute must-do.

Heading up the North Sea coast, Suffolk and Norfolk will confound expectations by the amount of open and wild spaces encountered. Orford Ness (Britain's 'Area 51'!) is arguably as remote a spot as you'll find in Britain, and the vast and stunning barrier coast of North Norfolk is among the best preserved natural landscapes in Europe. Inland, the Norfolk Broads have potential for sea paddlers in yet another unique environment.

Also worth noting is that wildlife is never far away. Common seals are for example ... well, common, with a huge population in the North Sea areas. Large cetaceans are not unheard of, and a killer whale was recently sighted off Norfolk!

Environment

Most of the south-east coast is heavily managed and protected, undoubtedly a necessary evil in such a densely populated region. The New Forest around the Solent is the first of three National Parks featuring in this book. Chichester Harbour is an AONB (Area of Outstanding Natural Beauty). The cliffs around Beachy Head are part of the South Downs National Park and are also included in the Sussex Heritage Coast. The finest shores of the eastern English Channel are within the High Weald and Kent Downs AONBs, and two adjacent Heritage Coasts – Dover-Folkestone and South Foreland – cover the Dover Strait.

Suffolk's wilder shores are also Heritage Coast, alongside the Suffolk Coasts and Heath AONB. The Broads National Park of course protects and manages this vast network of inland waterways, whilst the sublime shores of north Norfolk are included in both the North Norfolk Heritage Coast and North Norfolk AONB. A bewildering array of nature reserves and managed estates also serve to protect the south-east coast, run by the National Trust, RSPB and innumerable local wildlife trusts.

It is worth being aware of these layers of protection, preservation and management; many have rules and regulations which may impact upon your plans. Some arguably cross the line into draconian management; you be the judge.

Tides and weather

Sea conditions in the south-east should not be underestimated and all trips require careful planning. Tidal flow is always present and is often strong, as the waters of the English Channel and North Sea compress towards and through the Dover Strait. The fastest flows are found around the Solent and also the tidal Thames and its approaches. Mud flats and marshes are common in the region's estuaries and harbours, and are particularly extensive around the north Kent and Essex coasts; avoiding stranding is a very real consideration. The eastern English Channel is still exposed to Atlantic groundswells; surf can be encountered. Perhaps surprisingly, groundswell is also common along the north Norfolk coast, which catches swells originating inside the Arctic Circle. Many of the trips in this guide are on inland creeks and rivers; whilst ostensibly sheltered from the weather, they are also subject to dangerous fast flows and mud banks. A final factor is that the whole south-east coast sees heavy traffic, due to the numerous major ports. Large commercial vessels are a common sight; but not one best experienced up close.

Background reading

East Coast Pilot, Colin Jarman, Imray 2011, ISBN 1846233518

East Coast Rivers Cruising Companion, Janet Harber, Wiley Nautical 2008, ISBN 0470990929

Shell Channel Pilot, Tom Cunliffe, Imray 2013, ISBN 1846234468

Tidal Havens of the Wash & Humber, Henry Irving, Imray 2011, ISBN 1846232791

Further information

www.newforestnpa.gov.uk – New Forest National Park

www.conservancy.co.uk – Chichester Harbour AONB

www.southdowns.gov.uk – South Downs National Park

www.highweald.org – High Weald AONB

www.kentdowns.org.uk – Kent Downs AONB

www.suffolkcoastandheaths.org – Suffolk Coasts and Heath AONB

www.broads-authority.gov.uk – Broads National Park

www.norfolkcoastaonb.org.uk – North Norfolk AONB

Southampton Creeks

No. 1 | Grade A | 22 / 15 / 18km | OS Sheet 196

Tidal Port	Portsmouth
Start/Finish	△ ○ Hamble – Hamble-le-Rice (SU 485 067)
Start/Finish	△ ○ Itchen – Woodmill Centre (SU 439 152)
Start/Finish	△ ○ Beaulieu – Lepe Country Park (SZ 455 985) / Buckler's Hard Marina (SU 407 003)
Tidal Times	Tidal flows are very weak, however it makes sense to arrive in the upper reaches of each river around HW Portsmouth.
Coastguard	Solent, tel. 023 9255 2100, VHF Ch67, VHF weather Ch86 and Ch23 at 0130 UT, repeated every 3 hours.

Introduction

The tidal creeks in the Southampton area are interesting and varied, and offer options for poor weather as they are sheltered. The rivers Hamble, Itchen and Test flow into the expanse of Southampton Water. Just to the west along the Solent is the pretty Beaulieu River. This section describes the Hamble, Itchen and Beaulieu estuaries, each providing a unique experience. Whereas the Itchen is very urban with old dilapidated industrial dockyards along its banks, the Hamble and Beaulieu are rural, being bordered by deciduous woodland.

HAMBLE

The tidal Hamble has two contrasting sections:

Downstream of the M27 bridge is dominated by marinas and moored boats. Upstream of the bridge, the river is rural as it passes through unspoilt deciduous woodlands and salt marshes.

Eventually the river splits into two channels that go as far as Botley village and the Horse and Jockey public house respectively.

There is a pay and display car park next to a convenient beach at Hamble-le-Rice for access and egress. Adjacent to the car park is a handy café. We suggest the return trip between Southampton Water and the tidal limit of the Hamble. The tides are not strong but take note of local HW times. After the put-in, you pass through a huge number of moored private sailing boats until the M27 road bridge, giving the feeling that there is some money in these parts. Near the M27 bridge on a left hand corner is the popular Jolly Sailor pub.

Beyond the M27 bridge, the river suddenly becomes very peaceful and rural with deciduous woodland and luscious green salt marshes. Eventually the river narrows and divides into two tributaries – it is worth exploring both tributaries up to the tidal limit. The vegetation is lush and wildlife plentiful along both creeks. I once spotted five kingfishers within ten minutes (or the same kingfisher five times – I was never quite sure).

Hamble-le-Rice

This is an affluent village with an attractive cobbled street, public houses and restaurants. The village does not have any tourist attractions as such, but has large sailing club and marina, and thousands of expensive yachts moored up. It was the location for the filming of *Howard's Way* in the 1980s.

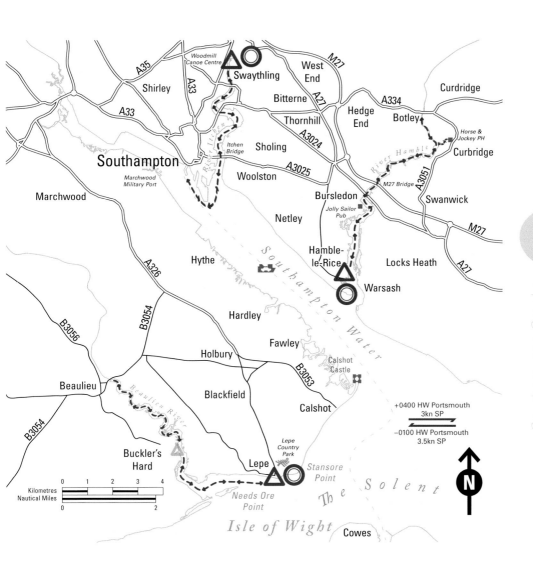

ITCHEN

You can put in just adjacent to the Woodmill Centre at the tidal limit of the Itchen. There is free car parking nearby. For the first 2km, the Itchen meanders through deciduous woods and has quite a rural feel. The river soon opens out and becomes increasingly urban, industrial and maritime as Southampton Water is approached. The river passes under a few bridges before the final, massive, concrete Itchen Bridge.

On reaching Southampton Water, it is worth exploring the Southampton docks to the right, before returning up river. The moored tankers and cruise ships are gigantic! It's very intimidating to paddle anywhere near to these as you're never quite sure when one will suddenly start up. It is a good idea to listen to the local VHF channel for shipping traffic movements. For a longer trip, it is worth crossing Southampton Water to Marchwood Military Port and Hythe for good views back to Southampton docks. Take care crossing Southampton Water as it is a busy shipping lane.

BEAULIEU

The Beaulieu River passes through oak woodlands and the meadows of North Solent Nature Reserve. There are marinas, country houses, Beaulieu village and Buckler's Hard to look out for. The river is the only privately owned stretch of tidal water in the UK, and permission must be sought from the Harbour Master before getting on the water. The trip is best done as a return trip between the Solent and Beaulieu village (at the tidal limit). There are two suggestions for starting: Lepe Country Park on the Solent or Buckler's Hard on the river. The former offers a

slightly longer and more interesting trip, but it may be challenging paddling across the open water of the Solent in windy weather. The latter allows the use of various amenities at Buckler's Hard (shower, changing rooms).

We recommend putting on at the marina of Buckler's Hard which has changing facilities (showers) and the Harbour Master's office to obtain permits. From the road at the top of Buckler's Hard, there is a lane with an entrance barrier that takes you to the marina area. Drive through the barrier, park in a large car park near the marina, and obtain a pass from the Harbour Master's office. There is a shallow, grassy bank and beach adjacent to the car park for getting in. The tidal flow is fairly weak and do not worry about paddling against the flow for parts of the trip. Ideally you should use the flood tide to help from Buckler's Hard to Beaulieu. At Beaulieu, wait for the tide to turn and use the ebb flow to paddle back to the Solent. Then wait for the flood tide again at the Solent, though you might be waiting a long time. It is best just to paddle against the tide back to Buckler's Hard.

Tides and weather

The tidal flow on the Beaulieu River is weak compared to the longer tidal creeks such as the Arun. As long as you do not venture out into the Solent, the Beaulieu is a good option for very windy conditions.

The Beaulieu Estate

Beaulieu House, Abbey and National Motor Museum are the big tourist draws in the area. The Motor Museum has an impressive collection of cars and motor bikes, with various displays and an interactive ride about all aspects of motoring. There are cars from the James Bond films, Top Gear, Harry Potter, world speed record attempts, and vintage periods back to the 1890s. On a completely different theme is the Beaulieu Place House, home to the Montagu family, dating from the 18th century, of which some parts are open to the public. Nearby there is the Abbey Parish Church and remains of the Cistercian Abbey. A monorail provides transport around the site with a good view of the pretty gardens.

Beaulieu village is a quaint olde-worlde village with gift shops and tea rooms. It is situated next to the tidal river and the pretty freshwater lake above the tidal barrier. There is a 3km walk from the village to Buckler's Hard, with a slightly longer riverbank option.

Although it doesn't look like it now, Buckler's Hard was a shipyard from Elizabethan times until the 19th century. Oak from the New Forest was used to build man-of-war boats such as Nelson's *Agamemnon*. The large hotel and restaurant was the home of Henry Adams, the master builder responsible for the Trafalgar fleet. At the top of the village, the Maritime Museum presents the history of the shipyard, and has some model buildings preserved in their 18th-century form.

With its Georgian cottages running down to the river, Buckler's Hard is part of the 9,000 acre (36km^2) Beaulieu Estate.

The hamlet, originally called Montagu Town, was built by the second Duke of Montagu, and was intended to be a free port for trade with the West Indies.

Buckler's Hard, under the control of Master Shipbuilder Henry Adams, was responsible for building many famous British naval vessels during the late 18th and early 19th centuries including ships which participated at the Battle of Trafalgar in 1805. Shipbuilding declined in the 19th century and today the village is primarily a tourist attraction, with a maritime museum and a yachting marina. During the Second World War, the village was used to build motor torpedo boats and the river was a base for hundreds of landing craft for the Normandy Invasion Operation Overlord. Buckler's Hard was where Sir Francis Chichester started and finished his single-handed voyage around the world in *Gipsy Moth IV*.

Portsmouth

No. 2 | Grade B | 24km | OS Sheet 196

Tidal Port	Portsmouth
Start/Finish	△ ○ Langstone Harbour entrance (SZ 686 997)
HW/LW	HW Langstone Harbour entrance is the same as Portsmouth. LW is 10 minutes after Portsmouth.
Tidal Times	Slack water in the harbour entrances coincides with HW/LW.
Max Rate Sp	5 knots.
Coastguard	Solent, tel. 023 9255 2100, VHF Ch67, VHF weather Ch86 and Ch23 at 0130 UT, repeated every 3 hours.
	Ch11 Call 'QHM' (Queen's Harbour Master).
	Ch12 Call 'Langstone Harbour Radio'.

Introduction

The circumnavigation of Portsea Island is a unique trip; where else can you paddle around a major city in an afternoon? Portsmouth Harbour is one of the world's great naval bases, and a commercial port. The trip is not without hazards as the busy harbour entrance can be a daunting place on a summer weekend.

Description

Starting from Langstone Harbour entrance offers access to the water at all states of the tide and free parking behind Eastney Sailing Club (SZ 684 995). For a clockwise circumnavigation you'll need to exit Langstone Harbour against the tide. An eddy along the western shore of the entrance will assist you, but a disused sewage outfall obstructs the inshore route. Negotiating this obstruction involves paddling into the full force of the flood tide. To avoid this on springs leave the harbour by 4hrs before HW (3hrs after LW) for a leisurely six-hour trip, otherwise leaving around one hour before HW works well. At neaps, the tidal issues are rarely a problem.

On the south-eastern corner of Portsea is the impressive 18th-century Fort Cumberland. The semi-derelict Fraser Gunnery Range sits between the fort and Fraser Beach which, although not officially a naturists' beach, is recognised as such by the council. The 400m long stretch of WWII anti-tank blocks (280 in total) along the beach have been granted Grade II Listed Monument status.

Heading west the beach gets busier, and its character changes to a classic British seaside resort. About 500m before the pier is the Submarine Wall; this submerged barrier is a row of concrete blocks extending out to Horse Sands Fort, one of the 1860's Solent Forts. There is a marked passage through the wall about 200m offshore, or you can paddle between the blocks.

Give South Parade Pier a wide berth as it is a popular fishing spot. There is no safe passage underneath.

At the south-western end of Southsea beach is a small black-and-white lighthouse sitting atop Southsea Castle. The 1544 castle is the site from which Henry VIII watched his flagship *Mary Rose* sink.

The route now heads north-west towards Portsmouth Harbour entrance. The seafront here is lined by a series of memorials, the Portsmouth Naval Memorial being most prominent. At the southern end of the beach is Southsea Hoverport; services run to Ryde approximately every 15 minutes. Watch out, hovercraft have an unnerving habit of travelling sideways towards you. Immediately after the hoverport is Clarence Pier, a once elegant Victorian pavilion rebuilt post-war in the kiss-me-quick style. Portsmouth Harbour entrance is guarded by Fort Blockhouse to the west and the Round Tower to the east. Entering the harbour must be done through the Small Boat Channel which is on the western side of the entrance. The crossing of the harbour entrance to this channel may only be done south of No. 4 Bar Buoy (port marker). Cross to the No. 4 Bar Buoy from just south of the hoverport. The final obstacle to getting into the harbour is the busy Inner Swashway; this channel runs parallel to the Haslar shore. Cross the channel by the port

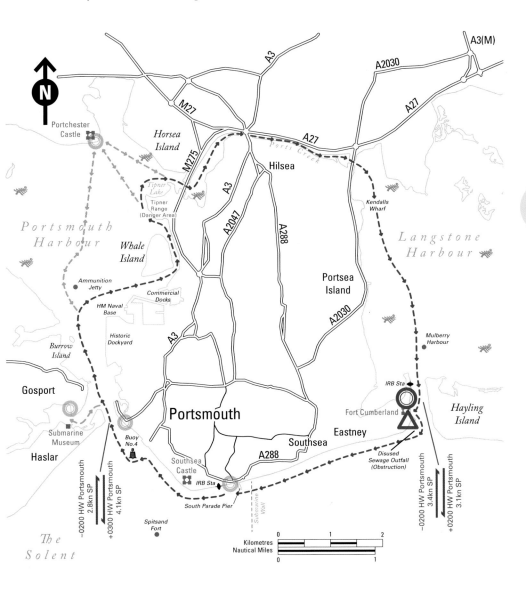

beacon, just outside the harbour entrance and hug the wall of Fort Blockhouse so you are out of the Small Boat Channel quickly. Inside the entrance there can be a surprisingly strong back eddy, so don't hug the wall too tightly. Inside the harbour, initially keep to the western shore. The first point where you are permitted to cross to the eastern shore is at the Ballast Beacon, a port marker opposite Gunwharf and north of the Haslar Channel.

To the east as you enter the harbour you pass Spice Island, a reference to the Caribbean spice trade. You can't fail to notice the 170m Spinnaker Tower, to the north at Gunwharf Quays.

On the west side of the entrance after Fort Blockhouse is Haslar Lake. On the northern shore is Haslar Marina, which unusually has a green lightship for its restaurant and shower block. To the south is Fort Blockhouse, formally HMS *Dolphin*, a Royal Naval submarine base. The 40m concrete tower is a swimming pool for submarine escape training. At the western end of the lake is the Royal Navy Submarine Museum. The primary exhibit sits proudly on the shore; HMS *Alliance*, a 1945 'A' Class submarine.

Heading north past Ballast Beacon, keep a lookout for the Gosport Ferry. You may also get a visit from the Volunteer Harbour Patrol; they have no legal powers, their role is to assist and advise only. The Ministry of Defence Police however do have legal powers (and guns), and will pay you a visit if you stray close to any naval vessels. You must stay at least 50m from naval ships and 100m from submarines.

As you approach the Naval Docks you will see HMS *Warrior*. She was launched in 1860 and was Britain's first iron-hulled warship. The *Warrior*, HMS *Victory* and the *Mary Rose* are three of the major exhibits in the Historic Dockyard. Next to the *Warrior* is a slipway you can land on,

near a convenient kiosk selling fish sticks and cups of tea. Toilets and the tourist information office are also nearby.

The western shore is largely occupied by a series of marinas and jetties, the exception being small wooded Burrow Island, locally referred to as Rat Island. Stay clear of the Ammunition Jetty particularly when ships are moored.

Heading north directly ahead is Portchester Castle. This 11th-century castle built within a former 3rd-century Roman fort is the best preserved of the south-east's eleven Saxon shore forts (see boxed text on page 106). Landing at the castle is recommended.

Back on the eastern shore after the Naval Dockyard is Portsmouth Commercial and Continental Ferry port. North of the commercial ports is Whale Island, home of the Royal Navy training establishment HMS *Excellent*; the training ship HMS *Bristol* is permanently moored south of the island. The more interesting, but longer, route is east of Whale Island. Stay alert and keep close to the island as there is very little room for ships to manoeuvre here.

The character of the trip changes as you enter the Portsmouth Harbour SSSI. Tipner Ranges are directly north of Whale Island; the signs imply that you can pass through even when the range is active. Rounding Tipner Point you are confronted with the dirty end of the harbour; the green hill to the north is Horsea Island, a landfill site. Pounds Ship Breakers occupies the north shore of Tipner, set off by the M275 as backdrop. Contaminated land has thus far thwarted attempts to redevelop this area, allowing the wildlife, which is less worried by the aesthetics, to move in. Tipner Lake is now part of the SSSI, and included in the Portsmouth Harbour Special Protection Area (SPA) which is listed as a Wetland of International Importance.

Passing under the M275 takes you into a lake with the Richard Farrington 'Jackstar' sculpture at the centre. This leads to Ports Creek running between Portsmouth and the mainland; the A27 dominates the northern shore for its entire length. At Hilsea Roundabout the creek squeezes through two tunnels. On a spring tide about two hours after HW you will find a significant westward flow; at neaps the water is generally stagnant.

Hidden amongst the trees on the southern shore is Hilsea Lines, constructed as part of the same fortifications as the Palmerston Forts on Portsdown Hill. The rail bridge crossing the creek can have insufficient headroom at HW springs. With a stand of about an hour at HW, you may have a long wait if you get your timing wrong.

Entering into Langstone Harbour, you thankfully turn your back on the A27 and enter into an altogether different world. Kendalls Wharf is an active commercial wharf but has an almost rustic charm.

The final stretch back to the harbour entrance is a time to relax and let the ebb tide do the work while you watch the wildlife. The channel runs down the unnaturally straight east coast of Portsea, the result of a combination of salt production and subsequent land reclamation.

The final few hundred metres run alongside the shingle spit of the western side of the harbour entrance, marked by the elegant lifeboat station and the Hayling ferry which crosses from the jetty at the northern end. The tide is exceptionally swift along this shore; mooring buoys partially submerge on the ebb, a potential hazard. There is an eddy at the base of the launching slipway, so the tide should not be an issue whilst landing.

Tides and weather

The ebb tides in both Portsmouth and Langstone Harbour entrances are stronger than the flood. At Langstone the spring ebb tide is 3.4 knots (anecdotally 5 knots) and at Portsmouth 4.1 knots. At HW the tide stands for approximately one hour.

Ports Creek is navigable 3hrs either side of high water, except at HW springs when there may not be sufficient clearance under the rail bridge. At springs, a slight westward current flows from about one hour after HW, particularly noticeable under the Hilsea roundabout bridges.

Approximately 2 to 3hrs after HW, an inshore current flows east along Southsea seafront. There is also an eastern flow along Eastney Beach on the flood tide. Both cause an overfall on the disused sewage pipe.

Additional information

Make sure you are familiar with the harbour regulations.

www.qhm.mod.uk/portsmouth – Harbour rules and regulations

Variations

The circumnavigation is possible in both directions; however going anticlockwise you'll finish the day paddling into Langstone Harbour against the ebb.

Alternative launching points for the trip are: Southsea seafront, next to the lifeguard club (IRB Station) (SZ 649 980), and Old Portsmouth on the beach below Round Tower (SZ 6929 993) (harbour regulations add a slight inconvenience to launching here). Take in the views from the top of the tower if launching here. Gosport has a couple of launching options; the slipway by Haslar Bridge (SZ 619 994) has good parking and is accessible at all states except LW springs.

The Royal Oak at Langstone | Mark Rainsley

Hayling Island

No. 3 | **Grade A** | **24km** | **OS Sheet 197**

Tidal Port	Portsmouth
Start/Finish	△ ○ Inn on the Beach (SZ 706 988)
HW/LW	At Chichester Harbour entrance, HW springs are 10 minutes before, and neaps are 5 minutes after, HW Portsmouth. LW springs are 20 minutes after, and neaps 15 minutes after, LW Portsmouth.
	Langstone Harbour HW as Portsmouth, LW is 10 minutes after Portsmouth.
Tidal Times	Slack water in the harbour entrances coincides with HW/LW.
Max Rate Sp	6.4 knots.
Coastguard	Solent, tel. 023 9255 2100, VHF weather at 0130 UT, repeated every 3 hours.
	Ch14 Call 'Chichester Harbour Radio'.
	Ch12 Call 'Langstone Harbour Radio'.

Introduction

Hayling Island lies between Langstone and Chichester harbours. In the past it was best known for salt production and shellfish farming. These days it is probably best known for dinghy sailing,

27

beach holidays and the invention of windsurfing. Within the harbours there is plenty to see, including a couple of good pubs. You'll see a huge variety of waders and wildfowl, and seals if lucky. All but a three kilometre stretch of the island's coast is within an SSSI.

Description

The circumnavigation is best done in an anticlockwise direction, entering Chichester Harbour on the flood tide, arriving at Langstone near to HW, and exiting Langstone Harbour on the ebb tide. Along the south coast of the island, the inshore tide flows east for the majority of the time, and a weak tide under Langstone Bridge tends to flow west at the start of the flood, so again this works for an anticlockwise circumnavigation.

Leaving around two hours before HW, head east from The Inn on the Beach. The shingle shoreline is capped with clusters of beach huts. This is rudely interrupted by the tacky funfair that is Beachlands. Housing dominates between Eastoke and Eastoke Point. On the flood tide you are likely to meet seas breaking in several directions over the West Pole spit, normally avoided by sticking close to the shore.

Sandy Point Nature Reserve sits on the south-eastern tip of the island; this is the last remaining part of Eastoke Common. With the flood tide carrying you into Chichester Harbour, Sandy Point quickly passes and you are whisked past the Hayling RNLI lifeboat station on to Black Point, dominated by the multi-million pound buildings of Hayling Island Sailing Club. Entering Stocker's Lake and the start of the Emsworth Channel, Mengham Rithe is to your left, offering a scenic detour to the wonderfully named 'My Lord's Pond'. If you plan to explore Mengham

Rithe, continue up the Emsworth Channel a little way before turning left to avoid a strong back eddy behind the spit at Black Point.

Continuing up the Emsworth Channel, you pass Mill Rithe to your left; this inlet is an important area for roosting wintering birds. Shortly after on the opposite shore is Marker Point, the most westerly corner of Thorney Island. The channel continues north alongside Thorney Island to Emsworth; our route turns north-west into Sweare Deep.

The spire of Warblington Church and the single remaining turret of Warblington Castle can be seen to the north as you pass Northney Marina. Langstone village lies beyond the prominent black stub of a windmill. The mill complex included both a wind and tide mill, and the mill ponds are now a nature reserve. Before Langstone Bridge are two pubs with convenient slipways, The Ship Inn and the Royal Oak; either makes a good lunch stop. The slipways are only accessible for about half the tide, so don't spend too long in the pub!

Prior to the bridge's construction in 1824, access to the island was either by boat or the kilometre-long 'Wadeway'. Intriguingly, the route of the Wadeway is still marked on OS maps as

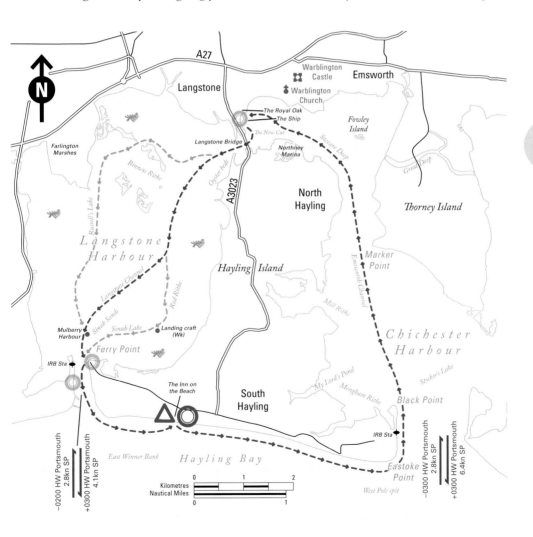

a public right of way. This is not a recommended crossing, as in 1821, the 'New Cut' (part of the Portsmouth to Arundel Canal) severed the causeway. Immediately after passing under Langstone Bridge there are the remains of a rail bridge built in 1865 as part of the Hayling branch line, affectionately named The Hayling Billy after the small 'Terrier size' locomotives. Today the branch line has been converted into the Hayling Billy Coastal Path, part of the National Cycle Network.

Entering Langstone Harbour, a vast area of open water appears before you, with the Portsmouth skyline on the horizon. Langstone Harbour is deceptively shallow, and taking the shortest route will inevitably lead to you running aground on Sinah Sands. On the west shore of Hayling Island are the Langstone oyster beds (West Hayling Nature Reserve), an important seabird habitat. The beds owe their current configuration to a mix-up between Ordnance Datum and Chart Datum in a 1980 planning application. The resultant abandonment of the enterprise to re-introduce shellfish farming left the Borough Council clear up the mess.

The buoyed main Langstone Channel takes you straight to the harbour entrance; however there are other choices of route. A southerly route takes you south of Sinah Sands via Rod Rithe into Sinah Lake, past the wreck of a WWII landing craft at SU 702 006, visible at most states of the tide. Nearby, buoys mark the 'Sinah Circle' an early fishing structure, circa AD 980. The northerly route for the bird spotters takes you through the RSPB reserve via Binness Rithe to Farlington Marshes, then out to the harbour entrance via Russell's Lake.

At the western end of Sinah Sands is a Mulberry Harbour section, a Phoenix Caisson (type C), which is one of the smaller breakwater sections. The caisson was constructed on Hayling Island but abandoned, having broken its back after launch. Exiting Langstone Harbour, the Mulberry construction site can be seen on the foreshore south of the Ferry Inn, consisting of a row of concrete slips visible in the shingle.

Solent Seals

Seals frequent the coast between Southampton and Selsey Bill, being seen most frequently in Langstone and Chichester harbours. They've been around since a lone seal pup was found on Chichester Harbour's East Head in 1993. There wasn't thought to be a breeding population, but in 1994 a pregnant female with a damaged flipper hauled out with two males in Chichester Harbour. Numbers have since steadily increased. Starting in 2008, the Solent Seal Tagging Project conducted counts and fitted GPS radio tags to five seals to better understand the seals' behaviour. By 2009 the common seal population was estimated at 23–25 and there are also one or two grey seals. The common seals have two regular haulouts in Langstone and Chichester harbours. The foraging range of the seals varies; while one tagged seal remained almost exclusively within the harbour system, another made a two-day Selsey Bill excursion. UK common seals account for approximately 40% of the world population. Their numbers have recently been in steep decline, making this small vulnerable Solent population especially important.

Hampshire and Isle of Wight Wildlife Trust's Code of Conduct: www.hiwwt.org.uk/solent-seals-project

The ebb tide demands respect as you exit the harbour past Ferry Point; eddies form behind the Mulberry section and there are numerous moored boats to avoid. The harbour entrance can get very busy; with a mix of pleasure craft, the occasional small (80m) coaster, and a passenger ferry running across the entrance.

East Winner Bank lies immediately outside the harbour entrance; this can produce breaking waves, of particular attraction to jet-skiers. You can normally avoid the surf (and jet-skis) by keeping close inshore, as there is a deeper water channel inside the sand bank. The final stretch back to the start is alongside Sinah Common, the quietest corner of the seafront.

Tides and weather

Significant swell can create dumping surf; consider a sheltered start from Ferry Point in Langstone Harbour entrance.

Both Chichester and Langstone Harbour entrances have significant tidal flows on the ebb tide; 6.4 and 5 knots respectively, but significantly less if you hug the shoreline. Watch out for partially submerged buoys in Langstone Harbour entrance on the ebb tide.

The sand bars at the west and east ends of the island (East Winner and West Pole) can have breaking surf.

Additional information

There are free car parks behind Eastney Sailing Club (SZ 684 995) and at The Ship at Langstone (SU 719 047). At LW springs it is possible that the latter will be guarded by mud.

www.conservancy.co.uk – Chichester Harbour Conservancy.

www.langstoneharbour.org.uk – Langstone Harbour Board.

www.havant.gov.uk – a surprisingly good source of information about the Langstone oyster beds and the Hayling Billy.

Our Changing Coast (ISBN-10: 1902771141, ISBN-13: 978-190277114) – Immensely detailed account of what's in the mud of Langstone Harbour.

Variations

Although it is easiest to complete the circumnavigation near HW, with a bit of thought a trip near LW can be more rewarding. With the mud banks exposed you will get a very different view of the island and harbours; seals hauled out on the mud, wading birds, wrecks and other intertidal archaeology. This trip is longer; you may have to go round East Winner sands.

Chichester Harbour 🔘🚣

No. 4 | Grade A | 17km | OS sheet 197

Tidal Port	Portsmouth
Start	△ Emsworth (SU 748 055)
Finish	◯ Dell Quay (SU 834 028)
HW/LW	At Chichester Harbour entrance, HW springs is 10 minutes before, and neaps are 5 minutes after, HW Portsmouth. LW springs and neaps are 20 minutes after LW Portsmouth.
Tidal Times	Tide times within the harbour are within a maximum of fifteen minutes difference from HW/LW at Chichester Harbour entrance. Slack water coincides with HW/LW.
Max Rate Sp	2.4 knots (6.4 knots Chichester Harbour entrance).
Coastguard	Solent, tel. 023 9255 2100, VHF Ch67, (Ch16 should only be used for emergency and urgent calls.) VHF weather Ch86 and Ch23 at 0130 local time, repeated every 3 hours.
	Ch14 Call 'Chichester Harbour Radio'.

Introduction

Chichester Harbour Area of Outstanding Natural Beauty (AONB) is a wildlife haven and a sailing Mecca. The harbour offers sheltered paddling, with views of historic, picturesque villages with the backdrop of the Sussex Downs. During summer weekends you'll share the harbour

with hoards of dinghies, windsurfers and keel boats. In autumn and winter you'll be able to appreciate the harbour's natural beauty at its best; it is also the best time to see waders and wildfowl, their numbers boosted by overwintering species. Brent Geese litter the mud flats from October to March.

Description

Emsworth is a small picturesque town at the north-western corner of Chichester Harbour. It was once a major port, the centre for oyster fisheries, and home to a number of shipbuilders. *Terror* is often moored here; a sailing boat built around 1890, she is believed to be the last remaining boat of the Victorian oyster fleet. Now Emsworth is mostly associated with sailing and a few exclusive restaurants.

Although the slipway is not accessible at all states of the tide, Emsworth makes a good starting point for a variety of trips in the western part of the harbour. It is worth exploring the river to The Old Flour Mill (one of Emsworth's two tide mills) and the boat yard (SU 753 056); beautiful wooden boats are often being restored here.

Heading towards the Emsworth Channel, the evidence of the former oyster industry is still to be seen, most notably towards LW when the Fisherman's Walk is visible. This causeway once ran most of the way to Fowley Island. North of Fowley Island, the channel is joined from the west by the Sweare Deep. The combination of these channels can produce a surprisingly swift flow between Hayling and Thorney Island, reaching 2 knots.

Oysters

A handful of fisherman still dredge for oysters in the harbour, but this is a shadow of the former industry which pre-dates Roman times. Emsworth was the centre of the industry ... until it was brought to an abrupt end by the Great Oyster Scare of 1902. Guests at a Winchester banquet became ill and the Dean of Winchester died from typhoid attributed to eating Emsworth oysters. Inspection of the oyster beds revealed gross sewage contamination. Oyster sales immediately slumped and the industry never recovered.

To the east is Thorney Island, a bleak and desolate place from the sea. The *'Welcome to Hell'* graffiti on the seawall further compounds this image! Thorney is however part of the AONB and the beautiful Church of St Nicholas at West Thorney (confusingly on the east of the island) is a major redeeming feature. The island has been connected to the mainland since 1870; the

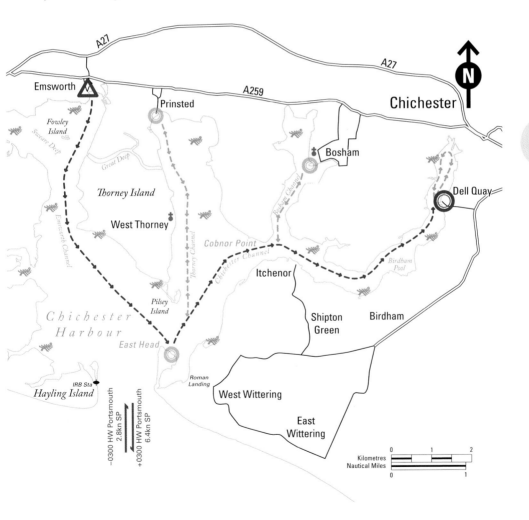

channels that once separated the island from the mainland are now regulated by sluice gates. Eames Farm is the most important site in the harbour for nesting waders and wildfowl, an area of reclaimed land forming a coastal grazing marsh habitat. South of the Great Deep, the island is an MOD base. Access is controlled by 'signing in' at the security gates. Walkers are permitted to walk the Sussex Coast Path round the perimeter of the island and visit the church. Landing by kayak is unlikely to be challenged, providing you don't stray inland.

To the south of Thorney Island on the eastern side of Chichester Harbour entrance is East Head, an important mobile sand dune feature, sand dunes being something of a rarity on the south coast. An SSSI managed by the National Trust, its habitat supports specially adapted maritime plants such as sea holly, sea bindweed and marram grass. There are several scarce invertebrates living here, and nesting in the dunes are ringed plover, skylark and meadow pipit. The sand spit has moved significantly since the 18th century when it pointed south-west into the Solent.

The northern tip of East Head provides a busy anchorage for yachts in the summer. It is an excellent place to stop for a leg stretch. The walk round the sand spit is about 2.5km. At the southern end is The Hinge (SZ 765 984), where the salt marshes of the harbour are perilously close to the open sea. Departing East Head, a potentially muddy but entertaining diversion is to explore the creeks through the salt marshes towards Roman Landing.

Heading north-east up the Chichester Channel, to the north is the RSPB reserve Pilsey Island. Attached to the southern peninsula of Thorney Island by a causeway, the island's undisturbed habitat is home to an impressive variety of unusual plants, spiders and insects. Three species of tern including the rare little tern sometimes breed here. The terns lay their eggs on shingle, so exploring on foot is strongly discouraged.

North of the Chichester Channel is a 2km line of broken piles, interrupted briefly by the Thorney Channel which leads to the alternative launch or landing at Prinsted.

After Chidham (Cobnor Point) is the Bosham Channel, which leads to the picturesque and historic village of Bosham. There is a slipway here, accessible at all states of the tide except when the road to it floods near HW. Bosham features in the Bayeux Tapestry, showing King Harold praying at the church before sailing on his ill-fated 1064 mission to Normandy; the rest as they say is history. The Holy Trinity church is one of the earliest in Sussex; the prominent Saxon tower is the oldest part. The legend of King Canute also relates to Bosham, the King's daughter is alleged to have drowned in the millstream and to have been buried at the church.

Continuing east into Itchenor Reach, the channel is flanked by yacht moorings. The shingle hard at Itchenor provides a launch point at all states of the tide.

The moorings continue up the channel almost as far as Birdham Pool, the north shore obstructed by a number of private hards and jetties which cross the mud flats from expensive-looking houses. Birdham Pool marina was reputedly the first purpose-built marina in England, developed in the late 1930s from tidal mill pools; the old mill building still stands at the entrance lock.

The Portsmouth and Arundel Canal enters the harbour at Salterns Lock. The canal is not navigable for the first 2.5km as it is used for houseboat moorings, but the short Chichester branch has been restored. The large, modern Chichester Marina is of little interest to the discerning paddler.

The channel becomes more rural in the final stretch to Dell Quay. This quieter section attracts huge numbers of birds. It is worth continuing for a further 1.5km beyond Dell Quay to get a unique view of Chichester Cathedral, the only cathedral visible from an English harbour.

At the top of the harbour is Fishbourne. Although not accessible by kayak, it is worth visiting the remains of the Roman Palace, which includes the largest collection of in-situ Roman mosaics in Britain.

Dell Quay has a quiet boatyard and quay on the eastern shore, and The Crown and Anchor Pub is conveniently located just behind the quay.

Additional information

Launching points and car parks:

Emsworth slipway: Accessible HW +/- 3hr, loading/unloading permitted on the hard shore by the slipway (SU 749 055). Pay and display car park in town 100m away.

Bosham: Launching at all states of the tide from the slipway; you will be charged if you take your car onto the quay, but otherwise it's free. Launch from the road at HW as the road floods. With good timing you don't have to carry the boat! (SU 805 038). Free parking on the road below HW mark. Pay and display car park in village 200m away.

Itchenor: Launching is possible from a shingle hard or slipway (SU 799 014) at all states of the tide. Pay and display car park 200m from the slipway.

Prinsted: Launching is possible two hours either side of HW from a small shingle launching area at the end of Prinsted Lane, Southbourne (SU 765 050). Limited roadside parking.

Dell Quay: Launching is possible three hours either side of HW from a shingle launch hard and slipway (SU 835 028). Limited roadside parking.

Langstone: Free car park at The Ship at Langstone. Launching possible at all states of the tide except LW springs. Three hours either side of HW the slipway adjacent to the car park is accessible; at other times a longer carry to the slipway at the base of the east side of the Langstone Bridge.

www.conservancy.co.uk – Chichester Harbour Conservancy

www.emsworthonline.co.uk – local information

www.emsworthheritageproject.org.uk – local history

Variations

Emsworth to Prinsted 14km (via East Head) – a short one way trip, optionally via East Head and/or Itchenor. The shuttle is 2.5km by foot and can be done almost entirely on footpaths.

Emsworth to Bosham 15km (via East Head); there is better parking at Bosham than Dell Quay.

Tidal River Arun

No. 5 | Grade B | 39 / 13km | OS sheet 197

Tidal Port	Dover
Start/Finish	△ O West Beach car park, Littlehampton (TQ 028 012)
Start/Finish	△ O Pulborough (TQ 046 185)
HW/LW	LW Littlehampton is 1 hour 10 minutes before LW Dover.
	HW Littlehampton is 30 minutes after HW Dover.
	HW at Amberley is 2 hrs after HW Littlehampton.
	HW Pulborough is 4 hrs after HW Littlehampton.
Tidal Times	At Littlehampton the in-going stream (flood) begins 2 hours after LW Littlehampton.
	At Pulborough the in-going stream (flood) begins around 3 hours after LW Littlehampton.
Max Rate Sp	6 knots.
Coastguard	Solent, tel. 023 9255 2100, VHF Ch67, VHF weather Ch86 and Ch23 at 0130 UT, repeated every 3 hours.

Introduction

The tidal River Arun is the longest tidal creek in South East England. It is 36km from the sea at Littlehampton to the tidal limit at Pallingham Quay. The river passes through several

geological areas and the occasional town. Travelling inland from the sea there is Littlehampton, the coastal plains, Arundel town, the South Downs hills, Amberley village, the Low Weald plains, Pulborough town, and finally the Greensand Ridge near the tidal limit – a lot of variation! Two sections of the tidal Arun particularly stand out for scenery: between Arundel and Amberley, and between Pulborough and Pallingham Quay.

Description

This section describes two trips:

1. Littlehampton to Amberley (return)
2. Pulborough to Pallingham Quay (return)

Arundel and Amberley have numerous tourist attractions including a large castle and an industrial heritage museum. There are several public houses and tea shops en route for refreshments. It can be difficult to get out on this river at low tide due to steep muddy banks.

LITTLEHAMPTON TO AMBERLEY

To avoid driving through Littlehampton, there is the convenient West Beach car park on the opposite side of the river for egress (there is a 2.06m height restrictor that could be an issue for higher vehicles). You can put on at the beach or if the sea is rough on the river near the yacht club.

With the powerful tidal currents, the return trip to Amberley is easily possible in a day. The tide flows very fast (up to 6 knots), and tidal planning is essential to avoid paddling against the tide. We recommend starting at Littlehampton two hours after low tide. If you get on any earlier, the ebb tide will still be flowing out of the Arun, and you will have to wait for the flow to reverse.

As you enter the mouth of the Arun estuary at Littlehampton, on the right-hand side there are new quayside developments, and on the left-hand side the boats of the yacht club. The Look & Sea Visitor Centre, the distinctive building on the right, has a museum, lifeboat station, and viewing tower; well worth a visit if you have time. The town of Littlehampton extends along the

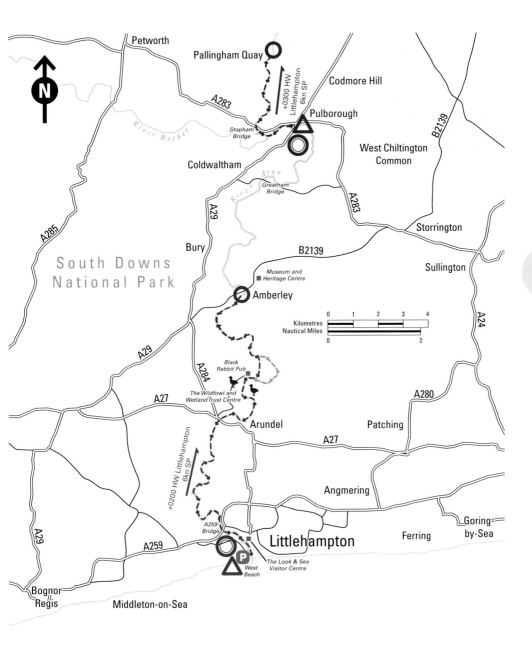

river until the A259 road bridge (2km) is reached. The river then passes through flat farmlands of the coastal plain and has steep artificial canalised banks until Arundel (9km), and is the least interesting part of the trip.

The river is considerably more scenic once Arundel (see opposite) and the South Downs are reached. Arundel is a very prominent town, being built on the first hill of the South Downs, and has an impressive castle and cathedral. The river passes under two bridges in Arundel – the ugly A27 road bridge and the slightly prettier bridge in the town centre. The river is narrow and flows very fast through the town, and the many moored boats present a significant hazard. Just after the town centre bridge to the right is a café, worth stopping at for a cream tea.

The river from Arundel to Amberley is very pretty with the rolling South Downs hills, deciduous woodlands, tall reeds, and high muddy banks; certainly the most interesting part of the trip. Soon after Arundel, the Wildfowl and Wetland Trust Centre, hidden by a high bank, and then the Black Rabbit pub (12km) are reached. The pub nicely overlooks the river on a bend and has steep slippery steps for egress. Just past the pub, there is a backwater to the right that can be explored if time permits – but it is a fairly lengthy extension to an already long trip. Amberley (18km) has a café and pubs, a pretty bridge and the Museum and Heritage Centre. In the latter, you can find out about the varied industrial heritage of the south-east, and a visit can easily occupy a whole day. The village marks the end of the South Downs and beginning of the Low Weald plains. It takes about two hours to get to Amberley from Littlehampton, paddling non-stop with the tide. The tide starts ebbing at Amberley two hours after HW Littlehampton. Amberley is a good place to wait for the tide to turn, with a tea shop and two pubs.

Arundel

As you journey up the river Arun, Arundel eventually comes into view as a collection of grey buildings on the first hill of the South Downs, with a large cathedral and castle. The town was established in Roman times, continued as a small town during the Saxon period (post 500 AD), and then William the Conqueror built a castle in 1067.

Much of the present castle was created by the 15th Duke of Norfolk in the late 19th century, although there are a few Norman features, such as the gatehouse and the moat. The castle is still the family home, passed down through the same aristocratic family since 1138. Inside the castle there are very opulent furnishings, making the castle well worth visiting when it is open between April and October.

There are three other notable attractions in Arundel: the Roman Catholic Arundel Cathedral, the ten-day Arundel Festival at the end of August, and the WWT Arundel Wetland Centre.

There is a public footpath that takes you through the vast estate of Arundel Castle and passes by the pretty Swanbourne Lake.

The river between Pulborough and Pallingham Quay passes through the pretty Greensand Hills and becomes increasingly narrow towards the tidal limit. It is less serious than the lower section (described above) due to being more sheltered and having a weaker tidal flow.

There is a convenient slipway near the A29 road bridge at Pulborough. You should park in the small car park on the opposite side to the river from the slipway. A tea room provides refreshments, should they be needed. The best put-on time is around 3 hours after HW Littlehampton, although tidal planning is not as essential as the tidal effect is weak this far upstream. From the A29 bridge to the A283 bridge, the river becomes progressively more scenic with deciduous trees lining the banks. Next to the A283 road bridge is the historic Stopham Bridge dating from 1423. The river then gradually becomes more narrow and reed-infested until the tidal limit about 6km upstream of the put-on at Pallingham Quay. Above the tidal limit, the river is too shallow to paddle at normal summer levels.

Tides and weather

This trip is a good option for windy days, although it can be hard going as the wind tends to channel through the Arun Valley in the South Downs. Accurate tidal planning is essential to avoid paddling against the very powerful currents – the speed of the river is breath-taking in places, especially through Arundel.

Variations

If time is short, the best part of the trip is the 9km section between Arundel and Amberley; though it can be quite tricky getting on at Amberley due to the steep muddy banks.

Amberley Chalk Pits

The South Downs is made of mainly chalk (a form of limestone) mixed with a small amount of flint. The chalk (calcium carbonate) is a sedimentary rock formed roughly 90 million years ago by the compression of the shells of micro-organisms (coccolithophores) that settle on the sea bed as sediment.

At Amberley the chalk was converted into slaked lime which is used for building mortar and agricultural use. There was a large chalk quarry and kilns, named Peppers and Sons, that was worked from 1840s to 1960s. It was adjacent to today's railway station and the area now forms the Amberley Heritage Museum. Rocks were blasted with gunpowder or gelignite, a rather dangerous job that involved exact positioning of the explosives (or else!). The chalk was carted by horses to the kilns, mixed with coal, and burned to form quicklime (calcium oxide). The quicklime was then turned into slaked lime through the process of hydration by adding water.

The museum is a very good day out. As well as the information about the chalk quarrying industry, there are exhibitions regarding telecommunications, domestic appliances, electricity, transport, road making, televisions, radios and much more. It has a narrow gauge railway and bus service to take you around the site.

Shoreham to Seaford ▰▰▰

No. 6 | Grade B | 27km | OS sheets 198 and 199

Tidal Ports	Shoreham and Dover
Start	△ Shoreham Harbour (TQ 235 049)
Finish	○ Seaford esplanade (TV 478 989) with alternative finish at Cuckmere (TV 516 977)
HW/LW	HW Shoreham is 9 minutes after HW Dover.
	HW Seaford is 4 minutes after HW Dover.
Tidal Times	The E going stream for this stretch of coast begins approximately 6 hours after HW Dover. The W going stream begins approximately 1 hour before HW Dover.
Max Rate Sp	Coastal streams can reach 1.3 knots easterly and 1.2 knots westerly. Flood and ebb flow through Shoreham Harbour entrance can be higher.
Coastguard	Solent, tel. 023 9255 2100. Shoreham, tel. 01273 452 226 (not 24hr), VHF weather 0110 and 0130 UT, repeated every 3 hours.

Introduction

This journey will take you between the principal ports of West and East Sussex. Its start being Shoreham, at the mouth of the River Adur to the west of Brighton, and the finish at Seaford, a short distance east of the entrance to Newhaven where the River Ouse meets the English

Channel. Despite the constant backdrop of the South Downs there is ever-changing scenery through a spectrum of industrial landscapes, Regency opulence, classic British seaside scenes, and unspoilt chalk cliffs.

Description

Shoreham Lighthouse is the landmark that best identifies the launch site. Building of the lighthouse commenced in 1842 and it was first used with an oil lamp in 1846. If that's not a reassuring enough feature from which to venture out to sea, the newly constructed RNLI building adjacent to it will do the job. Parking is available in the area above the beach between the lighthouse, rowing club and RNLI station.

The launch area is Kingston Beach, which stretches between the lighthouse and the lifeboat station. The beach is shingle with timber groynes, one of which has a handy ramp to assist with launching. At low tide there is an area of soft mud extending from the edge of the shingle.

The entrance to Shoreham Harbour splits, with the River Adur flowing from the west and the eastern area of the harbour enclosed with locks. Vessels entering or leaving the locked area are managed by a series of lights situated in front of the lifeboat station. The harbour entrance is wide, with safe areas on either side where smaller craft can remain clear of the main channel.

As you set out the National Coastwatch lookout station can be seen on the western side of the entrance. Turning east towards Brighton, a south cardinal marker can be seen guarding the east side of the harbour entrance. Fishing boats are often seen close inshore in this area. This could be associated with an outlet known locally as the 'Hotpipe' (TQ 247 046). This area is a favourite with the surfing community, both board and kayak. Carats Café is also located on the sea wall above this area of beach. If you decide to play in the surf or just stop early to fuel up, the breakfast is one of the best on the south coast.

As the industrial landscape of the docks begins to pass by, a cluster of beachfront houses known locally as 'Millionaires' Row' can be seen. Shoreham gives way to Southwick and Portslade, then Hove marks the change to a more opulent vista of refined architecture and rolling green lawns. Hove then melds into the mixture of Regency and café/bar culture of Brighton.

This stretch of coast is infamous among the windsurfing and sailing community for its shore dump in south-south-westerly blows. Waves rebounding from the Brighton Marina walls in South Westerlies can be uncomfortable. The entrance to Brighton Marina can also provide confused seas. Care should be taken, and a wide berth considered, if such conditions prevail. Roedean School can be seen on the chalk cliffs above the marina, followed by St Dunstan's, a centre that cares for blind ex-service men and women. Rottingdean Windmill and village are now visible and mark an ideal lunch/rest area at what is effectively the halfway point of the passage. Bouldered breakwaters enable a safer landing on the beach below the High Street at Rottingdean (TQ 370 021). Easy access to the road via a tarmac slipway, and plenty of parking, would also enable the journey to be shortened at this point.

The section from Saltdean and on to Telscombe Cliffs is far less populated, with a mixture of pebble beach and rising chalk cliffs. Peacehaven is the next area where buildings can be seen above the chalk cliffs. As you pass along Peacehaven seafront the arm of Newhaven's harbour entrance will come into view. The port is a busy ferry terminus (Newhaven–Dieppe) with an active fishing fleet.

The piers

West Pier, now all but destroyed by fire and the ravages of weather and time, can just be seen before you reach the still-thriving Marine Palace Pier. It comes complete with kiss-me-quick hats, slot machines and some, not for the faint-hearted, rides situated on the sea-most end.

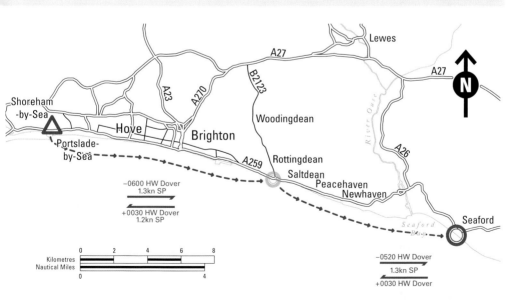

Once the harbour entrance has been safely negotiated, the beach at Seaford can be seen stretching out towards Seaford Head. The shelter of the harbour provides suitable landing along the length of Seaford Beach. An ideal focal point for landing and access to parking is the junction of Marine Parade, The Esplanade and Dane Road (TV 478 989).

Tides and weather

Timed correctly, the east flow will assist you for most, if not all, of the passage.

Additional information

Shoreham Harbour Radio VHF Channel 14.

The volunteer Coastwatch team at Shoreham is available via the duty watch keeper who can be contacted for local weather and sea conditions on 01273 463292.

Variations

Cuckmere Haven is an ideal extension to this journey, reached by paddling around Seaford Head and providing a more sheltered and picturesque landing (TV 516 977). A short section of the River Cuckmere can be navigated after a short portage over the beach to the Golden Galleon pub car park (TV 514 993). Cuckmere could also be used as a stopover/camp, if combining passages six and seven.

Sussex Ouse

No. 7 | **Grade B** | **40km** | **OS sheet 198**

Tidal Port	Dover
Start/Finish	△○ Seaford (TV 469 995)
HW/LW	HW at Newhaven is 13 minutes after HW Dover.
	LW at Newhaven is 68 minutes before LW Dover.
	HW at Barcombe is 2 hours 15 minutes after HW Newhaven.
Tidal Times	At Seaford the in-going (flood) stream begins about 2 hours 30 minutes before Newhaven.
Max Rate Sp	Up to 6 knots.
Coastguard	Solent, tel. 023 9255 2100, VHF Ch67, VHF weather Ch86 and Ch23 at 0130 UT, repeated every 3 hours.

Introduction

The Ouse is one of the five tidal creeks that cuts through the South Downs National Park. The river is continuously interesting with pleasant scenery, varied wildlife, two contrasting towns, and fast tidal currents.

Description

The tidal Ouse is a long, narrow river that stretches 20km inland and has very fast tidal currents (6 knots in places). Tidal planning is therefore essential to avoid paddling against the strong current. We recommend starting the trip at the seaside town of Seaford, just to the east of Newhaven, about 2.5 hours before high tide. Seaford has ample free parking at the seafront and a shingle beach to launch from. Alternatively, launch in Newhaven if the sea is too rough or likely to become rough later. There is a sheltered, sandy beach with a car park just inside the harbour walls underneath Newhaven Fort. (Note there is a 2m height restrictor that might be an issue for cars loaded with kayaks.)

From Seaford, it is an easy 2km paddle to the mouth of the Ouse at Newhaven. As you paddle around the pier and into the harbour, beware of the huge cross-channel ferries and look out for people fishing from the pier. If you get the tide times correct, the tide should be flooding and a brisk current will take you inland along the river. Although Newhaven is not a particularly pretty place, it adds variety to the trip and has a few notable tourist attractions. Heading up the river through Newhaven, you will see the hillside fort, large docks, the A259 road bridge, Denton Island, and the incineration plant. The main tourist attraction is the fort, worth a full day of exploration in itself.

After Newhaven, the river becomes very rural with big open views of the South Downs hills. Soon the village of Piddinghoe (4km) is reached, notable for having the only remaining bottle-shaped brick kiln in the country. After 12km, Lewes is reached with the distinctive white chalk cliffs to the right. Lewes has a castle, pretty river front, the Harvey's brewery and much else. The river now changes character, with reed-lined banks surrounded by gentle wooded hills. Look out for a narrow, overgrown backwater to the left (15km), worth exploring for its abundance of wildlife (especially kingfishers). After much meandering, Barcombe Mill (20km) is eventually reached at the tidal limit. As this is a nature reserve, you should egress at the road bridge 200m before the mill. You should now wait for the tide to turn before returning in the Newhaven direction. One possibility to pass time is to walk or paddle 2km upstream along the now non-tidal river to the Anchor Inn. It is perhaps best to walk to the pub to avoid the long, awkward portage around the mill. The inn hires out canoes to further explore the non-tidal river if you have more energy to burn.

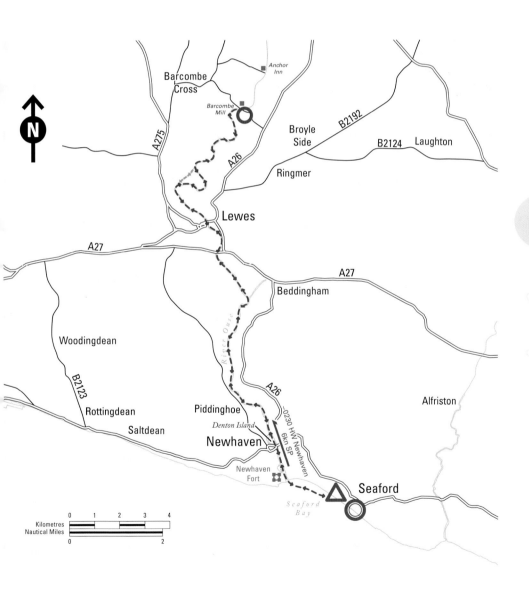

Tides and weather

The trip is mostly sheltered and is a good option for a windy day. However, the valley channels the wind and a few stretches may be hard going against a headwind. If the sea is rough, or likely to become rough through the day, you should launch from Newhaven or Piddinghoe.

Like all the South Downs tidal creeks, the Ouse has strong tidal currents, especially between Newhaven and Lewes. Good tidal planning is necessary to avoid paddling against the tide. At low tide it is difficult to exit the river due to the steep muddy and reedy banks.

Newhaven Fort

Newhaven is a busy ferry port and not exactly noted for being a tourist hot spot. Newhaven Fort, overlooking the entrance of harbour, is definitely worth a visit, with enough to keep the whole family busy for the day. It was built in 1871 by Lieutenant Ardagh as one of the Palmerston forts to guard against the French invasion that never came (hence a 'Palmerston Folly'). The fort then played a significant role in the First and Second World Wars. It has tunnels, gun embattlements, a radio room and various displays about the World Wars and Newhaven's role. Below the fort inside the harbour walls is a fine sandy beach.

Variations

For a shorter trip, the section upstream of Lewes to the tidal limit is well worthwhile. The Ouse is paddleable above the tidal limit at Barcombe.

Lewes

Lewes has a castle, museums, shops, and the Priory ruins and much else. The castle (£7.20 entrance in 2015) is about 1km westwards uphill along the High Street from Lewes Bridge. It is a Norman castle built by William the Conqueror, being famous for the Battle of Lewes between King Henry III and Simon de Montfort (1264). The main castle tower offers impressive views over the town, the river and surrounding downs. Lewes Priory, an extensive set of ruins spread over grassland, is downhill to the south of the castle. Just near to the priory is the Anne of Cleves House Museum. Anne of Cleves House is a 15th century timber-framed Wealden hall house that formed part of Anne's divorce settlement from Henry VIII in 1541. The house contains wide-ranging collections of Sussex interest, including Sussex pottery, and the bedroom and kitchen are furnished to reflect an earlier period.

The High Street is very pretty with many olde-worlde buildings. Harvey's brewery is the oldest independent brewery in Sussex.

Martello towers

The Napoleonic Wars (1793–1815) saw Britain at risk of French invasion. Although Bonaparte's Grand Armée never arrived, the danger was real enough during 1803 when he made plans to cross the "mere ditch". The response was the largest fortification scheme since Henry VIII, based around a simple tower design. In 1794 a small Corsican tower named Torre di Mortella had fended off two British warships. In 1803, engineer Captain Ford proposed stopping the French with similar 'Martello' towers. Construction began in 1804, each tower requiring over half a million bricks and costing £7,000. They were oval in plan, with a single door 6m above ground and sometimes a ditch. Their internal diameter was 14.6m with 4m thick walls at the base, tapering to 12.2m and 1.8m respectively at the roof parapet, 10m above. Each was designed to accommodate 24 men, trained to use the rooftop gun. By 1829, there were 103 Martello towers between Suffolk and Sussex. Inter-visible groups of towers guarded key ports and beaches, leaving undefended gaps along cliffs. In the event of French attack, the towers were to work in unison with floating gun platforms. The towers' strength is attested by the fact that 47 survive in the south-east alone; Dymchurch in Kent is an example open to visitors. Martello towers were subsequently constructed as far afield as Orkney and Pembrokeshire.

Contributed by Mark Rainsley.

 # Seven Sisters

No. 8 | **Grade C** | **17km** | **OS sheet 199**

Tidal Port	Dover
Start	△ Seaford esplanade (TV 478 989)
Finish	○ Eastbourne 'Wish Tower' (TV 983 613)
HW/LW	HW Seaford is 4 minutes after HW Dover.
	HW Eastbourne is 5 minutes before HW Dover.
Tidal Times	The E going stream begins approximately 5 hours 20 minutes before HW Dover. The W going stream begins 30 minutes after HW Dover.
Max Rate Sp	Coastal streams range from 0.4 knots along the coast to 2.6 knots at Beachy Head. In bad weather there are overfalls off the Head which, in such conditions, should be given a berth of 2m.
Coastguard	Solent, tel. 023 9255 2100, Dover, tel. 01304 210008, VHF weather 0110 and 0130 UT, repeated every 3 hours.

Introduction

This journey will provide views of some of the most spectacular coastal scenery to be found in the South of England. The dramatically undulating Seven Sisters reach their peak at Beachy Head, complemented by the natural inlets of Cuckmere Haven and Birling Gap.

Description

Seaford Beach is a relatively open area of shingle from which to launch. South Westerlies will create wave action that makes launching difficult. If conditions are challenging at the launch point they are likely to be more so around Beachy Head, and alternative routes should be considered.

Paddling east from the beach around Seaford Head the chalk cliff descends to reveal Cuckmere Haven. This natural feature was used extensively by smugglers throughout the 16th, 17th and 18th centuries. At low tide the Cuckmere River and valley are very difficult to make out from the seaward side, and the banked up shingle reduces the flow to a fast running stream dispersing over the pebbles. The beachhead and riverbank is a mixture of shingle, sea kale and grass, making it ideal for a stopover.

From here the Seven Sisters to the east appear compressed as though viewed through a telephoto lens. As you paddle towards Birling Gap each section of rolling downland opens up, revealing its true grandeur. Here the chalk cliffs descend to beach level providing a fascinating inlet where Vikings are thought to have landed to capture a nearby castle. On a more contemporary and reassuring theme it is now home to the Birling Gap Safety Boat Association (www.bgsba.org.uk). The association runs a lookout and rescue service which includes the use of kayaks. The beach landing at Birling Gap is not as sheltered as Cuckmere Haven, but provides a useful exit point should the conditions not look ideal for the passage around Beachy Head. Once you have negotiated the shingle beach and chalk/shale ledge via a large metal staircase, a car park area with hotel, café and ice cream van caters for most needs.

Smugglers

In January 1833 a struggle between the coastguard and a gang of smugglers took place by the Wish Tower. Four hundred smugglers had just landed their cargo when the coastguard arrived and opened fire on them. Local residents became alarmed as fire was returned. The smugglers fled, but not before coastguard George Pet had been killed and three other officers seriously wounded.

The Belle Tout Lighthouse, the original Beachy Head Light, can be seen on the section of downs west of Beachy Head. Construction started in 1831 and it became operational in 1834. The Belle Tout was moved fifty metres back from the cliff edge in 1999, because of coastal erosion. Due to prevailing mist and low cloud enveloping the Belle Tout light, a new lighthouse was built in the sea below Beachy Head. Standing at forty-two metres in the traditional red-and-white colours, it has been operational since 1902, and was fully automated in 1983.

The most prominent feature of the passage is the imposing Beachy Head. Rising to 162 metres (530ft) above sea level it is the highest chalk sea cliff in Britain. Since the 17th century Beachy Head has acquired a reputation as an infamous location from which to commit suicide. In recent years regular patrols by a chaplaincy team have done much to reduce the numbers of fatalities.

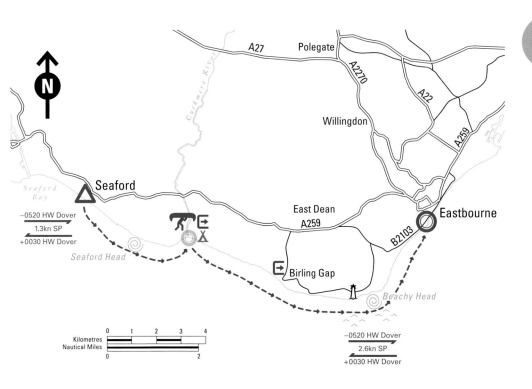

Beachy Head also features in many pieces of literature and film making from Charlotte Turner Smith's poem 'Beachy Head' to more contemporary films, documentaries and rock/pop videos. The paddle around Beachy Head itself will bring you into the lee of the prevailing south-westerly winds. Care must be taken to ensure the tide and weather conditions are ideal for you to enjoy this awesome section of the passage.

Beachy Head

The name Beachy Head appears as 'Beauchef' in 1274, and was 'Beaucheif' in 1317, becoming consistently Beachy Head by 1724, and has nothing to do with beach. It is a corruption of the original French words meaning 'beautiful headland'.

Once around the headland and lighthouse the town of Eastbourne can be seen stretching from the foot of the downs on the west to Langney Point in the east. The paddle from the lighthouse to the western edge of Eastbourne, known as The Meads, will take you past a landscape of huge flat sections of chalk with dramatic rock falls, evidence of the constant eroding effect of weather and sea. In 2001 heavy rainfall followed by freezing temperatures lead to the movement of large sections of these chalk cliffs.

The finish point is the conspicuous Wish Tower located on lawns on the western portion of Eastbourne seafront. The Wish Tower is Martello Tower No. 73, one of the best documented of the south coast Martello towers built to protect the coast from invasion. Currently a museum, the Wish Tower has easy access from the road to a sloped area leading from the beach making this a user-friendly exit point.

Tides and weather

Timed correctly the east flow will assist you for most, if not all, of the passage. The tidal gate at Beachy Head is critical in the planning of this passage. In poor weather overfalls will be experienced at Beachy Head.

Variations

The passage can be extended along Eastbourne's seafront to Langney Point or beyond to Pevensey Bay. This may be a consideration if camping overnight as quieter locations can be more easily found here.

Hastings to Cliff End

No. 9 | Grade B | 8.5km | OS sheets 189 and 199

Tidal Port	Dover
Start	△ Hastings (TQ 825 093)
Finish	○ Cliff End (TQ 889 132)
HW/LW	Hastings and Cliff End are 5 minutes before Dover.
Tidal Times	The NE going stream flows from 3 hours before HW Dover to 1 hour after HW Dover. Slack water is from 1 hour after HW Dover to 3 hours after HW Dover. A negligible SW going stream begins 3 hours after HW Dover. The SW flow gets going from 4 hours after HW to 4 hours before HW Dover.
Max Rate Sp	1.1 knots.
Coastguard	Dover, tel. 01304 210008, VHF weather 0130 UT, repeated every 3 hours.

Introduction

This is a shorter trip with some challenging tidal features if the conditions are right. An extension up to Rye and Camber Sands is also possible.

Description

The ideal place to start this trip would be by the lifeboat station to the east of the Harbour Arm at Hastings, although there are plenty of alternatives places if conditions are suitable, as Hastings has a couple of miles of shingle beach to choose from. At very low tides the beach becomes sandy and makes for a smoother, less steep launch. It is recommended to avoid Pelham Beach which has been designated as a family beach close to the town centre, and is to the immediate west of the Harbour Arm.

The ideal start time is from three hours before high water to one hour after high water. The later start time within this period will result in paddling at slack water towards the end of the trip.

Travelling north-east from the shingle beach, outcrops of rocks are encountered before passing beneath cliffs. At high tides the sea can generate challenging conditions over these rocks and tidal races can occur. Hastings Country Park is situated at the top of these cliffs with views across the English Channel. It is possible to land at the foot of these cliffs at low tides in an emergency and walk to Cliff End or Hastings, but allowance must be made for the incoming tide. The cliffs are exceptionally loose and we suggest wearing helmets as a precaution if landing at the base of the cliffs.

The next point of interest is Fairlight Glen which forms part of Hastings Country Park. This is a wooded area which leads to Covehurst Beach which is listed as a naturist beach but shared by other users. This beach is again mainly shingle with patches of sand at low tide. There are no facilities at this beach, nor in the country park, apart from parking. It is a steep climb of at least 20 minutes to the park from the beach and due to the erosion of the cliffs some scrambling is required to reach the top.

Fairlight Cove is an important location for archaeology and has been described as the best site outside of the Isle of Wight for dinosaur remains. This area has yielded fish, plants, and reptile remains mostly in fragments and is very popular with fossil hunters. The cove is accessed via Fairlight Country Park, although parking immediately by the beach is limited. The easterly part can be accessed via Cliff End where it is best to park in the small village of Pett Level near the Smuggler Inn, or get permission to park in the pub car park itself. There are toilets about 50 metres away from the pub. It should be noted that there is limited mobile phone signal in this area. At Cliff End there is another long stretch of shingle beach with a road running parallel to the shore, which is where our route ends.

Variations

As an alternative, continue eastwards towards the Rother estuary at Rye. Portage to the Royal Military Canal is possible at Rye, and in poor conditions the canal provides a sheltered but unique alternative to paddling on the sea. It is possible to follow the canal through Rye and on to its other end at Seabrook near Hythe. The easterly section requires a licence from Shepway District Council.

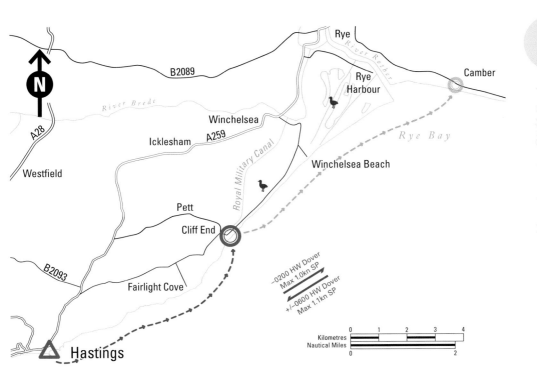

Entrance to Rye Harbour can be challenging. There are a large number of buoys and underwater constructions, and eddies can form around the groynes and various features. To the immediate east of the estuary entrance lies Camber Sands which is a wide flat sandy expanse giving rise to good surf at ideal tidal and weather conditions. There is a signalling system in the entrance to the harbour which must be followed. Once into the estuary the Rother meanders through mud flats and becomes very shallow in places at low tide.

Additional information

Hastings: www.visit1066country.com

Fairlight Cove: www.discoveringfossils.co.uk/fairlight_fossils.htm

www.fairlight.ukfossils.co.uk/

Royal Military Canal: www.royalmilitarycanal.com

Folkestone to Kingsdown

No. 10 | **Grade B** | **22km** | **OS sheet 179**

Tidal Port	Dover
Start	△ Folkestone (TR 235 361)
Finish	◯ Kingsdown (TR 380 482)
HW/LW	HW Folkestone is 10 minutes before Dover. HW Kingsdown is 15 minutes after Dover.
Tidal Times	SW going stream starts 5 hours after HW at Dover. NE going stream begins 1 hour before HW at Dover.
Max Rate Sp	At South Foreland 2.5 knots SW and 4.1 knots NE.
Coastguard	Dover, tel. 01304 210008, VHF weather 0130 UT repeated every 3 hours.
	Dover Harbour Board (for crossing ferry terminal) 01304 240400, call sign Dover Port Control on Ch74.

Introduction

This is a lengthy paddle which passes along the famous White Cliffs. The views are spectacular and, when seen from a kayak, give a perspective that few have observed. Caution is required in the region of Dover Harbour as this is a busy port leading into the busiest shipping lanes in the

world. However with some careful planning this should not limit the enjoyment of this trip. The journey can be broken down into several shorter paddles as there are a number of access points at strategic places of interest.

Description

At Folkestone the natural choice for a starting point is Coronation Parade which leads to a sandy beach. Toilet facilities are available at the beach café (open during summer months) and also just along on the parade. There may be a need to carry the kayaks some distance to the sea at low tide.

Paddlers need to be aware of any boats using the outer harbour entrance. Following an ESE bearing will bring you out from the beach and around the rocks at the base of the cliffs. To the north a Martello tower can be seen at the top of the cliffs overlooking the harbour.

Heading east, following the cliffs, you will pass the village of Capel-le-Ferne high above on the cliff tops where the Battle of Britain memorial attracts thousands of visitors each year. Care needs to be taken if planning a stop along this section as there are numerous rock outcrops and sea walls.

The route then passes Samphire Hoe. This is the longest stretch without a place to stop, and consists of 1.6km of sheer wall protecting the interesting ecology which has flourished on the reclaimed land following the construction of the Channel Tunnel. In an emergency there is a small sandy beach to the immediate west of the wall which is reached through rocks. There is little or no mobile phone reception here, although there is a ranger's office and vehicular access at the visitors centre.

From Folkestone to Dover the railway runs through the cliffs and can be seen emerging to the north of Shakespeare Beach. This beach is the official start point for cross-channel swim attempts, and care needs to taken in the summer months to avoid boats flying the blue and white 'Alpha' flag (diver or swimmer in the water), especially on neap tides. Conversely this shingle beach is often deserted in the colder months despite its proximity to Dover. It is also the first place to take a break after Samphire Hoe, and access is possible via Bulwark Street where there is also a car park.

The next stage of the trip crosses the port of Dover. If launching from Shakespeare Beach it should be noted that the currents and winds may suddenly increase once emerging from the shelter of the harbour wall. You must remain in constant contact with the harbour authorities on VHF Channel 74 if crossing less than one mile offshore, and permission must be obtained to cross the harbour mouth. The Admiralty Pier marks the western-most harbour entrance to the cruise liner terminal. This then leads to the main harbour wall which protects the outer harbour. The busiest part of the port is the Eastern Docks which lies east of the main harbour wall, and this houses the cross-channel ferry port. Care is essential here as the ferries produce large wakes and turbulence, and attention must be paid to harbour authority instructions.

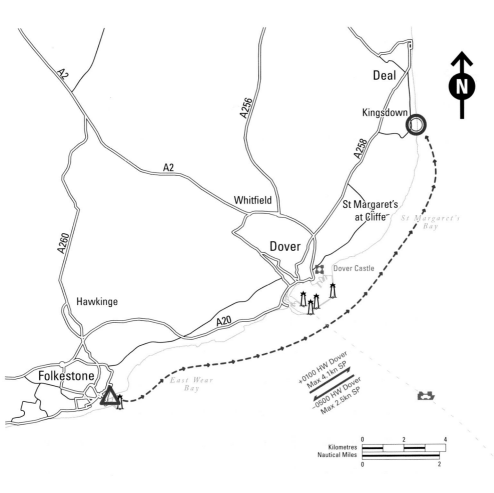

Heading past the lighthouse at South Foreland will bring the trip to St Margaret's Bay, a sheltered bay with ready vehicular access, pub and café open in the summer. Although it is a shingle beach with groynes surrounded by rocks and cliffs, landing is easy. However this part of the coast is buffeted by onshore breezes when the wind is in the north to east which can make for a lively landing. Under these conditions keep out of the way of the local surfers.

Moving north-east around the small headland you will arrive at Kingsdown. There are groynes here, but the beach offers a selection of landing places along a stretch of shingle beach. Access by car to this stretch of coastline is easy and there are plenty of pubs to choose from. Be aware that strong north-easterly winds bring about a challenging landing on the steep pebble beaches.

Samphire Hoe

Samphire Hoe was made from the rubble dug out from the Channel Tunnel. It is located on the seaward side of the White Cliffs to the west of Dover, and is home to all sorts of creatures from birds of prey to adders and insects. It also a popular place for fishermen who cast out from the sea wall. Visitors can enjoy walking along the mile-long sea wall, or follow paths across the grassland which is used as grazing for sheep. Access is via a tunnel cut into the cliffs leading to a car park, warden's office, toilets and small café.

Variations

There are a number of places to start and finish shorter trips along this stretch. It could also be lengthened by starting at Seabrook near Seapoint Canoe Centre where the Royal Military Canal meets the sea via a sluice gate.

Further information

White Cliffs Countryside Project www.samphirehoe.co.uk www.whitecliffscountry.org.uk

Dover Harbour Board www.doverport.co.uk

www.discoverfolkestone.co.uk

St Margaret's Bay and St Margaret's at Cliffe, www.firstlightcoast.com

Stour Estuary & Pegwell Bay ▬◉▦◪

No. 11 | Grade A | 25km | OS sheet 179

Tidal Port	Dover
Start/Finish	△◯ Sandwich (TR 333 582)
HW/LW	HW Sandwich is 1 hour after HW Dover. HW at the bar (Stour river mouth) is 15 minutes after HW Dover. HW Ramsgate is 19 minutes after HW Dover.
Tidal Times	At the bar, the ingoing (flood) stream begins around 4 hours and 50 minutes before HW Dover. The outgoing (ebb) stream begins around 2 hours after HW Dover.
Max Rate Sp	Even the Admiralty Pilot is unsure(!) but all agree that flows are strong.
Coastguard	Dover, tel. 01304 210008, VHF weather 0110 UT, repeated every 3 hours.

Introduction

The tidal River Stour from Sandwich town to Pegwell Bay and then across Pegwell Bay to Ramsgate offers a surprisingly interesting and varied trip. To avoid long car shuttles, the trip is

best done there and back. En route, you will encounter wildlife (seabirds and seal colonies), a seaside resort (Ramsgate), a pleasant riverside town (Sandwich), a fast tidal river, and an open water crossing (Pegwell Bay).

Description

In Sandwich there is a slipway 200m downstream of the road bridge for access to the tidal River Stour. There is a pay and display car park next to the slipway. You should aim to get on 1 to 2 hours after high tide, when the river is ebbing fast and the deep mud banks are still covered. Because the river is flowing very fast here, you should give moored boats and overhanging trees a wide berth. Initially the Stour is narrow with trees and reed-lined banks. The Discovery Park business park soon comes into view on the left bank; until 2012 this was the massive Pfizer Pharmaceutical Research Centre, employing 3000 people. Along the river, seal colonies and many types of bird may be spotted. There is plenty of birdlife to see along the river and estuary. As you progress, the river becomes wider and the banks turn from mud to sand, and then it empties into Pegwell Bay.

When crossing Pegwell Bay to Ramsgate, you should follow the navigation buoys to keep to the deep channel, otherwise there is a real chance of grounding if the tide is ebbing. Take care when crossing the entrance of Ramsgate Harbour and keep a look out for big cross-channel ferries. There is a nice sandy beach to land at Ramsgate for lunch and a rest before the return journey, which should commence soon after LW.

Sandwich

Sandwich was once a medieval port on the Wantsum estuary but, due to silting up over the centuries, now lies inland on the River Stour. It is surrounded by nature reserves containing diverse birdlife in the varied terrain of sand dunes, salt marshes and chalk cliffs (these include the Sandwich and Pegwell Bay Nature Reserve). The medieval port linked England with the continent, and as a consequence was heavily fortified. The Fisher Gate, built in 1384, is one of the only surviving medieval gates in Britain. Thomas à Becket (running from Henry II) and Richard the Lionheart (journeying to the Crusades) are said to have passed through Sandwich.

There is a pretty toll bridge across the river (no toll payable these days) that is occasionally raised to let sailing boats through. The Elizabethan Town Hall houses the Guildhall Museum, which gives the history of Sandwich.

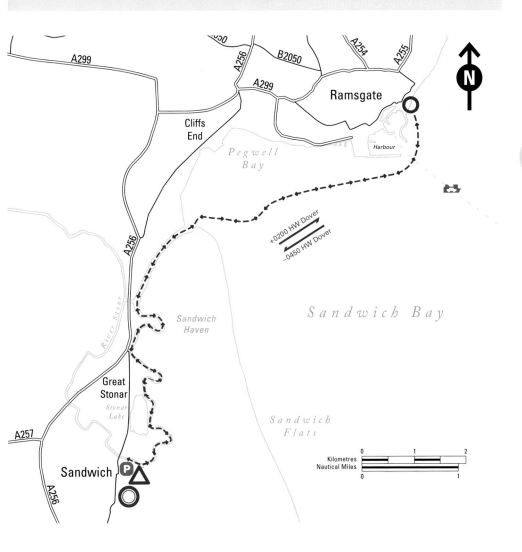

Sandwich and Pegwell Bay Nature Reserve

Indeed much of the land around the estuary is a National Nature Reserve (NNR) and Site of Special Scientific Interest (SSSI). There are bird observatories in the reserves but from a kayak you can get much closer to water birds in their own environment. Around Sandwich you see river birds such as coot, swan, mallard and great crested grebe, but the species seen change as you move towards the sea, introducing lapwing, oystercatcher, little egret and dunlin. Then, as the river opens into the estuary, there are shelducks, various waders including curlews, and a whole host of gulls and terns including, if you're lucky, the Sandwich tern of course – named after this locality.

Contributed by Peter Statford.

Tides and weather

The flood tide lasts between three and five hours, dependent upon freshwater flow in the river. At LW large parts of Pegwell Bay are dry, and you are restricted to marked channels.

The Stour has strong tidal currents that present a hazard around moored boats and overhanging trees. The river is relatively sheltered from the wind and offers a good option in windy weather. The Pegwell Bay crossing is quite open and exposed and best avoided on windy days. Due to the shallow water, the bay may have patches of breaking surf that can be surfed by the brave.

Variations

This trip is just one of many variations. On windy days, a trip completely on the river is perfectly feasible. One possibility is from Sandwich to Fordwich and back using the tides.

The 'coastal crust'

Under threat of Nazi invasion during WWII, the splendidly-named General Ironside created the 'coastal crust', the most extensive defensive network Britain had ever seen. By 1941, volunteers had completed a defensive landscape of 28,000 concrete pillboxes along the south and east coasts. Around 5000 survive, often alongside concrete 'dragon's teeth' tank traps. The 'coastal crust' was backed up further inland by 'stop lines' of pillboxes.

It was envisaged that this would stall invaders long enough for the Royal Navy to intervene. However, when General Brooke replaced Ironside in July 1940, he reviewed the plans and concluded that static defences might actually hinder victory against the Wehrmacht's highly mobile 'blitzkrieg' tactics. Stop lines were abandoned and whilst the 'coastal crust' remained (manned by Local Defence Volunteers, the so-called 'Dad's Army'), it was secretly acknowledged as a strategic white elephant. Churchill's claim, "We shall fight on the beaches", was merely rhetoric.

Contributed by Mark Rainsley.

Isle of Thanet ▨▨▨

No. 12 | Grade B | 26km | OS sheet 179

Tidal Port	Dover
Start/Finish	△ ○ Ramsgate (TR 390 653)
HW/LW	HW Ramsgate is 20 minutes after HW Dover.
	LW Ramsgate and LW Dover are at the same time.

Tidal Times
Between Ramsgate and North Foreland, the NE going (ebb) stream begins 1 hour and 40 minutes before HW Dover. The SW going (flood) stream begins 4 hours and 20 minutes after HW Dover.

Between North Foreland and Foreness Point, the tide flows NW between 1 hour 20 minutes before and 45 minutes after HW Dover, but is then 'irregular with considerable turbulence' *(Admiralty Pilot)* until 4 hours and 40 minutes after HW Dover. A SE going stream then lasts until 4 hours and 50 minutes before HW Dover, when flows become 'weak and irregular' until the NW going stream begins.

Between Foreness Point and Margate, the W going (flood) stream lasts from 4 hours and 50 minutes before HW Dover, until 45 minutes after HW.

Max Rate Sp
2.75 knots off North Foreland.

Coastguard
Dover, tel. 01304 210008, VHF weather 0110 UT, repeated every 3 hours.

Introduction

Welcome to 'Planet Thanet'! The Isle of Thanet coast offers a pleasant mixture of sandy beaches, seaside resorts, secluded coves, stacks, arches, and chalk cliffs with caves. The 'Isle' refers to the peninsula at the eastern extreme of Kent, which was an island until the River Wantsum silted up in the 17th century.

This trip follows the coastline between Ramsgate and Margate (13km), and is best undertaken as a return trip. There are plenty of sandy beaches to rest along the route, with cafés, pubs and toilets.

Description

We recommend starting at the East Cliff at the eastern side of Ramsgate town centre where there is a convenient car park and beach. You can also start at the western side of Ramsgate Harbour by parking on the seafront road. You should aim to put on 2 hours before low tide to catch the remainder of the ebb flow from Ramsgate to Foreness Point. The tides are quite complicated along this section of coast – the ebb tide flows from Ramsgate northwards and from Margate eastwards, both meeting at Foreness Point! You cannot avoid paddling against the tide for some of the trip, generally not an issue if you stay close to the shoreline.

Ramsgate was one of the great seaside resorts of the 19th century, and is now a large cross-channel ferry port. The harbour walls dominate Ramsgate seafront with a large commercial ferry terminal and a private boat harbour. At the east end of the harbour is the Ramsgate Maritime Museum, housed in the distinctive 17th century clock tower building. The Thanet Wind Farm fills the horizon to the east, and is the world's third largest offshore wind farm, costing £900 million to build. As you paddle along the coast northwards from Ramsgate, there are stretches of continuous white chalk cliffs interspersed with sandy bays and seaside resorts. You pass by seven sandy bays en route, the so-called 'Jewels in Thanet's crown'. They are Dumpton Gap, Louisa Bay, Viking Bay, Stone Bay, Joss Bay, Kingsgate Bay and Botany Bay.

The chalk cliffs are the striking feature of the Thanet coast. At low tide, below the cliffs, there are sandy beaches and chalk reefs creating various habitats for wildlife.

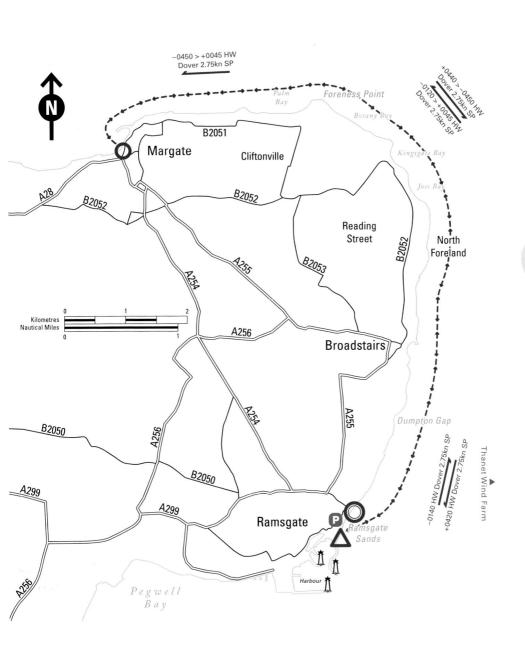

Dumpton Gap is the first sandy beach reached and has a café, toilet and a row of beach huts. Next is the pretty seaside resort of Broadstairs with its narrow streets, sandy beaches, Victorian and Edwardian buildings, and quaint shops. Dominating the north of the bay is Bleak House, where Charles Dickens stayed on his visits. Broadstairs celebrates the author with costumed events and parades.

There is sometimes surf at Joss Bay, especially with an east wind. A surf school and café are open during in the holiday season. The white North Foreland Lighthouse, just above Joss Bay, served to warn shipping about the treacherous Goodwin Sands. Its sister lighthouse, South Foreland, is located near to Dover and is open to the public; it is well worth a visit to find out about the Goodwin Sands and the two lighthouses. Only the North Foreland Lighthouse is still working.

Next is Kingsgate Bay with its impressive chalk formations of caves, stacks and a rock arch. Kingsgate Castle dominates the cliff top to the south of the bay. It was built in 1760s as an aristocratic residence and is now divided into privately-owned residences. The Captain Digby pub nearby is one of the oldest pubs on the Isle of Thanet, dating from between 1763 and 1768. Botany Bay is a Blue Flag beach and has a long continuous sand beach backed by white cliffs. The sand dunes formed under cliffs are a rather unusual feature.

As you round Foreness Point, the Margate coastline comes into view. When crossing Palm Bay you should keep outside the area marked for jet-skis. Margate is a traditional seaside resort with a large sandy beach, donkeys and amusement arcades etc. The town has become somewhat run down in recent years due to the closure of Dreamland Funfair, the derelict lido, and general tawdriness of the place. However the town is undergoing a renaissance. There is the new Turner Contemporary Gallery and the 2015 re-opening of Dreamland as an historic funfair.

Tides and weather

The tides are complicated and powerful in this area; two tidal streams meet at Foreness Point, resulting in rough water in certain tide and weather conditions. On ebbing tides, you will be with the tide from Ramsgate to Foreness and against from Foreness to Margate. Also, be aware that the sea state may change as you round Foreness Point into the large expanse of the Thames Estuary mouth.

In summary, as long as you keep close to the coast line between Ramsgate and Foreness Point, the tidal stream is quite weak. The stretch between Margate and Foreness Point has a stronger stream and requires some planning.

Isle of Sheppey

No. 13 | Grade B | 45km | OS sheet 178

Tidal Ports	Dover and Sheerness
Start	△ Queenborough (TQ 905 724)
Finish	○ Queenborough (TQ 905 724)
HW/LW	HW Queenborough is 1 hour and 35 minutes after HW Dover.
	HW at the Harty Ferry Is 1 hour and 25 minutes after HW Dover.
Tidal Times	In the Thames Estuary, the E going stream begins at HW Sheerness, and the W going stream begins 6 hours after HW Sheerness.
	At the mouth of the Medway, the outgoing stream begins 30 to 60 minutes before HW Sheerness, and the ingoing stream begins around LW Sheerness.
	Tide flows in the River Swale are erratic and variable, but the ingoing stream begins from both east and west at around 5 hours and 55 minutes before HW Sheerness, meeting near Fowley Island (near Conyer Creek). The outgoing tide begins in both directions around 1 hour and 5 minutes after HW Sheerness, but the point of separation varies considerably. Around Milton Creek, the outgoing (NW) flow continues for just 3.5 hours, and at the western entrance to the Swale, the outgoing (N) tide runs for 6.5 hours.
Max Rate Sp	1 knot at the mouth of the Medway.
	4 knots near Kingsferry.
Coastguard	Thames, tel. 01255 675518, VHF weather 0110 UT, repeated every 3 hours.

13

Introduction

The circumnavigation of the Isle of Sheppey is a challenging trip with various coastal terrains including mud cliffs, mud flats, tidal marshes, and seaside towns. With careful tidal planning, the complete circumnavigation can be done in a day by a fit person. It is about 35km in circumference and takes about six hours to paddle. Here we describe the circumnavigation in the anticlockwise direction, although it can be done as two shorter trips:

1. The north coast between Sheerness and Shell Ness
2. The Swale between Queenborough and Shell Ness

Description

A convenient starting point for the circumnavigation is Queenborough, a pretty, historic town on the bank of the Swale creek just before it joins the Medway. There is a slipway allowing access to the Swale at all states of the tide. To the south the Swale meanders around a small pier (with two cranes). Then there is a long straight stretch, known as Long Reach, before the impressive Kingsferry road and railway bridges are reached.

The Swale now becomes quite narrow, bends to the left, and passes the paper mill factories and the mouth of Milton Creek. The tidal currents are strong around here. Milton Creek is an optional extension to the trip. It goes through industrial estates into Sittingbourne town centre.

The Swale now becomes a 1km wide, open expanse with extensive areas of mud banks at low tide. In low water, carefully follow the navigation buoys in order to keep to the deeper water channel. At low tide, the channel is narrow (about 100m wide) with nowhere to land (unless you want to sink into deep mud). In high water, there are side creeks through the tidal marshes to the north to explore, for example Dutchman's Island.

Conyer Creek is another optional extension. It takes you to the pretty village of Conyer and its marina complex. There is a pub in the village but it can be difficult to get out.

Further along the Swale, the Oare old ferry crossing slipway is reached which allows access to the Swale in all tides. On the mainland side, there is a small car park and nature reserve. On the Sheppey side is the famous Ferry Inn.

Just past the ferry crossing slipway is another tidal creek, worth exploring if time permits. It splits into two branches. The right branch takes you to the village of Oare, the left takes you to the pretty market town of Faversham.

Eventually, you reach the eastern extremity of the Isle of Sheppey at Shell Ness. The beach at Shell Ness is made of shells (hence the name). At low tide the beach now becomes very wide, and it will involve a long walk if you wish to explore Leysdown-on-Sea or Shell Ness village. The coastal terrain is flat until Warden.

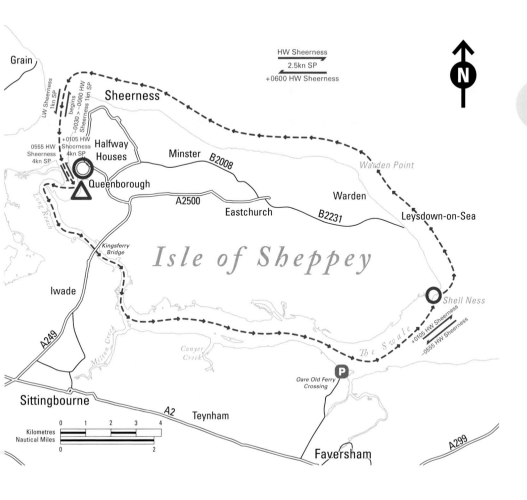

At the town of Warden, clay sea cliffs suddenly start and continue to Minster. The gun emplacements on the beach at Warden Point were at the top of the cliffs during WWII. After a few miles, a collection of rusty sunken ships and the remains of the so-called 'Thames Boom' are reached.

Minster has an historic abbey which cannot be seen from the sea. Instead you see a shingle beach, grass bank and row of houses. At Barton's Point (TQ 941 748), just west of Minster, there is a car park and easy access to the sea across a shingle beach; this is an alternative egress point to Queenborough.

Eventually the mouth of the Medway estuary is reached. There are strong currents at the mouth, which can be hazardous around the moored boats and jetty. After about 2km, the town of Queenborough and Swale Creek are reached on the left, completing the circumnavigation.

Swale Nature Reserve

The site has an outstanding assemblage of scarce plants. The area is best visited in the spring and early summer for breeding birds (particularly waders), or in the winter for ducks, geese and waders.

Tides and weather

To circumnavigate the Isle of Sheppey from Queenborough, start at Queenborough two hours before HW. Paddle along the Swale to Milton Creek using the remaining flood tide. When you get to Milton Creek, the ebb tide should take you to Shell Ness (with plenty time to explore Conyer, Milton and Oare creeks en route). At Shell Ness, wait for LW and use the flood tide to paddle along the north-east shore of Sheppey, and then along the Medway back to Queenborough. This makes for a fairly long day! This is just one possibility; another alternative would be to start and finish at the Oare ferry.

Eddies form either side of Garrison Point, depending upon the tide direction. Flow times and directions in the Swale are particularly unpredictable, as the point where the two outcoming currents separate tends to shift around.

Variations

The north coast of Kent between Seasalter and Reculver passing Whitstable and Herne Bay en route has some interest. Just west of Seasalter, there is a free car park on the seafront for the put-on – it is best to put on at high tide as the tide goes out a long way along this coast.

Lower Medway Estuary

No. 14 | Grade B | 39km | OS sheet 178

Tidal Port	Sheerness
Start/Finish	△ ◯ Barton's Point, Sheerness (TQ 945 745)
HW/LW	HW Upnor is 15 minutes after HW Sheerness.
Tidal Times	At Short Reach, the ingoing stream begins 6 hours and 5 minutes before HW Sheerness, and the outgoing stream begins 5 minutes after HW Sheerness.
Max Rate Sp	1 knot at the Medway mouth. 2.5 knots through Rochester Bridge.
Coastguard	Thames, tel. 01255 675518, VHF weather 0110 UT, repeated every 3 hours.

Introduction

The trip described here is the lower Medway Estuary between Rochester and Sheerness. There is also the upper estuary between Aylesford and Rochester, but it is less interesting. To avoid a time-consuming car shuttle, it is best to do the journey as a return trip. The lower Medway Estuary has open expanses of water surrounded by flat, salt marshlands. It becomes a vast expanse of deep mud at low tide, making it difficult to get out. There are salt marsh islands, old sunken ships and Victorian forts to explore. Large noisy flocks of sea birds inhabit the islands. Hoo and Darnet Islands have two Victorian forts; the latter can be explored *inside* by boat because its base has been flooded.

Description

We recommend starting at Sheerness, using the flood tide to paddle up the estuary, and arriving at Rochester at high tide. This takes about 3 to 4 hours. Then wait at Rochester for the tide to turn and return to Sheerness using the ebb tide flow. You should start four hours before high tide at Sheerness. There is an accessible beach with parking at Barton's Point east of Sheerness about 3km from the mouth of the Medway Estuary. Sheerness itself has a high sea defence wall, which can be crossed using steep steps, but this is awkward with sea kayaks.

Paddle westwards for 3km along the shingle beach of Sheerness to the mouth of the Medway. There are strong currents at the mouth, which are hazardous with the moored boats and jetty. The distinctive Grain Tower, built in 1855 as a Martello tower, can be seen just across the river mouth. On the west side of the river is the dominant Grain Power Station, which gets its coal from a local mine. You should now roughly follow the green or red buoys, avoiding straying into the shipping channel. The banks of the estuary are very different in character. The right (north) bank is much more industrial with power stations, cranes and jetties. The left (south) area comprises numerous salt marsh islands. If time permits and the mud banks are covered, it is worth exploring the backwaters around the islands.

Deadman's Island and Burntwick Island are the first islands to be reached. When the area was riddled with contagious diseases, they used ships as accommodation and put those sufferers on board. Their bodies were then buried at Burntwick Island or Deadman's Island. On the opposite bank, the London Thamesport, with its massive cranes, is a container seaport serving the North Sea.

Eventually the circular Darnet and Hoo Forts are reached, built on facing islands. They were completed in 1871 after significant construction challenges due to the ground subsidence.

The river bends to the left opening up in a long, straight section with Chatham Historic Dockyard (east bank) and Upnor Castle (west bank). The dockyard has three historic ships and a museum.

Eventually the river then bends to the right, and Rochester is reached with its historic castle and cathedral. The castle is one of the best preserved in the UK. Beware of the very fast currents under Rochester Bridge. Just before the bridge is a rusty half-submerged submarine. The *Black Widow* ex Russian Foxtrot B-39 (U 475) Hunter Killer Class Submarine was built in 1967 and prowled the oceans until 1994. The submarine was used to train mainly Libyan, Cuban, and Indian submariners, and spent its time playing cat and mouse with NATO. When it was fully armed it could hold 22 torpedoes, including two with low-yield nuclear warheads.

It is recommended to stop at Rochester and wait for the tide to turn for the long return journey to Sheerness.

Tides and weather

There are many hazards in the estuary including mud banks, the possibility of being stranded on islands, powerful currents, large shipping traffic and remoteness.

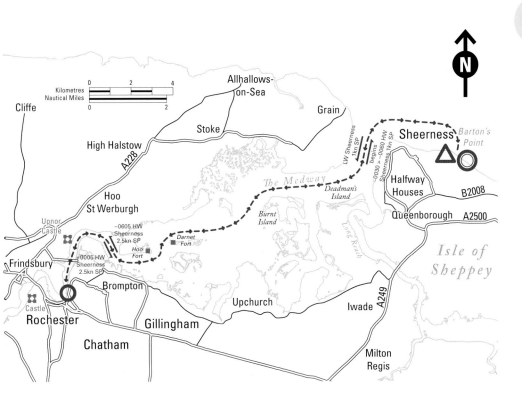

Variations

Rather than paddle the full length of the estuary in one go, it is worth spending a few hours exploring the salt marsh islands in more detail. Two islands have some history; Deadman's Island and Burntwick Island. These can be explored as an easy, return trip from Queenborough on the Isle of Sheppey (TQ 905 724). During the summer months the islands are havens for migrating birds. Be careful not to disturb their nests, and beware, some birds may dive bomb you.

Deadman's Island, just 500m across the Swale from Queenborough, was used to isolate victims with contagious diseases, and many human bones are buried below the surface. Though you are not allowed to land on the island, there is a narrow channel between the mainland and island that can be paddled from mid-tide upwards. The channel is marked with wooden posts that are sea defences – the island is slowly being lost to the sea.

Burntwick Island is 3.5km west of Queenborough and worth circumnavigating. The island has remains of WWII barracks, a pier and sunken ships, and also was an isolation camp for victims with contagious diseases. It is worth landing near to the pier as this area was used as a glass bottle dump during Victorian times. Bottles of many shapes and sizes can be seen here just lying on the surface. Please do not dig down to find bottles, there are enough to see on the surface.

The Thames Forts

No. 15 | Grade B | 30km | OS sheet 178

Tidal Port	Sheerness
Start/Finish	△○ Barton's Point, Sheerness (TQ 941 748)
HW/LW	As for HW Sheerness.
Tidal Times	The E going (ebb) stream begins at HW Sheerness, and the W going (flood) stream begins at 6 hours after HW Sheerness.
Tidal Rates	Around Red Sands Fort, flows reach 2.5 knots.
Coastguard	Thames MRCC, tel. 01255 675518, VHF weather 0110 UT.

Introduction

Far out in the Thames estuary and its approaches lurk a chain of fortifications dating from WWII. Few people know about the Thames Forts, and far fewer still have visited them. The *Guardian* described them as, *"some of Britain's most surreal and hauntingly beautiful architectural relics"*. Paddlers who have visited them tend to be less articulate, muttering descriptions like, *"something out of War of the Worlds"* and, *"those walking things from Star Wars"*. What they do agree on is that this trip is something unique and special.

Description

Sheerness is a good launch point for Red Sands Fort. Although the fort is 10km from the nearest land (at Warden), the 15km paddle from Sheerness is aided by tidal flows and allows an easy and mud-free launch. The Thames estuary is barred from view by a huge seawall, but 2km east of Sheerness, the road rises up onto the seawall at Barton's Point (TQ 941 748) where there is parking and a convenient shingle beach. Note the tall masts sticking out of the water at an angle, surrounded by warning signs and buoys, 3km NNW. This is the *Richard Montgomery*, an American cargo ship which drifted aground in 1944. The wreck contains 1500 tons of explosives, enough apparently, if detonated, to reduce Sheerness to rubble.

Confronted by an open estuary, care needs to be taken with your navigation. Just north of the direct route ENE to Red Sands Fort is the Medway Channel. This leads from Sheerness Docks and is joined by the Yantlet Channel, the shipping route from the Thames. There is constant large commercial traffic, straying into their path would be disastrous. With only shipping buoys to guide you, it's recommended that you carry a chart. Brave paddlers could find their way to Red Sands Fort by staying out of the shipping channel and following the buoyage along the south side of the Medway Channel, taking extreme care not to stray north of the buoys.

Your destination is located at TR 077 795, and you won't miss it. Seven towers rear 30 metres from the seabed, each consisting of a rust-stained steel box measuring 12m x 12m and weighing 300 tonnes, supported on four concrete legs. The towers were originally linked by bridges, one of which has been restored. One tower has a restored landing platform; landing from a kayak is possible but probably dangerous. Your only company will likely be the gulls. Make what you will of this remarkable place, and then turn around and head back towards Sheerness.

Tides and weather

Consider timing your launch to ride the last hours of the ebb tide to the forts, and then return on the flood tide. The waters around the forts are four to twelve metres deep, shallow enough to generate small tide races and to whip up choppy waves in wind against tide conditions.

Additional information

Project Redsand (www.project-redsand.com) has carried out surveys and early restorative work, with a view to eventually opening the towers to the public. Artist Stephen Turner completed the Seafort Project (www.seafort.org) in 2005, involving 36 days of solitude at Shivering Sands Fort. His book *Seafort* gives an interesting perspective.

Variations

From Red Sands Fort, Shivering Sands Fort can be seen 6.5km further out, virtually identical but with one less tower surviving. If this extension is not challenging enough, Knock John Tower is a further 9km. Knock John is very different, being a 'navy fort' (see boxed text). If venturing this far, landing on the Essex coast will probably be easier than returning to Kent.

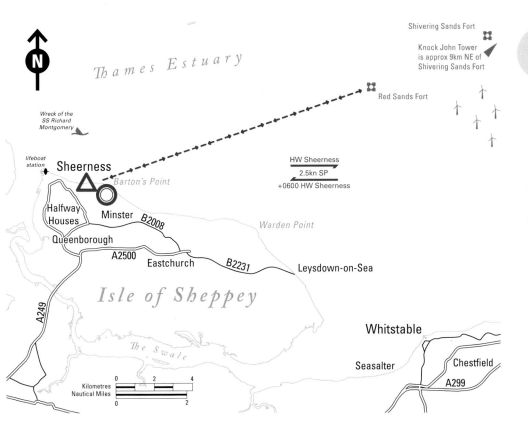

The Maunsell Forts

The Thames Forts are examples of WWII 'Maunsell Forts' built 1942–3 by engineer Guy Maunsell, who later went on to build the first North Sea oil rigs. Seven Maunsell Forts were built off the east coast, and three more around the Mersey.

Red Sands is one of three 'army forts' located in the Thames to cover the blind spot in London's anti-aircraft defences. These were constructed at Gravesend, towed into position and sunk onto the seabed. Each consisted of seven towers supported by four metre-thick concrete legs, interlinked by wire bridges. One tower was armed with two 40mm Bofors cannons, four more with anti-aircraft guns, and another with searchlights. These were arranged in a semi-circle around a control tower housing radar and accommodation facilities. Each fort was manned by 165 personnel, increasing to 265 during the 1944 'doodlebug' (V1 Flying Bomb) attacks. The men served shifts of four weeks in these isolated outposts, being credited with shooting down 22 planes and 30 doodlebugs.

The four 'navy forts' were totally different, basically a concrete platform supported by two tubular towers. They were manned by 123 personnel and also carried anti-aircraft guns, but were intended to protect ports and shipping from U-boats and minelayers. Tongue Sands Fort actually sank a U-boat.

The forts suffered varying fortunes after the war. Nore Army Fort was dismantled in 1959 after a ship collision which killed four civilian contractors. Shivering Sands lost a tower through a ship collision in 1963. From 1964 to 67, both surviving army forts were home to 'pirate' radio stations, utilising their offshore location to evade broadcasting restrictions. They also featured in a 'Doctor Who' episode where seaweed monsters attacked the towers!

Two of the navy forts are gone; Sunk Head was demolished in the 1960s, and Tongue Sands collapsed in 1996. In 1967 Rough Sands (11km off Felixstowe) was declared 'The Principality of Sealand' by resident Roy Bates, and hence outside UK legal and tax jurisdiction. Sealand's 'official history' at www.sealandgov.org will boggle the mind.

Thames Tideway

No. 16 | Grade B | 70km | OS sheets 176 and 177

Tidal Port	London Bridge
Start/Finish	△○ Ham House near Richmond (TQ 170 732)
HW/LW	HW London Bridge is 2 hours and 33 minutes after HW Dover.
	HW Richmond is 61 minutes after HW London Bridge. LW Richmond is 2 hours and 50 minutes after HW London Bridge.
	HW Greenwich is about 10 minutes before HW London Bridge. LW Greenwich is about 15 minutes before LW London Bridge.
Tidal Times	At Richmond the outgoing (ebb) stream begins around local HW.
	At Greenwich the ingoing (flood) stream begins around local LW.
Max Rate Sp	6 knots.
Coastguard	London, tel. 020 8312 7380.

Introduction

To see the sights of London from the perspective of a small kayak in the Thames is a unique experience. You *could* board a river ferry and do the trip in comfort at speed. However the kayak

gives unobstructed 360° views and is much more exciting (think of large fast boats and rough water). You need to repeat the trip two or three times to fully appreciate all the sights: Houses of Parliament, London Eye, Millennium Bridge, St Paul's Cathedral, Tower Bridge, The Shard, Canary Wharf, Royal Naval College, to name but a few. The Tideway is a hazardous environment with powerful tidal currents and large fast boats, particularly between Westminster and Tower Bridges. For whitewater enthusiasts, there may be a few standing waves under the bridge arches in some states of the tide.

Description

We suggest two alternatives for a Tideway trip:

1. Putney Bridge to Thames Barrier and return – this is a shorter trip for the less adventurous and short winter days.

2. Ham House (near Richmond) to Greenwich and return – this is a long trip for summer days.

The description given here is for the longer trip.

Ham House, upstream of Richmond, is a convenient place to start, with a handy free car park next to the river (TQ 170 732). You should start just after high tide and use the full duration of the ebbing tide for the long paddle (35km) to Greenwich. You should choose a day when high water at Richmond is early morning (before 8am) so that low water at Greenwich is around 1 to 2 pm. At Greenwich there should be a short wait for the tide to turn; a good opportunity to rest, have lunch and visit some tourist attractions.

After putting on, Ham House is soon seen on the right bank, slightly hidden in the trees. It was built in 1610 and enlarged in 1670s by the Duke and Duchess of Lauderdale. On the left-hand bank, the white Marble Hill House was built from 1724 to 1729 in Palladian style for Henrietta Howard, mistress of King George II when he was Prince of Wales.

The river meanders to the left just below Richmond Hill with its distinctive Royal Star & Garter Home for disabled ex-service men and women.

Richmond Bridge (2km) comes into view and is the oldest bridge across the tidal part of the Thames, built in 1777. The Riverside development (1984–87) immediately after the bridge to the right is a re-creation by Quinlan Terry and comprises of a variety of new buildings in different classical styles from the 17th to the 19th centuries.

Richmond half-tide lock (2.5km) is only a lock in low tide conditions and you can paddle through any of the arches in high water. The lock was built in 1890 to maintain a navigable depth of water upstream of Richmond. For two hours each side of high tide, the sluice gates which make up the barrage are raised into the footbridge structure above, and river traffic can pass through the barrage unimpeded. For the rest of the tidal cycle the sluice gates are closed, and ships and boats must use the lock.

The pretty Isleworth Island and riverfront (4km) soon follows on the left. Then there is a long stretch of rural river with Syon House and Kew Gardens to the left and right respectively. Just after Kew Bridge (7km) there is Kew riverfront to the north and eventually Chiswick Bridge (9km). A wooden marker post at Chiswick Bridge marks the end of the Oxford and Cambridge Boat Race course, and the next stretch of river is very popular with rowers, especially on Sunday mornings. Be careful to keep out of the way of rowers as they can be very fast and creep up

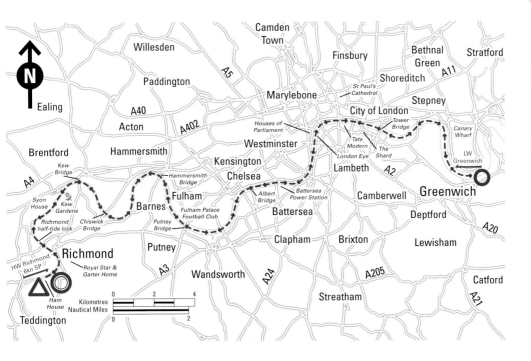

quietly. They follow the outside of the river when rowing against the flow, and the centre when rowing with the flow. This is different from the non-tidal Thames where the rowers keep to the right-hand side.

Hammersmith Bridge (13km), designed by Sir Joseph Bazalgette and opened in 1887, is a stylish, green-painted suspension bridge, a landmark in the Boat Race. Harrod's Depository (1913), immediately to the right, is a ludicrously grand building used as a furniture warehouse. It is five storeys high, designed in the 1890s in neoclassical style by William Hunt.

Heading towards Putney Bridge, the Fulham Palace Football Club can be seen on the left, and Putney with its numerous rowing clubs on the right. After Putney Bridge (16km), the river becomes more urban, with upmarket (expensive) apartment complexes overlooking the river.

Albert Bridge (20km) is a striking pink-and-white painted suspension bridge with fairy lights at night. The central buttress was put there in the 1970s to strengthen the bridge. Chelsea Embankment to the left is a very desirable neighbourhood, containing the former residences of many famous people such as Oscar Wilde and John Constable. On the Embankment, Chelsea Old Church, the Physic Garden, and the Chelsea Pensioners Home are visible from the river. On the opposite side is Battersea Park with its Peace Pagoda, one of many erected worldwide by Japanese Buddhists in response to the Hiroshima and Nagasaki bombings.

Battersea Power Station (22km) is a disused coal-fired power station, one of the best-known landmarks in London, and features on the cover of Pink Floyd's 1977 album *Animals*.

Lambeth Palace (24km), opposite the Houses of Parliament, has been the London home of Archbishops of Canterbury since the 13th century. In contrast, Millbank Tower is a 118m high sky-scraper in the City of Westminster, used as the Labour Party's campaign centre in the mid-1990s.

The Houses of Parliament (25km) comprises the House of Commons and House of Lords. Don't stray across the line of buoys! It is a neo-Gothic style building built by Charles Barry and Augustus Pugin in 1840. The most famous feature is the clock tower, commonly known as Big Ben, and recently named Elizabeth Tower to mark the Queen's Diamond Jubilee.

The London Eye, the 135m-high observation wheel, is one of the more successful of the millennium projects. It is the tallest Ferris wheel in Europe.

St Paul's Cathedral (27km) is Sir Christopher Wren's masterpiece, finished in 1697. It is one of the largest cathedrals in the world, being only outdone by a few Italian cathedrals such as St Peter's in Rome. It has held important funerals (e.g. Lord Nelson and Winston Churchill), and famously avoided being flattened in WWII. On the direct opposite bank is the Tate Modern, formerly Bankside Power Station, which now houses London's largest modern art gallery. The Millennium Bridge (a.k.a. Wobbly Bridge) is a low-profile walkway that connects Tate Modern and St Paul's Cathedral.

The Shard, to the right near London Bridge, is the tallest building in Europe at 309m and the highest point in south-east England. It is higher than Leith Hill in the North Downs by 19m. It completely dominates the view south of the Thames and can be seen for miles. Beneath The Shard, the WWII Cruiser HMS *Belfast* is permanently moored.

The Tower of London is a medieval castle dating back to William the Conqueror (1066 to 1087). It is famous for its beheadings, for example Henry VIII's wife Anne Boleyn, and is the home of the British Crown Jewels.

Tower Bridge (29km) is perhaps the most recognised structure on the Tideway. Built in 1894 in neo-Gothic style with twin towers, it is an awe-inspiring sight from river level. The bridge is quite regularly lifted in summer. This is the last bridge until the Queen Elizabeth II M25 road bridge, 41km downstream.

Immediately following Tower Bridge is London Docklands with its numerous docks and wharfs which have been transformed into desirable riverside residences.

Canary Wharf (32km) is London's version of Manhattan's skyscrapers; One Canada Square, HSBC and Citigroup are the tallest.

Greenwich (35km) has the *Cutty Sark*, Royal Naval College, Royal Observatory, and Queen's House, all visible from the river.

At low tide, there is a large stony beach just below the *Cutty Sark,* to get out for lunch and wait for the tide to turn. Beware of sharp objects such as hypodermic syringes and broken glass on the Tideway beaches and make sure you have good footwear. Although the Thames is supposedly clean, you should always wash your hands before eating food.

The tide turns suddenly, so be ready to catch it for your return trip.

Tides and weather

The tide flows out for around 7 hours, and in for around 5 hours.

The Tideway should not be underestimated; treat it like any exposed sea trip. Places to get out are infrequent and often awkward. The water can be rough and the tide flows immensely powerfully, taking little heed of fixed obstacles such as buoys and ships. The river ferries are fast, merciless and kick up large wakes. Central London is patrolled by police boats which may visit your group and offer advice; heed it!

Useful information can be found at the Port of London Authority (PLA) website.

Variations

There are several options for shorter trips such as:

Putney Bridge to Thames Barrier and back. Parking is relatively easy at Putney. This is a good option to see the main highlights of the Tideway without being a full-on endurance test.

Shadwell to Cheswick Bridge and back. This is the route of the London Kayakathon which takes place at the same time as the London Marathon.

East Thames Tideway

No. 17 | **Grade B** | **70km** | **OS sheet 177**

Tidal Port	London Bridge
Start/Finish	△ ◯ Gravesend (TQ 656 743)
HW/LW	HW Gravesend is 1 hour 43 minutes after HW Dover.
	HW Greenwich is about 10 minutes before HW London Bridge. LW Greenwich about 15 minutes before LW London Bridge.
Tidal Times	At Gravesend the ingoing (flood) stream begins around local LW.
	At Greenwich the outgoing (ebb) stream begins around local HW.
Max Rate Sp	4 knots.
Coastguard	London, tel. 020 8312 7380.

Introduction

Although not quite as impressive as the Thames Tideway trip through central London, the river east of Greenwich still has much to offer.

The highlights are The Millennium Dome, Thames Cable Car, Thames Barrier, and the Queen Elizabeth II road bridge as well as the varied bird life. This is a serious trip due to the deep mud banks, possible pollution, few escape points, and the large ships.

Description

We describe the section between Gravesend to Greenwich, and recommend doing it as a return trip using the tides; it would be very time consuming setting up a car shuttle for a one way trip. This is a long trip (70km return) taking at least 8 hours, and best left for a long, summer day.

There is a free car park to the east of Gravesend town centre on the river front which has a convenient wooden slipway to the water's edge. You should aim to start at low tide, and use the full duration of the incoming tide for the long journey to Greenwich (35km upriver). It typically takes 3 to 4 hours to paddle to Greenwich with the tide, where there should be only a short wait before the tide turns. There are numerous attractions and refreshments in Greenwich to keep you occupied while waiting.

Gravesend was a popular seaside resort in Victorian times, when people would arrive from London on large steamer boats. The distinctive iron pier and many of the town centre buildings date from this time.

Tilbury Docks (3km, north bank) are soon reached, which is a major container port from where very large ships start their journey to the sea. These ships should be given a wide berth by keeping a good distance from the port entrance.

At Grays (6km, north bank), look out for *The Gull* lightship, the second oldest in existence, built in 1860.

The dramatic Queen Elizabeth II bridge (10km) carries the M25 high above the Thames. It is the latest road bridge to be constructed across the Thames, opened in 1991, and the only bridge downstream of Tower Bridge.

Rainham Marshes (18km) on the north bank are ancient medieval marshes and were opened to the public in 2000 as an RSPB nature reserve. It has a visitor centre with a shop and café, and numerous boardwalks across the marshes. In the area, look out for wading birds and wild ducks. Cormorants and shags are very common, and will be perched on anything that vaguely pokes out of the water.

Erith (16km) is home to a large cable works (now Pirelli). There was a large Vickers works that manufactured guns and ammunition during the First World War. Since 2000, the river front has been re-developed with the building of new flats.

Thamesmead (23km, south bank) is famous for its modernist/brutalist social housing estates comprising high-rise flats and terraced housing – it all adds to the interest of the trip.

Barking Creek Flood Barrier (24km, north bank), which protects the River Roding from tidal flooding, is a notable feature.

Woolwich Arsenal (26km, south bank) carried out armaments manufacture, ammunition proofing and explosives research for the British armed forces. Much of the area has been converted into residential and commercial buildings.

Look out for the Woolwich Ferry (27km), a vehicle ferry with a long history which takes vehicles across the river.

The Tate and Lyle sugar refining factory (28km, north bank) is the mass of buildings in North Woolwich that makes, among other things, the world-famous golden syrup.

The Thames Barrier (29km) is part of London's flood defence against sea surges from the North Sea, possible due to a combination of a strong easterly wind and large flood tide. The flooding risk is increasing as London is slowly sinking, and a new larger barrier will need to be built in the future. Paddling through the Thames Barrier is one of the highlights of the trip, a privileged opportunity to see the iconic silver domes of the barrier at close quarters.

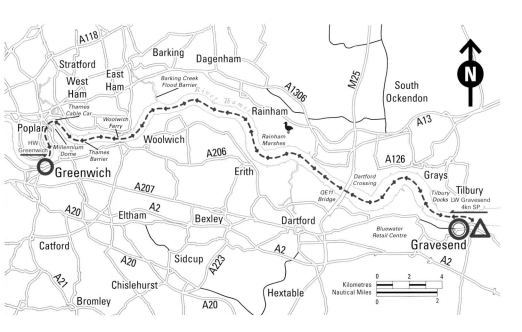

Just before the Millennium Dome, is the new Emirates Air Line cable car crossing between North Greenwich and Blackwall. The £60 million cable car rises to a giddy 50m above the Thames, and gives impressive views over London. In 2014 it was reported that a grand total of zero Londoners were using it to commute.

The Millennium Dome (31km), now the O2 Arena, looks like a huge marquee and is one of the most recognisable buildings in the world. It has twelve 100m high, yellow support towers, and is 365m in diameter. For the best views of the Dome, you should paddle over to the opposite side of the river near the lighthouse at Trinity Buoy Wharf. There is now a precarious walkway over the Dome that requires the walkers to be harnessed to a steel cable.

Canary Wharf (32km) is a collection of distinctive skyscrapers, including Canada Place.

Greenwich (35km) is a very popular tourist attraction and worth a day of exploration. It is notable for the Royal Naval College, Royal Observatory and Queens House, all visible from the river. The renovation of the *Cutty Sark* has been completed recently, following a serious fire in 2007.

When you arrive at Greenwich, it should be near to high tide, with the water level right up against the river walls. This can make finding places to get out quite difficult. One option is to use the hard ramp adjacent to Poplar Rowing Club.

Tides and weather

There are quite a few hazards associated with the Thames Estuary. This part of the Thames is a major shipping channel. As the large ships create big wakes, a closed cockpit kayak is essential to avoid getting swamped. It is safer to keep close to the river bank, although the tidal stream will be slightly slower. River police and customs officers closely monitor the river for possible illegal activity (e.g. smuggling). A police boat may occasionally come over to you and ask a few friendly questions. Debris is a constant hazard on the river. The banks are deep mud at low tides making it difficult to get out of the river for long stretches.

Useful information can be found at www.pla.co.uk – the Port of London Authority (PLA) website.

Variations

It is possible to start and finish in inner London at high tide, though car parking and access points are difficult to find.

Walton Backwaters

No. 18 | Grade A | 12km | OS sheet 184

Tidal Port	Walton-on-the-Naze
Start	△ Dovercourt, Harwich (TM 251 306)
Finish	○ Naze Tower, Walton-on-the-Naze (TM 265 233)
HW/LW	HW Stone Point is 40 minutes after HW Dover.
Tidal Times	At Stone Point, the outgoing (ebb) stream begins 40 minutes after HW.
Max Rate Sp	Flood 1.7 knots.
	Ebb 2.4 knots.
Coastguard	Thames, tel. 01255 675518.
	VHF weather 0110 UT, repeated every 3 hours.

Introduction

The Walton Backwaters are a protected site of special scientific interest and a haven for wildlife including herring gulls, black-backed gulls, redshanks and black-and-white avocets, as well as a breeding colony of little terns. Not to forget the seventy plus colony of grey and harbour seals! It is a place to escape from civilisation and commercialism. Many will have 'visited' the Walton

Backwaters as children when reading Arthur Ransome's *Secret Water*, and for some, the magic kindled by the book never went away. Much of the Backwaters are within sight of Felixstowe docks and the tower on the Naze.

Description

The launch site at West End Beach, Dovercourt (past the Harwich & Dovercourt Cricket Club) offers a small (but free) parking area with a pay and display car park a mere 50 metres away, and a public toilet to boot. There is a lovely field of green grass to lay out and pack your boats, before carrying 50 metres to the beach (sandy at two hours either side of high tide).

The waters here are shallow, so getting some distance off the beach towards the navigation buoys is recommended, and keep an eye out for the plentiful mudflats prevalent all around the east coast. Heading SSW for 3km, you'll pass Irlam's Beach on your right, sandy at high tide and muddy and unlandable 2 hours either side of a spring high tide.

Health warning!

Stay out of the mud! It'll suck you down to your knees at best and to your waist at worst. A 'waist submersion' will require a rescue by the emergency services, hopefully before the tide rises. Cold, uncomfortable, usually embarrassing, and can be deadly!

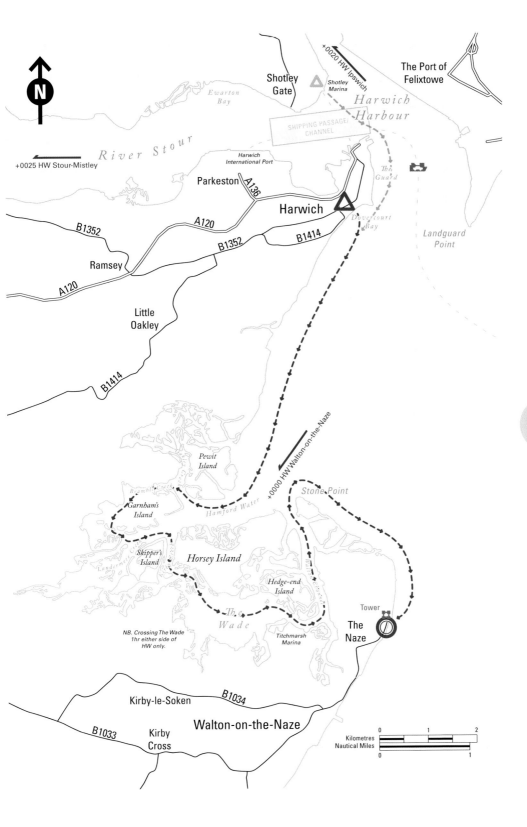

N

+0020 HW Ipswich

Shotley
Gate

Shotley
Marina

The Port of
Felixtowe

*Ewarton
Bay*

*Harwich
Harbour*

SHIPPING PASSAGE/
CHANNEL

River Stour

+0025 HW Stour-Mistley

Harwich
International Port

Parkeston

A136

*The
Guard*

Harwich

*Dovercourt
Bay*

Landguard
Point

A120

B1352

B1414

B1352

Ramsey

A120

Little
Oakley

B1414

+0000 HW Walton-on-the-Naze

*Pewit
Island*

Stone Point

Bramble Creek

*Garnham's
Island*

Hamford Water

*Skipper's
Island*

Horsey Island

Landermere

*Hedge-end
Island*

Tower

NB. Crossing The Wade
1hr either side of
HW only.

*The
Wade*

*Titchmarsh
Marina*

The
Naze

Kirby-le-Soken

B1034

Walton-on-the-Naze

B1033

Kirby
Cross

0   1   2
Kilometres
Nautical Miles
0   1

Two kilometres due south lies Stone Point and the entrance to Hamford Water with the deep water boating channel clearly marked with port and starboard navigation buoys. The Backwaters do not reveal themselves until much closer in but be patient, all will be revealed as you make your approach. Entering the channel, beware of the shallow water to your right. It's a matter of judgement as to how far offshore you want to paddle, whilst keeping an eye out for mudflats, their presence betrayed by feeding curlew sandpipers. If on an ebb tide, paddle towards the navigation buoys and keep a sharp eye out for yachts under sail. On a summer's day the area is swarming with all manner of leisure boats. The Backwaters is a strong tidal area, particularly close in to Stone Point in the main boating channel, and you should be cautious on your ferry glide on your return from visiting the seal colony.

Paddle up into Hamford Water with Walton Channel on your left (also known as the Twizzle), and continue up past the sunken Thames barges scuttled to protect the north side of Horsey Island. Landing is restricted on this beach with tern nests all along this stretch, so please stay well away from the beach. With a strong south-westerly and a flood tide, a large swell works this short shoreline, and nipping in to the leeward of the barges will provide some shelter. Don't get in too close to the beach; this will scare the terns off their eggs which then get poached by seagulls and crows, or just get cold and die. Head for the east cardinal buoy at the entrance to Bramble Creek and pass Garnham's Island where you'll find both common or harbour (*Phoca vitulina*) seals and grey seals (*Halichoerus grypus*). The best time to view the seals is at or near low tide when they bask on the mudflats, and you'll notice the russet colour on some of the older cows. This colour is due to the iron ore in the mud which stains their coats, and the darker the red, the older the cow.

The seals of Bramble Creek

Keep your distance here as the seals are skittish and scaring them into the water reduces the blood flow across their skin, limiting their ability to produce a thick winter coat. Keep your distance and keep the noise down – turn your VHF right down.

Now you can make your way to the left and on up Bramble Creek, and on a spring high work your way through the mudflats and into Landermere Creek with Hamford Water deep water channel on the left. Continue on over the oyster beds with Skipper's Island on your right. Landing here is restricted without a ranger from the Essex Wildlife Trust accompanying you. The next section of your journey is only recommended on a spring high tide or two hours either side. This is a beautiful part of the trip due its shallow waters; you'll probably be the only person within sight. This whole area is an internationally important wetland for birds. It is on the migration route for many bird species, and provides wintering grounds for brent geese, godwit, redshank, shelduck, teal and avocet, and breeding grounds for terns. You'll notice a wooden pier to the left in the distance with a causeway running right across the stretch of water; this is the access road from the mainland to Horsey Island which is privately owned. The owner doesn't mind paddlers landing here as long as they are responsible and low impact. Keep your kayaks together and take your litter out with you! To the right, just over half a mile off is the entrance to Titchmarsh

Marina (Channel 80). You could stop here for lunch at the Harbour Lights Restaurant (01255 851887) which offers reasonable food and service, with lovely views over the marina from the deck on a summers day.

Re-launching from the slip be wary of the muddy sides, there is no hard bottom here and it's very easy to sink in deep, so stay to the centre of the slip to be safe.

Back in deep water, take a right and you'll find yourself at the top of the Twizzle, hopefully on an ebb tide which will take you down past the moored yachts and on to your lunch stop at Stone Point. This beautiful sandy beach offers wonderful views of Felixstowe and Harwich to your right and Hamford Water to the left. Enjoy your stop here and remember to take your rubbish out with you. Currents in the deep water channel on the leeward side of Stone Point run very fast, and launching directly off the beach into the eddy is good fun, with a clear run around the beach and south-east towards Walton-on-the-Naze. The Walton Backwaters are well protected by Pye Sand, a large expanse of hard sand best avoided in strong wind and a flood tide, unless you enjoy paddling in a washing machine. Tides here can run to 2 knots on an early ebb tide. Follow along the beautiful stretch of beach which is a nature reserve; indeed the whole of the Backwaters is a Site of Special Scientific Interest (SSSI), so care should be taken throughout the whole area. The lie of the land will change from sandy beach on your right to the green of Walton Hall marshes. Watch for obstructions in the shallow waters around this bend towards the Naze Tower, everything from bits of steel girder (Second World War defences) to bits of wood. Continue up past the fast-eroding cliffs on your right, popular for fossil hunting.

Tides and weather

The tides are strong but manageable, with some compression in places and a lot of shallow water and mudflats. With some careful planning, the tidal flow will assist you all along this route. The prevailing wind here is usually a south-westerly, and you'll notice it when you stop at Stone Point beach. As we all know English weather is changeable and with a strong wind against tide, the usually flat waters become very choppy with a big swell off the barges on a spring tide and strong winds.

Additional information

Further information about the Walton Backwaters can be found at www.visitmyharbour.com

Variations

An alternative extension to this route is to launch from Shotley marina (opposite Harwich Harbour) on the Shotley peninsula. Permission should be gained from the duty harbour master to launch from the outside of the outer pontoon, and get in touch with Harwich VTS who control these busy commercial waters to let them know your intentions. This will add an additional six kilometres to the trip. There's plenty of free parking, clean toilets and a good pub (The Ship Wreck), and the marina staff are very helpful with weather and tidal updates available upon request (www.shotleymarina.co.uk, tel. 01473 788982).

Stour Estuary

No. 19 | Grade B | 18km | OS sheet 168

Tidal Port	Dover
Start	△ Car park, Wellington Road, Harwich (TM 264 322)
Finish	○ The Walls, Manningtree (TM 109 319)
HW/LW	Harwich is a standard port. HW Manningtree is 20 minutes after HW Harwich.
Tidal Times	E going stream begins HW Harwich. W going stream begins LW Harwich.
Max Rate Sp	2 knots (1.5 knots at neaps).
Coastguard	Walton-on-the-Naze, tel. 01255 675518, VHF weather 0710 UT, repeated every 3 hours.
Port Control	Harwich VTS on VHF Ch 71.

Introduction

The River Stour tidal section runs from Manningtree to the sea at Harwich and Felixstowe, making this one of the busiest ports in the country. The port splits into three distinct areas; Felixstowe is a major container port, Harwich and Parkeston is a major ferry and cruise ship terminal also servicing the offshore wind farm industry, and the River Orwell leads up to the port of Ipswich.

This means that commercial traffic can be encountered almost anywhere, so it is important to notify Harwich VTS on VHF Channel 71 before crossing any of the shipping channels.

The trip from Harwich to Manningtree is approximately 18km and should take about 3 hours.

Description

The launch point is a sandy beach accessed from the car park on Wellington Road, Harwich. The best time to set off is approximately 3 hours before HW Harwich.

Once launched, head north across the front of the Pound. This is the Harwich pilot boat harbour, so best to give VTS a call as the pilot boats operate at about 20 knots. Just past the entrance to the Pound there is an area of the quay used by the wind farm support craft. At the end of the quay (known as Navyard Wharf) turn into the Stour and continue up past the lifeboat station and the Lightship Museum to Halfpenny Pier, and the Trinity House Pier, where there are often one or more buoy tenders in, and a collection of buoys on the quay. Just past here is the old train ferry pier and Bath Side Bay beyond.

At this point it is worth crossing to the Shotley (north) side of the river, to keep clear of Parkeston Quay ferry terminal which is also now used as a base for the wind farm construction work. The old HMS *Ganges* naval training base is visible at Shotley, with its abandoned buildings and mast above.

There is also the possibility to start this trip from Shotley, either launching on the upriver side of the pier in front of the Bristol Arms pub (TM 245 335), or from Shotley Point Marina who normally give permission to use their pontoon outside the lock gates. Please do not use the sailing club slipway as they are not that welcoming to kayakers.

Once on the Shotley side the next target is Erwarton Ness about a mile away across the bay. The bay is very shallow with sandbanks up to half a mile offshore, especially opposite Brick Yard cottages, which can be seen on the shore about halfway across.

Erwarton Ness has the remains of an old barge quay, and is one of the few places on the river where a landing is possible at most states of tide. There are no facilities here, although there is room to pitch a couple of small tents. We are now past all the commercial quays. The south side of the river is an RSPB bird reserve all the way up to Wrabness, which has moorings, a sandy beach, and loads of beach huts. As we reach Wrabness the large expanse of Holbrook Bay is opening up on the north side, with the imposing sight of the Royal Hospital School at the head of the bay, with its large clock tower and expansive playing fields.

For the next couple of miles the channel meanders back and forth across the river until it reaches Mistley marina and the quay beyond. Landing is difficult here as the whole of the quay is sheet piled with a fence at the top (the fence is a sore subject with the locals, and there are attempts being made to get it removed). Mistley is famous for once being headquarters of Matthew Hopkins, the Witchfinder General; from here he sent many people to Colchester to be tried.

Once past Mistley the channel heads again for the north bank before turning south again to Manningtree (the smallest town in England). Landing is possible near high tide along The Walls, with parking along the road. If you have arrived early in the tide you could continue up towards the sailing club where there is a hard usable for about 3 hours either side of HW.

Variation

At Manningtree the river splits into two channels, the southern one leading up to a large sluice gate, and the northern one leading to Brantham. At Brantham there is another sluice with a set of boat rollers, meaning that access can be made into the freshwater Stour and a canoe trail that leads all the way to Sudbury, twenty-odd miles inland.

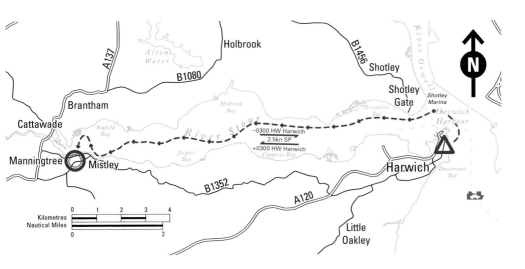

Saxon Shore Forts

A unique chain of Roman forts was built along the south-east coast during 200–300 AD. The 'Saxon Shore Forts' were described c. AD 395 in 'Notitia Dignitatum', an Imperial register, under the command of the 'Count of the Saxon Shore'. The eleven forts located beside river mouths and natural harbours, from Brancaster in Norfolk (route 25) to Portchester in Hampshire (route 2), are among the largest and best-preserved Roman remains in Britain. Strikingly similar to castles built 900 years later, most were square with massive stone walls 3 to 4m thick and up to 8m high. Pevensey was the largest, with 760m of wall. They are a bit of an enigma; the name 'Saxon Shore Forts' and the 'Count' title misled historians to interpret them as a defence network against Saxon invaders. They do seem to have partly been naval bases, but they don't follow typical Roman fort design. Archaeologists have demonstrated that they were mainly occupied by civilians and their construction also predates any Saxon attacks. It seems likely that the 'Saxon forts' were actually secure depots for grain awaiting export. The surviving forts are well worth a visit, to appreciate the scale and complexity of their construction.

Contributed by Mark Rainsley.

Orford Ness

No. 20 | **Grade A** | **33km** | **OS sheet 156 and 169**

Tidal Port	Dover
Start/Finish	△○ Slaughden (TM 463 555)
HW/LW	HW at the mouth of the River Ore occurs 15 minutes after HW Dover. HW on the River Alde at Slaughden occurs at 1 hour and 55 minutes after HW Dover.
Tidal Times	East of Orford Ness, the SSW going stream begins 5 hours and 50 minutes before HW Dover, and the NNE going stream begins 20 minutes after HW Dover. At the mouth of the River Ore, the ingoing and outgoing tides begin 1 hour after local low and high water, respectively.
Max Rate Sp	East of Orford Ness, rates reach 2.5 knots going SSW, and 3 knots going NNE. At the mouth of the River Ore and upstream, rates can reach 6 knots on ebb, 4 knots on flood.
Coastguard	Thames MRCC, tel. 01255 675518, VHF weather 0110 UT.

Introduction

Hidden in a remote corner of Suffolk is a 16km shingle spit called Orford Ness, known locally as 'The Island'. It's an important and impressive geological and ecological feature, but what those who journey to this obscure spot will best remember is the Cold War legacy; until recent times, Orford Ness was a top-secret military site. There is perhaps no stranger landscape in the entire UK.

Description

A full circuit of Orford Ness is best achieved from Slaughden quay, just south of Aldeburgh; Slaughden was actually Aldeburgh's port in the 16th century, until cut off by longshore drift. There is a car park here and the water here is accessible for most of the tide.

Planning carefully, you can ride a powerful tidal flow downriver to the sea, and back up the seaward side of the spit.

Paddling down the River Alde, you are barely two hundred metres from the North Sea across the narrowest point of the spit. The first landmark is a 'quatrefoil' (clover leaf-styled) Martello tower on the spit. Coastal erosion means that its days are numbered, but in the meantime it's possible to rent it from the Landmark Trust. Beyond the tower, signs on the spit ask walkers to turn back. This advice is consistently ignored (especially by fishermen) and the little tern colonies beyond are in decline as a result.

The river is canalised with embankments as it passes the transmitter masts which until 2011 were used by the BBC World Service. When this was the site of 'Cobra Mist' (see boxed text), at this point you'd probably have been arrested as a spy.

Passing King's Marshes, the Alde becomes the River Ore and Orford (TM 425 496) is reached. There is a car park 150 metres behind the quay, and this is the obvious spot from which to launch if you only want to paddle across the river and explore Orford Ness by foot. Orford was another thriving port prior to the growth of the spit, and its maritime wealth was guarded by the 12th-century Orford Castle, which still dominates the landscape.

South of Orford, a crossroads is reached; the river splits either side of the low embankments of Havergate Island, whilst Stony Ditch leads east. Stony Ditch reaches 2km into the former Atomic Weapons Research Establishment (AWRE), one way to view the famous 'pagodas' close up; don't get stranded! Havergate Island is an RSPB reserve of brackish lagoons where avocets and terns breed. Landing is forbidden. Following the west side of the island allows access to Butley River, whilst the east side is known as Main Reach, leading to The Narrows where, as you might imagine, the tidal flow is particularly strong. The two channels rejoin after 3km at Dove Point; the landward shore here is Boyton Marshes RSPB reserve.

The River Ore is mostly featureless along Long Reach, surrounded by mud flats and embankments. This is also a water-ski area. Things become more interesting at North Weir Point, where the North Sea is joined at Hollesley Bay. The shallows around the river entrance change continually, so much so that Trinity House surveys them annually; see www.eastcoastpilot.com for updated advice.

A kilometre south of the spit are the Martello tower and few houses of Shingle Street, worth a diversion for a lunch break. The hamlet of Shingle Street was requisitioned during WWII and used for bombing target practice.

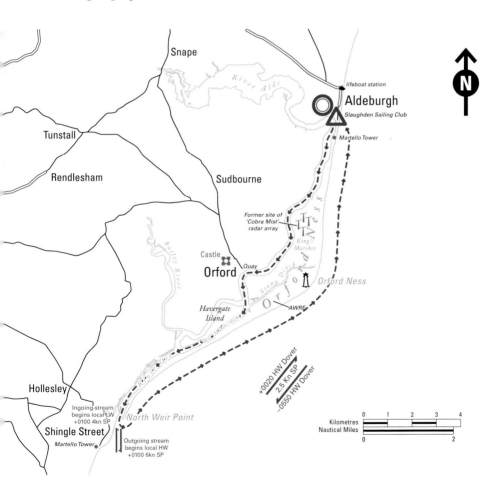

Turning north, it's a long haul along the monotonous shingle beach, back to Slaughden. The good news is that the tide can be utilised to give plenty of assistance. The interest comes from the assorted manmade structures. First reached, are the hulking remains of the AWRE laboratories, starting with the 'pagodas'. The wooden tower framework which follows was previously a military police lookout. The red-and-white striped lighthouse is then reached, alongside a boarded-up coastguard lookout. The lighthouse dates from 1792, but was finally switched off in 2013 due to coastal erosion. From offshore, you might also spot the concrete and brick Bomb Ballistics Tower (built in 1933 to study aerial bombardment), and the 'Black Beacon', an oddly attractive 1928 wooden tower which housed an experimental navigation beacon.

Groynes are reached and the shingle becomes less steep towards the car park at Slaughden. If the surf is dumping, note that the landing is almost sandy a short distance further at Aldeburgh

Tides and Weather

The River Ore entrance is potentially dangerous when onshore winds face an outgoing tide.

The shingle beach of Orford Ness shelves steeply, forming dumping waves in swell.

Additional Information

The National Trust office at Orford quay sells an excellent guide booklet.

The National Trust would like visitors to explore Orford Ness by foot only from the landing opposite Orford quay, sticking to marked paths, and having paid an entrance fee at their office

You can pay your fee and access the landing by kayak, but perhaps call ahead (01394 450900). It makes sense to respect these restrictions. Extensive and irreparable damage was inflicted by the military on the shingle ecosystems, and you will see how the delicate plant communities barely cling to survival. Merely landing on the seaward side of the spit could cause damage. Landing is not forbidden along the river between Stony Ditch and North Weir Point, but is discouraged.

Signs also claim that wandering freely is dangerous due to unexploded ordnance.

Habitats at Orford Ness

Orford Ness National Nature Reserve is the largest vegetated shingle spit in Europe, and extends sixteen metres in length yearly. It's the only one of Britain's three large shingle landforms with a 'nose'. The seaward side is shingle, whilst the landward side is an extensive tidal marsh. From atop the Bomb Ballistics Tower, it's possible to view successive ridges and swales of shingle, indicating how the spit has formed incrementally through centuries of longshore drift. Sea campion has colonised the ridges, although visible damage has been done to these communities by past military activity and more recently, morons on trail bikes. There are nesting colonies of little terns at the southern and northern ends of the spit, currently in decline. Two thousand pairs of herring gulls and 6,000 pairs of lesser black-backed gulls nest within Lantern Marshes and amongst the shingle at the southern end.

Variations

There is scope for exploration up Butley River, and also upstream of Slaughden quay through the lagoon of Long Reach to Snape Bridge.

A glance at the map will reveal the surprising wildness of the Suffolk Coast and Heaths Area of Outstanding Natural Beauty; road access is intermittent and there are few population centres. Affluent Londoners are in on the secret; they've bought up a third of the property in the attractive resort of Southwold. Spots to explore include Dunwich, where about a dozen buildings survive of what was once a town with eighteen churches.

Orford Ness and the Cold War

Orford Ness bears traces of military activity from 1913 onwards, but the oddest remains belonged to the Atomic Weapons Research Establishment which existed until the 1980s. Huge bunkers were half-buried into the shingle and used for stress-testing atomic weapons (yes, you read that right) and other highly secret functions. The most recognisable of the bunkers are the 'pagodas' which were built open-sided to release energy from explosions. The bunkers are usually out of bounds, but can occasionally be visited with guides.

The site was known as 'Cobra Mist', a vast experimental over-the-horizon radar system. This expensive project consisted of eighteen 600 metre arrays of linked masts, spread fan-like from a central hub. Cobra Mist was intended to detect Soviet missile launches, but was scrapped in 1973 after encountering insurmountable problems with background 'noise', suspected to have been caused by signal jamming from Soviet trawlers out in the North Sea. The site was later occupied by the BBC World Service masts. Incidentally, this spot has been associated with UFO sightings, and certain folk remain convinced that this is what Cobra Mist was really about ...

The English Heritage publication *Cold War* covers Orford Ness and is highly recommended for those wanting to learn more about our (dauntingly extensive) legacy of Cold War archaeology.

Norfolk Broads Circuit

No. 21 | Grade A | 46km | OS sheet 134

Tidal Port	Lowestoft
Start/Finish	△○ Mutford Lock, Lowestoft (TM 521 928)
HW/LW	HW Great Yarmouth entrance is 25 minutes before HW Lowestoft. HW at Haven Bridge in Great Yarmouth is 3 hours after HW Lowestoft.
Tidal Times	HW and LW relative to Haven Bridge in Great Yarmouth; at Oulton Broad, +0330; at Somerleyton, +0230; at St Olaves, +0130; at the west end of Breydon Water, +0100. At Great Yarmouth harbour entrance, water continues to flow out into the sea for between 30 minutes and 1 hour 15 minutes after local LW.
Max Rate Sp	Rates reach 3 knots on the coastal stretches. In the River Waveney, ebb flows can reach 6 knots at narrower spots.
Coastguard	Humber MRCC, tel. 01262 672317, VHF weather 0150 UT.

Introduction

Paddling this circuit is an eclectic experience, encompassing the tidal rivers of the southern Broads, the bustling ports of Great Yarmouth and Lowestoft, and Britain's easternmost point. You could take the whole lot on for a long and varied day, or break it down into several shorter trips, each interesting in its own right.

Description

OULTON BROAD AND THE WAVENEY

This trip begins at Oulton Broad in Lowestoft, where there is plenty of parking behind the children's park. On a summer weekend this will be a busy place, with many holidaymakers ashore and boats crowding the water. Powerboat races are regularly held here. You may be surprised how quickly this is all left behind. The western part of Oulton Broad is Carlton Marshes Nature Reserve, managed by the Suffolk Wildlife Trust. Follow Oulton Dyke for 2km until it joins the River Waveney. What you see here is what you'll see for a few hours ... a fast-flowing river hemmed in by reed beds. The surrounding landscape is mostly too flat to appreciate from kayak level, but you will no doubt learn to appreciate the reeds, a key part of the Broads economy, used for thatch. Some variation is provided by occasional windmills and pumping stations, built to drain water from the lower-lying marshlands. The brick chimney of Black Mill is the first such landmark, followed by the peculiar railway swing bridge at Somerleyton, where there is a pub and road access. Herringfleet windmill follows, built c. 1820 and still in working order.

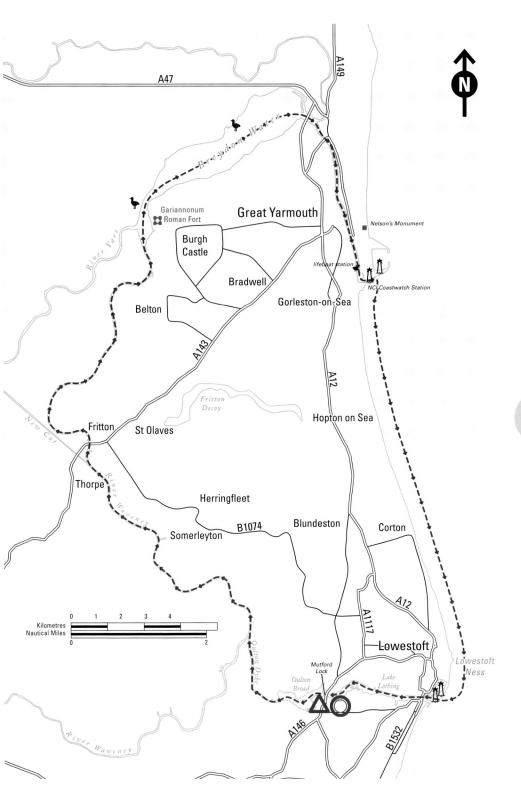

A47

A149

N

Breydon Water

Gariannonum
Roman Fort

Great Yarmouth

Nelson's Monument

Burgh
Castle

lifeboat station

Bradwell

NCI Coastwatch Station

River Yare

Belton

Gorleston-on-Sea

A143

A12

Fritton
Decoy

New Cut

Fritton

Hopton on Sea

St Olaves

Thorpe

River Waveney

Herringfleet

Blundeston

Corton

B1074

Somerleyton

A12

Kilometres
Nautical Miles

0   1   2   3   4

A1117

0   2

Lowestoft

Mutford
Lock

Lowestoft
Ness

Oulton Dyke

Oulton
Broad

Lake
Lothing

A146

B1532

River Waveney

Norfolk Broads Circuit

21

When you reach a fork in the river, keep right; the left channel is the New Cut, running straight as a die for 4km to the River Yare. St Olaves is a good spot to hop ashore, although this can be tricky with the tide running. There is a pub and it's possible to walk downstream and visit St Olaves Windpump; the key can be obtained from the Bridge Stores.

Five more windmills and some high pylons bring you to the Fisherman's Bar, amidst a large marina. Landing is again awkward, but this is the last stopping point before entering Breydon Water. A short walk downstream are the hefty walls of the 3rd-century Roman Saxon shore fort of Gariannonum (see boxed text page 106). When first constructed, this guarded a much more extensive estuary.

BREYDON WATER

As the Waveney widens into Breydon Water, the River Yare joins from the left. A short detour upstream brings you to the Berney Arms (a pub only accessible by water!) and the late 19th century Berney Arms Mill, Norfolk's tallest windmill. This was originally a grinding mill, but was used for drainage from the 1950s. It's occasionally open to the public. Landing is (again) a hair-raising affair; your best bet might be to slog past the mill to where a side creek enters.

Breydon Water (Scandinavian 'water broadened from narrow') is what remains of an estuary which once reached Beccles and Norwich. It's an RSPB reserve for the wildfowl and waders, and you'll spot hides on both banks. The deep channel is marked by buoys and a Navigation Ranger patrols by boat. In stiff wind, this is a lively place with waves breaking over shallows; don't underestimate this 6km open crossing! The concrete edifice of Breydon Bridge marks the entrance to Great Yarmouth.

The Norfolk Broads

The Norfolk Broads consist of about 200km of navigable waterways, linking shallow lakes known as 'broads'. These were actually formed by industrial activity, being pits formed by peat digging between the 9th and 14th centuries, and subsequently flooded. Until recent times the broads were worked by single-masted square-rigged sailing vessels known as wherries, which could carry 40 tons of cargo. Only seven of these survive. The broads were 'discovered' by leisure sailors in the nineteenth century, and have been a popular holiday destination ever since. Boat hire companies rent a wide range of powered and unpowered craft to all manner of folk; all human life is here, but it's also perfectly possible to find peace and solitude.

The Broads Authority is responsible for conservation, recreation and navigation – www.broads-authority.gov.uk

Two guidebooks are useful; *Complete Guide to the Broads* by Bridget Lely, and the *Norfolk Broads Waterways Guide* from Collins, which has excellent maps.

GREAT YARMOUTH

The River Yare flows rapidly through the heart of Great Yarmouth for 5km, first passing the quays and wharfs of the Heritage Quarter. There are various interesting places to visit ashore (e.g.

the Nelson, and Time and Tide Museums), but they'll have to wait for afterwards, as stopping and landing isn't especially practical along this working waterfront. You'll pass some big ships, so proceed with caution. One possible get-out is where Riverside Road briefly comes close to the right bank in the final kilometre, after you pass the Nelson monument on the left bank.

After passing the RNLI station, a sharp left bend (known as The Brush) leads you between piers and directly out into the sea. Turning south, your first good landing is Gorleston beach. If you want to break the trip here, there is parking beside the Pavilion Theatre.

GREAT YARMOUTH TO LOWESTOFT

Parts of the 11km coast to Lowestoft harbour are fairly grim, due to extensive remnants of failed coastal defences. All manner of shattered concrete and metal shards poke upwards at the water's edge; you won't want your kayak anywhere near this! Paralleling your course 2km offshore is the long spit of Scroby Sands, marked by wind farms and occupied by seal colonies. Approaching Lowestoft is an attractive section of coastal heath and dunes below the cliffs, before coastal defences again intrude, looking not unlike medieval torture implements.

LOWESTOFT

Lowestoft Ness is the easternmost point of Britain, but is sadly a bemusing let-down for paddlers and an enduring embarrassment to locals. Britain's tallest wind turbine (called 'Gulliver', 126 metres) overshadows the Ness, which is crowded with a gasworks, a sewage works, a waste tip and a fish processing plant. Occupying the actual point (and highlighted on the OS map as an

attraction) is the grandly named 'Euroscope', a nondescript plaque in the ground. You couldn't make this stuff up. Coastal defences make landing here impractical.

Entering Lowestoft Harbour, it is recommended to contact Harbour Control on VHF Channel 14 for advice. The inner harbour (Lake Lothing) is accessed by the Bridge Channel; the Harbour Bridge lifts up ten times daily, and traffic lights direct vessels passing through. Kayaks certainly won't need the bridge lifting, but as Harbour Control overlooks the channel, you'd best communicate with them before heading through. Note the lifeboat man statue on the left.

The 2km length of Lake Lothing is lined by marinas and commercial quays, leading to Mutford Lock, the entrance to Oulton Broad. Mutford Control can be contacted on 01502 531778 or sometimes on VHF Channel 9/14. They probably won't be keen to admit kayaks however, and in any case it will be quicker to portage around. You can either simply land and hop over the wall to the south of the lock, or land discreetly among the marinas further back on the south side (e.g. Lowestoft Haven Marina) and use a trolley. Either way, take care whilst crossing the busy road back to your start point at Oulton Broad.

Tides and Weather

Along the rivers of the southern Broads, paddler-unfriendly moorings, strong currents and mud make landing and launching an awkward and occasionally risky undertaking. Consider carrying mooring ropes and some form of fender.

The tidal range of the Waveney is 91cm at Somerleyton, and 1.15m to 1.25m at Burgh Castle.

Additional Information

The numerous campsites around Belton are mostly ghastly 'holiday parks', but Rose Farm Touring Park (www.rosefarmtouringpark.co.uk) is more conventional; it's 2km from the Burgh Castle waterfront.

Lowestoft Maritime Museum is a recommended diversion. www.lowestoftmaritimemuseum.org.uk

Variations

There is obviously much more paddling potential within the Broads. A good place from which to explore the wooded northern Broads is Wroxham, at the tidal limit of the River Bure.

An alternative upon leaving Great Yarmouth harbour is to turn north to sample the Pleasure Beach. With three pleasure piers and Britain's oldest working rollercoaster, how can you resist?

Sheringham
to Mundesley 🞑🞑🞑🞑

No. 22 | Grade A | 18km | OS sheet 133

Tidal Ports	Dover and Immingham
Start	△ Sheringham (TG 160 435)
Finish	○ Mundesley (TG 314 367)
HW/LW	HW Cromer is approximately 1 hour after HW Immingham.
Tidal Times	The E going stream begins around 5 hours before HW Dover. The W going stream begins around 1 hour after HW Dover.
Max Rate Sp	Around 2 knots.
Coastguard	Humber MRCC, tel. 01262 672317, VHF weather 0150 UT.

Introduction

In 1900 this area was promoted as, 'The Switzerland of East Anglia'. This was a reference to the Cromer Ridge, East Anglia's highest point (a breath-sapping 92 metres). The ridge is composed of

layers of sands and gravels laid down as terminal moraines by a glacier stretching along what is now the North Sea, around 700,000 years ago. It meets the sea as a line of crumbling 30 metre cliffs, extending between the resorts of Sheringham, Cromer and Mundesley. The Imray Pilot describes these as, *"perhaps the best cliff frontage and profile to be found between Flamborough and Beachy Head"*.

Description

Until the railway arrived in 1887, Sheringham was a busy fishing village with over 200 boats lined up on the beach. Now it's a resort with under twenty boats, but 50,000 kilos of crab are still landed each year. Sheringham was the first place in Britain to experience aerial bombardment; at 8.30pm on 19th January 1915, a Zeppelin airship dropped an incendiary bomb which passed through a house roof without exploding; a plaque in Whitehall Yard marks the spot.

A good place to access the beach is the wooden slipway at Beach Road (TG 160 435) which is used by fishing boats. Drop boats off, and perhaps park at the seafront car park a hundred metres west.

The pebble beach is backed by rocky reefs at LW. Look out for pieces of amber or jet, but note it is illegal to remove them!

On launching, mind your hull on the reefs which then crop up intermittently in the kilometres past Cromer. Even on calm days, they can surprise you with the occasional breaking wave.

The cliffs are made of boulder clay, crumbling and slipping to form mud slicks and tottering spires. They retreat several metres annually, and you'll spot the remains of walls and houses sticking out from their tops, or scattered halfway down. At least one WWII pillbox has travelled the full distance to the base of the cliffs, intact. At some points the cliffs are noticeably more vegetated due to sea defences on the shoreline, hopelessly trying to prevent the inevitable.

Two gaps in the cliffs denote West and East Runton. You might see tractors towing fishing boats to the water from these road heads. Much of the Runton cliffs are topped with endless acres of static caravans, the least inspiring architectural feature imaginable. More engagingly, the cliffs themselves are up to two million years old and regularly reveal fossils. Just past West Runton is the two metre thick 'Cromer Forest Bed', between 400,000 and 700,000 years old. This dark band has yielded remarkable remains from Runton's tropical past, most famously the 'West Runton Elephant', discovered in 1990. This complete (non-fossilised) skeleton was of an extinct species which was twice the weight of modern elephants. These cliffs are an SSSI, but this designation is also due to West Runton's unique rock pools, the only chalk shore between Yorkshire and Kent. At LW Springs, colourful anemones can be seen, with hermit and velvet swimming crabs scuttling for cover.

Cromer was originally a mile inland. During the 18th century, erosion provided it with a seafront and it became a resort. Cromer's name is synonymous with the three million crabs caught locally each year, allegedly the best in Britain. The pleasure pier was built in 1901, with a lifeboat station added on the end. The pier was breached in 1940, lest it aid a Nazi invasion. It was, apparently, then realised that the lifeboat station couldn't be reached, so it was bridged again! The current, huge RNLI shed dates from 1998. Past the pier, look out for the Henry Blogg Museum; Blogg was a lifeboat man who saved 873 lives in 54 years before retiring in 1947. Entry to the museum is free.

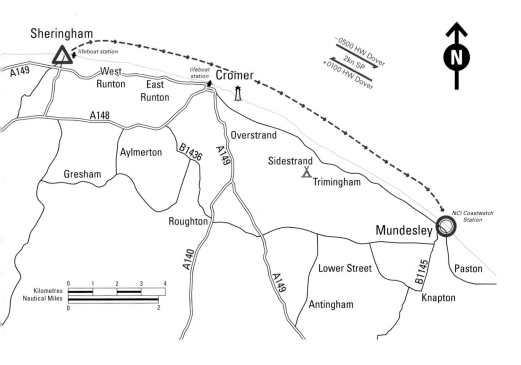

Leaving Cromer, you'll spot Cromer Lighthouse, 84 metres above. It was built half a mile inland in 1866, to replace a lighthouse which had tumbled into the sea. It guides ships past 'The Devil's Throat,' as the local waters are sometimes known.

The remaining coast is empty all the way to Mundesley. These beaches were heavily mined during WWII, and not deemed (reasonably) safe for years afterwards. Little is seen of the villages of Overstrand and Sidestrand from the water, although look out for the 'golf ball' radar of RAF Trimingham, 69 metres above sea level on Beacon Hill. This site tracked enemy shipping and aircraft during WWII and became an Early Warning station during the Cold War. It still features extensive underground bunkers to co-ordinate response to nuclear attack. If you are a foreign spy, please disregard the previous sentence.

Having lost its rail link in 1964, the resort of Mundesley now consists of little more than a few hotels. Land in front of the rows of colourful beach huts and carry up the path to the lookout tower which hosts a tiny Maritime Museum. There is parking directly across the road. Waiting for the shuttle, consider a round of crazy golf ...

Tides and weather

Surf is a possibility, given the reefs and exposure to swells from the north.

Additional information

Pond Farm Campsite (TG 260 392) at Sidestrand is both inexpensive *and* easy-going; few campsites in the region can boast either characteristic.

Be sure to purchase a copy of *Cley the Cromer Crab* from Tourist Information, a children's book by a local author (who happens to be my sister).

Variations

Past Mundesley, the cliffs recede and sand dunes lead to Great Yarmouth. One appeal of this coast is the large seal population, but huge rock groynes have been dumped offshore in places for beach defence. Happisburgh's cliffs have yielded Britain's earliest human traces, from 700,000 years ago.

Blakeney Point ▰▱▱

No. 23 | Grade A | 8 / 12km | OS sheets 132 and 133

Tidal Port	Immingham
Start/Finish	△◯ Blakeney (TG 028 442) or Morston (TG 006 443)
HW/LW	HW at Blakeney Quay is 50 minutes after HW Immingham. HW at Blakeney Point is 3 hours after HW Immingham.
Tidal Times	Off Blakeney Harbour entrance, the E going stream begins 2 hours before local HW.
Max Rate Sp	Rates reach about 3 knots within the Blakeney Harbour, and 5 knots at the entrance.
Coastguard	Humber MRCC, tel. 01262 672317, VHF weather 0150 UT.

Introduction

A vast spit, consisting of 82.5 million cubic feet of shingle is slowly extending westwards from Weybourne. It currently terminates in a succession of smaller finger-like spits at Blakeney Point, creating a natural sheltered harbour. This impressive landform was Norfolk's first nature reserve, and is a place of great natural beauty. Better still, the Point is home to large colonies of common and grey seals. However, whilst this is an idyllic spot for paddlers to explore, it must be noted that some things are very rotten in the state of Denmark ...

125

Description

You have a choice of launching from quays near National Trust car parks at either Morston or Blakeney. Launching from either should be possible for two hours either side of HW. Blakeney barely gets water at some neap tides.

Blakeney is now a silted backwater, but was among Britain's busiest ports during the 13th century. The impressive church of St Nicholas is evidence of former wealth. It was still a busy coasting port into the 18th century. In the early 19th century, £2000 was spent to cut new channels. Eighty-ton ships were still being constructed into the 1840s when the railway network bypassed the port, dealing a fatal blow.

Morston is closer to Blakeney Point, with a popular car park; this is the base for the seal boat tours.

This trip is a simple matter of paddling out through the naturally enclosed harbour to visit the seals basking on multiple spits at the seaward end. A powerful tide race forms around the outermost spit, and if you head out further you will encounter vast expanses of sandy shallows.

The seal colony at the outermost spit is mostly comprised of common seals. The local grey seals produce several hundred pups a year, but haul out on the more exposed beaches of the spit. For obvious reasons, do not paddle too close to the seals, and landing amongst them is certainly *verboten*.

After visiting the seals, a good way to sample the diversity of Blakeney Point's 1300 acre National Nature Reserve is to land at the disused lifeboat house. There are information displays, and paths lead from the salt marsh through the dunes to the outer shingle coast. Purple sea lavender adorns the marshes in summer, whilst the shingle is brightened by colonies of yellow-horned poppy. Stick to the paths, as populations of sandwich terns, common terns, little terns and Arctic terns all scrape out nesting spots hereabouts.

Tides and weather

There are powerful currents within the harbour and a significant tide race past the end of the spit. Large areas of salt marsh are covered and uncovered by spring tides.

The seaward side of Blakeney Spit is dangerous to land upon in swell, with dumping waves.

Additional information

Blakeney Harbour – A Good Practice Guide is a useful leaflet available from the visitor centre at Morston.

Variations

Cley (pronounced 'Cly') Eye (TG 048 453) is a possible launch or finish point to access the spits from seaward. The car park here overlooks Cley Marshes Nature Reserve, run by the Norfolk Wildlife Trust; the reserve's reed beds are home to a huge variety of birds.

It is possible on HW springs to explore upstream as far as Cley next the Sea, where there is an attractive windmill. The Cley Channel takes you through the Blakeney Freshes, an area of freshwater marshes and reeds; look out for marsh harriers.

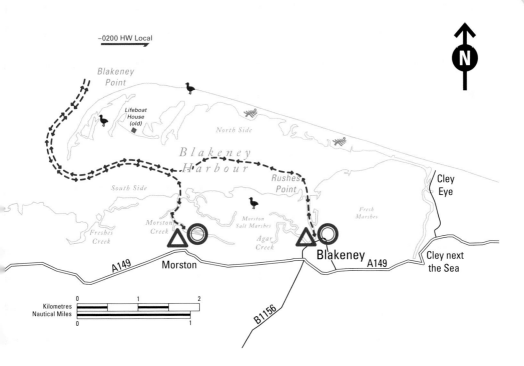

Ecotourism

Three of us were on the water early, visiting the common seals at Blakeney Point. We enjoyed quietly watching the hundreds of basking seals from an appropriate distance. Three or four swam out to the tide race to examine us, following our kayaks. Most continued to snore.

Tour boats began to arrive. We counted a dozen in 90 minutes. Each boat was 8 to 15 metres long, crammed with tourists. Each emitted diesel exhaust fumes and at least one had a loud hailer system with which to impart information to the customers. Many boats exceeded the harbour limit of 5 knots whilst ferrying to and from the colony. Every boat went right up to the seals, practically at point blank range. If you went this close in a kayak they would certainly be disturbed; clearly over the years they have become reconciled to this continual harassment.

This is apparently ecotourism.

Every single tour boat skipper who passed us, warned us away from the seals, claiming that kayaks disturbed or harmed them. They appear to lack a sense of irony thereabouts.

Another seal boat skipper passed us (kilometres from any seals) and – to our astonishment – responded to our wave of greeting by staring at us and repeatedly making throat-slitting gestures, standing behind his customers.

It's difficult to know what advice to give paddlers, faced with the current situation. There are a number of different issues to consider: the sustainability of the seal-watching industry in its current intense form, the ingrained misconceptions about kayakers and seals (which appear to be shared by some National Trust and Nature Reserve officials), and how best to react if challenged (or indeed threatened) whilst paddling. An obvious solution is to paddle at the rare times when the tour boats are not in operation. Either way, give thought to how you might politely respond to, or indeed challenge, misconceptions and hostility. Above all else, be careful not to do anything which might disturb the peace of the Blakeney seals any more than is already happening.

Brancaster Staithe to Wells

No. 24 | Grade B | 18km | OS sheet 132

Tidal Ports	Immingham and Dover
Start	△ Brancaster Staithe (TF 792 443)
Finish	◯ Wells-next-the-Sea (TF 921 438)
HW/LW	HW at Brancaster Staithe and Burnham Overy Staithe is 50 minutes after HW Immingham. HW at the Bar outside Wells is 20 minutes after HW Immingham. HW at Wells Quay is 1 hour after HW Immingham.
Tidal Times	The E going stream begins around 4 hours before HW Dover. The W going stream begins around 1 hour after HW Dover.
Max Rate Sp	Rates reach 2 knots.
Coastguard	Humber MRCC, tel. 01262 672317, VHF weather 0150 UT.

Introduction

This trip is a continuation of the amazing barrier coast outlined in route 25. The introduction to that route notes that everything in this landscape is on a *big* scale; in this adjacent section the

golden beaches, dunes and marshes are *even bigger!* Stunning Scolt Head Island is reason alone to be here.

Description

Launch from Brancaster Staithe within two hours of HW (see Route 25).

Paddlers have the choice of paddling out of Brancaster Harbour to follow the seaward shore of Scolt Head Island, or of taking the shorter inshore route. The outside passage passes the wreck of the *Vina* (see Route 25) and spits covered with cormorants, before turning east to follow the 6km-long lines of high dunes that protect the vast tidal marshes further inland. At the time of writing, the only landmark is a whale carcass. The 'inside passage' is only possible around HW when Norton Creek is passable, but experiencing the marshes makes for an interesting diversion. The village of Burnham Overy Staithe is hidden behind the marshes at the eastern end. Like Brancaster Staithe, there is parking and landing, and launching is possible for two hours either side of HW. Burnham Overy Staithe was a busy port until the 19th century, but silting forced it to finally cease trading in the 1920s. Close by at Burnham Thorpe in 1758 Rector Edmund Nelson's wife gave birth to their sixth child (of eleven), whom they named Horatio. Despite the area's obvious nautical influences, it seems likely that the victor of Trafalgar didn't actually set foot on a ship until he arrived at Chatham in Kent for naval training, aged thirteen.

The 9,768 acres of Holkham National Nature Reserve are part of the Coke family's huge Holkham Estate and encompass the beach, dunes, pine woods (planted to stabilise the dunes in the 1780s) and salt marsh. The sandy expanses of Holkham Bay are among our finest beaches, familiar from films such as *Shakespeare in Love* and *The Eagle Has Landed.* Terns nest in the dunes.

Scolt Head Island

Scolt Head Island is Britain's best example of a barrier island. Despite being 6km long, it is thought to be only around a thousand years old, having formed on a 'skeleton' of glacial shingle deposits. Natural coastal processes are allowed to continue without human intervention, and the island is valued by ecologists for its study potential. High dunes face the open sea, protecting salt marshes and mud flats on the landward side. This is a precious ecosystem, and paddlers should exercise care if landing. Orchids grow among the dunes. At the western end, between April and August, 3,000 pairs of sandwich terns (25% of the UK population), hundreds of pairs of common terns and some little terns nest and breed here. Through the rest of the year, geese rule the marshes; a third of the world population of pink-footed geese, alongside tens of thousands of brent geese (a record 68,000 were seen at once in 2002). This is as true a wilderness as any that this author has experienced in our country.

The western end is a nudist beach, but the vastness of the yellow sands means that you're unlikely to spot them from the sea. Even if you keep on looking really hard.

Wells-next-the-Sea is an exceedingly long way from the sea, unless you arrive around HW. The entrance to The Run leading to Wells is marked by single buoy. A channel (rather shallow at LW) winds south for 2km before reaching beach huts and a lifeboat station. There is a car park here, but it's recommended to continue a similar distance south again to Wells Harbour. Whilst negotiating this peculiar sandscape, you might hear a klaxon announcing the incoming tide.

Wells is a surprisingly bustling harbour, given how cut off from the sea it is. It is home to the *Albatros*, built in 1899 for the Baltic trade, and still delivering cargoes into the 1990s. This distinguished sailing ship now serves as a floating Dutch restaurant, but during WWII the *Albatros* smuggled Jews out of occupied Europe, and delivered arms shipments to the Dutch Resistance, under the Nazis' noses.

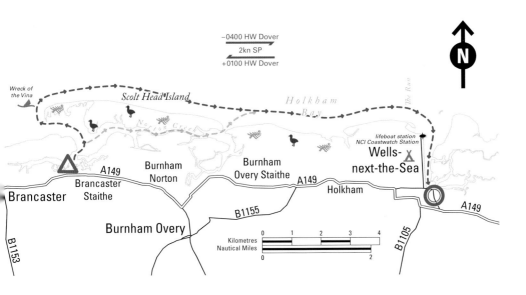

Note the flood heights marked on buildings surrounding the harbour; the 1978 storm surge deposited a 500 ton coaster on the quayside! There is a harbour car park, but this is awkward to access (and may involve a landing fee); perhaps the best spot to come ashore is just down the road past the overhanging warehouse.

Tides and weather

Locating the entrance to Wells Harbour (or any of the inlets) in poor visibility or surf could be a real problem.

Additional information

www.norfolkcoastaonb.org.uk is a useful source of information on this coast's very special ecology and geology.

Pinewoods Holiday Park www.pinewoods.co.uk is at the end of Beach Road in Wells. It caters mainly for caravans, but tents are allowed, and it's near the sea. For some alternative accommodation, consider bed and breakfast on the *Albatros*! (www.albatroswells.co.uk)

Variations

If you arrive at (or off) Wells around HW, consider continuing to Blakeney (TG 028 442), around 13km from the outer entrance to Wells. From here to the shelter of Blakeney Point (see Route 23) is more vast emptiness; 7km of sands extend 2km out from Stiffkey Marshes at LW. The only landmark is the pine trees on East Hills, the dune complex visible north-east of Wells.

Hunstanton
to Brancaster Staithe

No. 25 | Grade B | 17km | OS sheet 132

Tidal Ports	Immingham and Dover
Start	△ Hunstanton (TF 671 408)
Finish	◎ Brancaster Staithe (TF 792 443)
HW/LW	HW at Brancaster Staithe is 50 minutes after HW Immingham.
Tidal Times	The E going stream begins around 4 hours before HW Dover. The W going stream begins around 1 hour after HW Dover.
Max Rate Sp	Rates reach 2 knots.
Coastguard	Humber MRCC, tel. 01262 672317, VHF weather 0150 UT.

Introduction

This coast is special. Paddlers visiting this quiet corner of the Norfolk flatlands get to explore what is probably Europe's finest example of a 'barrier coast', a landform more commonly encountered

in places like Australia or the eastern USA. Mile after mile of startlingly wide beaches, backed by high dunes, front an extensive inner band of salt marshes and creeks. Natural England calls this coast "*a last true wilderness in lowland Britain*". Everything in this landscape is on a *big* scale, and the biggest feature of all is the Norfolk sky. Prepare to feel very small.

Description

Hunstanton ('Sunny Hunny') is the only east coast resort from which the sun can be watched setting into the sea. At LW it looks out upon the Wash's vast sand flats; consider launching around HW! Launching from near the car park at the south end of the town allows viewing of Hunstanton's amazing cliffs. These consist of Norfolk carstone chalk in two sharply contrasting colours; a lower red layer is topped by a thicker layer of dazzling white. Fulmars nest in nooks along the cliffs, whilst the rocky beach below is picked over by turnstones and oystercatchers. Above, on St Edmund's Point, is the Old Lighthouse, the only unmistakeable landmark on this trip. Built in 1844, it was used as a secret naval observation station during WWI, before closure in 1921. It's now a holiday home. Next to the lighthouse are the ruins of 13th century St Edmund's Chapel.

Past the cliffs, the kiss-me-quick paraphernalia of Hunstanton is left behind. Old Hunstanton is a marked contrast, a quiet former fishing village offering an alternative launch point. From the car park (TF 682 425) a trolley will come in handy to cross the beach to the water; you'll pass the RNLI station en route, which utilises a tractor and trailer to launch the lifeboat. Note that the beach could be a kilometre wide at LW.

The Wash

Presumably the Wash isn't high on many paddlers' wish lists. If so, they should re-consider. The shifting sands of this 600km square estuarine bay are home to Europe's largest common seal population (c. 3,000), who are in turn vastly outnumbered by the birds. Year-round, but especially during winter months, waders roost here in staggering numbers; a third of a million birds is common. At HW springs, these waders are squeezed to the fringes of the Wash; 10,000 pecking (or flying) dunlins make for an unforgettable spectacle, regardless of whether bird watching is your thing.

Of course, the Wash deserves respect. Legend has it that wild horses have been outrun by the incoming tide, and the converse scenario could rapidly strand you a long way from solid ground.

Leaving Hunstanton behind, you'll become more aware of the expanses of the Wash as you pass thousands of wading birds thronging the shore. A vast wind farm can be glimpsed far out to sea, but otherwise there are no landmarks until the pine trees of Holme Dunes National Nature Reserve, a kilometre past Gore Point. The reserve gained unexpected fame when 'Seahenge' was discovered in 1998. Norfolk Wildlife Trust runs a visitor centre a short walk inland. They serve tea but there are no toilets, and they may follow you around to ensure you don't disappear behind a bush. Really.

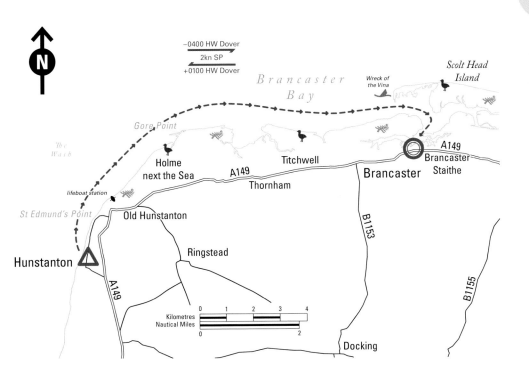

Directly east, a buoyed creek leads inland to Thornham; this was once an important harbour for exporting grain and importing coal, but is now silted. Behind the following dunes are the marshes of RSPB Titchwell. Over 300 species of bird have been recorded here, the most visited bird reserve in the UK. Traces of bunkers and pillboxes on the beach are a reminder that this was a tank firing range during WWII. The remains of two Covenanter tanks are occasionally visible in the intertidal area. Look out for pieces of ancient peat containing seeds and pieces of twig along the strandline; the dark peat reef exposed at LW is a remnant of a 9000-year-old forest.

The lone building next encountered is Royal West Norfolk Golf Club, beside a car park (TF 771 451) and slipway. A road leads inland to the village of Brancaster, best known for the remains of the 4th century Roman shore fort of Branodunum.

The wreck of the *Vina* is visible for much of the tide, guarding the entrance to Brancaster Harbour. This 1,021 ton cargo vessel was built in 1894, but met its end during WWII. It was to be blown up to block Yarmouth harbour entrance if invasion came, but in 1943 was moved to its current location out on the sands for aeroplane target practice. Bombing the *Vina* ascertained that 250lb bombs would be the most effective for use on D-Day, and indeed 523 tons of these were dropped on 6th June 1944.

Directly past the *Vina* are the westernmost spits of the remarkable Scolt Head Island. Brancaster Harbour is the inlet to the south of the island, leading the paddler to Brancaster Staithe, initially hidden away behind the tidal marshes. Incidentally, 'staithe' is Old Norse, referring to a small quay. Smuggling was big at Brancaster Staithe. Dutch smugglers offloaded contraband here from vessels armed with guns, leading to the stationing of a 'preventative boat' in 1710. In 1832, coastguards seized a single boat carrying 5,565 lbs of tobacco and 650 gallons of brandy.

There is parking here, and the village is accessible for landing and launching for around two hours either side of HW. Don't arrive late!

Tides and weather

Fog is common in the Wash.

With the most recognisable features (e.g. towns) hidden from sight kilometres inland, keeping track of your position can be challenging. Locating the entrance to the inlets in poor visibility or surf could be a real problem.

Additional information

The road east to Hunstanton from King's Lynn can grind to a halt in summer; be mindful of this, if you have a tide to catch.

This area is sometimes dubbed 'Chelsea on Sea', a clue to the demographic of visitors; food and accommodation are somewhat upmarket. Unless you wish to pay £130 a night to stay in a yurt, the best campsite is that recommended in route 24. Bunkhouse accommodation is available at Courtyard Farm near Hunstanton (TF 728 400) (www.courtyardfarm.co.uk).

www.norfolkcoastaonb.org.uk is a useful source of information on this coast's very special ecology and geology.

If you somehow fail to spot any seals on this trip, consider a visit to Hunstanton Seal Sanctuary (www.sealsanctuary.co.uk).

Variations

It's strongly recommended to also explore the coast continuing to the east (outlined in route 24); consider combining the two sections into an overnight adventure, or (if you can figure the tides out for the landings!) one long daytrip.

A crossing of the Wash to Skegness would be an attractive challenge, needing to be timed carefully to avoid grounding.

The Seahenge circus

In 1998, local man John Lorimer discovered a seven metre long oval of 55 oak posts in the tidal mud at Holme, encircling an inverted oak trunk (TF 709 453). This Bronze Age ritual site had been uncovered beneath an eroding ancient peat layer. Excavations began, before the site eroded away. The press showed an uncharacteristic interest in prehistoric archaeology, and (inaccurately) dubbed the site 'Seahenge'. An international media circus descended on this National Nature Reserve, damaging the ecology and disrupting local activity. Some New Age types also arrived and attempted to halt the excavation.

After the dust finally settled, studies of the oak remnants revealed that Seahenge was constructed on marshland behind sand dunes in 2049 BC, using exactly fifty axes. Seahenge is now displayed in Kings Lynn Museum. A second, larger monument was subsequently discovered close by, but kept secret! More 'Seahenges' from this ritual landscape will surface as the peat erodes, but if any are currently known of, be assured that no one local will tell you.

The Channel Crossing

Grade C+++ | 100+km

Introduction

Probably the ultimate paddling challenge within this guidebook's region, testing your fitness, navigation and rough water skills to extremes … whilst this epic crossing is as hard as you might imagine, you may be surprised by how many paddlers have successfully completed it.

Description

The first thought when 'channel crossing' is mentioned is of the narrowest part, the c. 35km-wide Dover Strait between Dover and Calais. Whilst this has seen a very large number of kayak crossings, in September 2009 the UK Coastguard and French *Préfet Maritime* jointly banned 'unorthodox' crossings of the strait, i.e. all crossings other than approved channel swims. Google 'Dover Strait unconventional crossings' for more details, but in short, if you want to paddle across the channel, you now have to do it the long way.

This crossing has been completed by various routes, with start/finish points ranging between Brixham and Portsmouth on the English side, and between the Channel Island of Guernsey and

Caen in Normandy on the 'French' side. Probably the longest crossing was that of a military group who in 2014 paddled folding kayaks from Portland Harbour to the D-Day landing beaches, c. 200km! The 'short' routes involve starting and finishing through the powerful tidal waters around Dorset's Portland Race and Normandy's Cap de le Hague (according to the *Imray Pilot*, *"possibly the most stream-lashed headland in the world"*); this is not simply an endurance challenge.

The rules and regulations are maddeningly ambiguous. Portland Coastguard will happily listen to and advise upon your plans. However, French regulations on sea kayaking prohibit offshore paddling, crossing of international borders and paddling at night. Enquiries to French officialdom have generally met polite refusal, re-direction to another agency, or have simply been ignored. We advise that whatever approach you make, you begin a long time in advance! The good news is that no group actually attempting the crossing appears to have encountered any interference … yet. Of course, if you paddle to or from the Channel Islands, none of the French restrictions apply.

Whilst there is no requirement for an escort vessel (another official grey area), this is strongly recommended. An escort vessel offers the chance of evacuation, but perhaps most usefully, it should provide radar capability and visibility. You will be crossing the busy waters of the Traffic Separation Zones. We barely saw any vessels during our attempt, but others tell horror stories of near-misses in fog. Finding an escort vessel requires resourcefulness. There is no ready-prepared commercial fleet as in the Dover Strait; you will need to ask around ports, negotiate price and then hold training sessions so that the crew are appropriately prepared and clear as to their role. More than one group in 2014 hadn't practised evacuation from the water until it actually became necessary.

If you've read this far, you may feel bemused (or conned) to learn that I haven't completed the crossing! I attempted it with a group in 2014, but various factors lead to us retreating onto our escort vessel in mid-channel. Regardless, this was a fantastic challenge which I hope to attempt again in the future. I commend it to all willing to commit to the very considerable time and effort needed to be fully physically and logistically prepared. When the dawn rises over empty seas stretching to all horizons, you'll know it was worth it.

Additional information

French authorities:

CROSS/ Centre Regional Operational De Surveillance et de Sauvetage Jobourg

DIRM/ La Direction Interrégionale de la Mer Manche est-mer du Nord

Préfet Maritime de la Manche et de la Mer du Nord

The chapter Sea Kayaking in France and www.brittany-kayaking.com have advice on interpreting French sea kayaking regulations.

How many paddlers have achieved this? The figure seems to be in the low dozens; information can be gleaned from www.ukriversguidebook.co.uk and www.performanceseakayak.co.uk.

A successful crossing

The 'How About Alderney' team crossed from Swanage to Alderney in 2014.

"I am very proud of the team. It took 19 hours of solid paddling. The last two hours were in lumpy seas in the biggest tide race in the world. We had to paddle as fast as we could to get on the right line for Braye Harbour. A tad one way and we would have missed the south of the island and a tad the other and we would have missed the north of the island. We had an amazing surf down huge waves right into Braye Harbour to a reception of boats cheering our arrival. It was like running a marathon to find you had a 400m hurdle race at the end! What a buzz!

An awesome and very challenging experience built on good training and trip planning. Most of the team were relative novices before starting training, testament to their determination and commitment. An RNLI chief gave us a 40% chance at the outset. I can only say that ordinary people can achieve extraordinary things when they put their mind to it."

Ian Smith

Telegraph Bay Alderney | Derek Hairon

The Channel Islands

When you arrive in the Channel Islands things look British. The cars drive on the left, people speak English, and all the usual high street retailers are in the towns. It all looks rather familiar. Gradually you notice that things are not quite the same. The currency is sterling but there is a watermark of a cow instead of the Queen on Jersey bank notes. Even more puzzling, the notes are different between the two largest islands. Car number plates carry long numbers and drivers seem to spend most of their time stopping to let people out of minor roads or playing, *"No no, after you"* at mini roundabouts called 'filter in turn'. The more you look, the more you realise that you are no longer in Britain.

Charts and maps

The Channel Islands are outside the British Ordnance Survey Grid, so there are a few changes to how to use this section of the book.

Jersey and Guernsey each produce their own maps. Where the OS sheet number would normally appear there will either be a 'J' or a 'G'.

J = Jersey 1:25,000 Official Leisure Map
G = Bailiwick of Guernsey 1:15,000/1:10,000 States of Guernsey Official Map

These are followed by the numbers of whichever of the following Admiralty Charts is needed:

60 Alderney and the Casquets
808 East Guernsey, Herm and Sark
1136 Jersey north coast
1137 Approaches to St Helier
1138 Jersey east coast
3654 Guernsey, Herm and Sark
3655 Jersey and adjacent coast of France
3656 Plateau des Minquiers and adjacent coast of France

The Admiralty publication *NP 264 Admiralty Tidal Stream Atlas – Channel Islands & adjacent coast of France* is helpful for planning most trips and essential for the open crossings.

Where French charts are useful they are listed under 'Additional Information'.

Start, finish, and other positions are given using the Jersey or Guernsey grid where possible, as it will be easier to find your way by road there using the local maps. Where the positions are not on these maps, or charts are more likely to be used, they will be given as latitude and longitude.

Language and place names

All the islands have their own languages based on ancient Norman French. Today you will be lucky to hear it spoken except on Sark or perhaps at a traditional event. However, there is a revival of interest in the teaching of both Jèrriais and Guernésiais.

Expect some fun and games, both when pronouncing names, and also working out which place is which. For example, ask directions to La Grande Route des Mielles and you will probably get a blank look, and then a flash of recognition, *"You mean the five mile road?"* Leave your car parked next to a sign saying, *"Ces premises sont terre à l'amende,"* in Guernsey, and you can expect to face a parking fine. There are variations both in name and spellings between the charts, maps and texts both within and between the islands.

Independence

Though the Channel Islands are geographically much closer to France than the UK, they are loyal to the British crown. In 1204 King John lost Normandy to the growing French kingdom. Jersey and Guernsey remained with the English crown. To all extents the islands were Norman and with Normandy visible on the horizon, it would have been easy for the islands to switch sides and join France. The geographical position of the Channel Islands made them a vital strategic asset. To keep the islands on the English side, King John poured huge amounts of money into their defence, and granted the islands a greater degree of independence. The islands owe allegiance to the Duke of Normandy – the English crown – not parliament. When laws are passed in either Jersey or Guernsey they must be ratified by the crown. Today this requires the approval of the Privy Council. Norman customary law forms the basis of the islands' constitutions.

Both Jersey and Guernsey are largely independent from the UK, and each set their own taxes (Sark has no income tax). Laws are based on Norman customary law. Do not assume the same legal principles or laws apply even between the islands, let alone with 'the mainland', which is how most locals refer to the UK.

Alderney and Sark are self-governing but are part of the Bailiwick of Guernsey. Both islands look to Guernsey to deal with health and other affairs, while retaining their independence. Sark remains more rooted to feudal times. It is only since 2008 that an island-wide mandate was implemented, and women only gained equal property rights in 1998. Until then a woman living on Sark could only inherit property if there were no male heirs. Sark however is changing, as the island copes with the demand to invigorate the economy and move, albeit grudgingly, into another century. Which century that might be is sometimes open to debate.

Health

In Jersey a reciprocal health agreement exists with the UK. This covers emergency treatment and ambulance travel, but not the costs of repatriation if a UK resident is taken ill in Jersey and cannot return on a conventional flight or ferry. Within the Bailiwick of Guernsey there is currently no reciprocal agreement with the UK, and you will be charged for medical treatment within a hospital, for the ambulance, and repatriation.

A travel insurance policy is advised. Ensure you have declared you are going sea kayaking as some policies consider this a risk activity.

The Channel Islands today

Jersey and Guernsey have developed in slightly different ways. Speak to a Guernseyman and he will usually describe Jersey as 'more commercial', while Jerseymen describe Guernsey as 'quieter' n the 19th century Guernsey developed a strong quarrying industry, while Jersey became a major player in the cod trade with Canada.

In the 20th century both islands benefited from being at the end of the line for the railway companies which operated the mail boats, and the islands became 'exotic' tourist destinations. By the 1960s Jersey was advertising itself as 'Britain's South Sea island' which fooled some visitors. I remember one couple arriving with just shorts and T-shirts, having thought they were heading to a Caribbean-like climate.

The arrival of long haul flights to warmer destinations in the 1990s resulted in the decline of tourism. On both Jersey and Guernsey agriculture has declined due to lower cost produce from southern Europe. There remains plenty of fresh, local produce sold on the islands, and it is still great fun to buy from roadside or 'hedge veg' stalls where you pay by popping your money into an honesty box. Buy local to support the islands' farmers and also to enjoy high quality and fewer 'food miles'.

The finance industry is the mainstay of the islands' economies though there is an increasing attempt to diversify by attracting new technologies. One result is that Guernsey has enormous internet capacity, and Jersey is installing ultra-fast fibre optic cabling island-wide as part of a digital strategy.

All the Channel Islands have a level of infrastructure which is considerably more developed than many towns with a similar-sized population in the UK. You will be spoilt for choice when deciding where to stay and eat, and for activities to do on the larger islands.

For the sea kayaker this means that the islands are ideal places to enjoy a kayaking trip and have a holiday. Not everyone wants to paddle every day. On both the main islands you can kayak in the morning, visit the many historical sites in the afternoon, chill out at your hotel, campsite, hostel or bed and breakfast, and then head into town for a meal or evening out.

Weather

Think south coast of England but a bit warmer. Sea temperatures can reach 19°C by September, and on a rising tide some bays may be even warmer.

Wind and swell can be a problem, but tend to move through rapidly. Many paddlers are surprised at how quickly conditions improve. Conversely, conditions can deteriorate quickly, so it is important to check local forecasts as the Bay of Mont St Michel (where the islands lie) generates its own micro weather systems. Jersey Met (www.gov.je/weather/Pages/Jersey-Forecast.aspx) provides Channel Island-wide forecasts and is the most reliable source. Jersey Met has recorded land and sea forecasts for both Jersey and Guernsey, as well as offering a premium rate direct line to the duty forecaster, tel. 090 5807 7777.

Tides

The tides are big, and around Jersey the spring tides will reach 12.5m. Think of the islands as being like rocks in a river which just happens to change direction twice a day. This means you may encounter overfalls (rapids), eddies, and river-like conditions off some headlands and coasts. Just remember the other riverbank may be 18km or more away. Paddle on a big tide and your trip will feel like you have stepped onto a travelator. One huge plus of the large tidal range is that the coastline is constantly changing. If you return on the same route, it will look completely different as rocks, reefs and sand appear that were not there at high water.

Expect to encounter tidal streams of 3 knots or more off most headlands around the islands especially during the third hours of the tide. Though this can appear daunting, providing you refer to the *Admiralty Tidal Stream Atlas – Channel Islands and adjacent coasts of France (NP 264)*, and use the trip guides, you will find it possible to paddle on even the largest tides. Modern editions of the *Admiralty Sailing Directions* (also referred to as *Pilots*) contain considerable information on Channel Island tidal streams though pre-1960 editions have more information. St Helier is the Standard Port for the Channel Islands and, because of the large tide range, only this port is used to reduce confusion.

Where to stay

Accommodation, ranging from campsites and hostels to five star luxury hotels can be found on all the islands, though the largest selection is obviously on Guernsey and Jersey. Wild camping is officially discouraged on the beaches and outside of designated campsites.

The use of caravans and motorhomes on Jersey requires an entry permit which is issued when you book with a local campsite. On Guernsey, caravans are not permitted, and motorhomes are limited to a maximum of fourteen. As in Jersey, an entry permit is issued when you book with a Guernsey campsite.

Eating and drinking

When it comes to eating and drinking the choice on all the islands is impressive. Even the smallest islands have excellent restaurants. Locally caught fish and shellfish is a delicacy, along with fresh local produce. The islands also have a beach and water sports culture, so you will find many small beach cafés producing excellent food.

Things to do

"You can do it here," might well be the answer to most questions about what to do in the Channel Islands. If you enjoy water sports, the islands are a Mecca. There is a sophisticated, cultural scene and no shortage of heritage sites.

Distances are small, so it is easy to pack a lot of activities into your stay. If the conditions are not good on one section of coast, it is easy to switch venues.

Getting to the islands

Regular high speed and conventional ferries operated by Condor Ferries depart from Poole and Portsmouth. The option of not taking a vehicle, and wheeling your kayak onto the ferry, is currently not possible but this may change. The islands are served by regular air services from many regional airports, so within a couple hours of leaving home you can be out kayaking.

The main islands have a few kayak outfitters, though they may want to see your paddle skills on a trip before letting you hire a kayak for an unguided trip.

Inter-island travel

Inter-island travel is not as easy as you might expect. Ferries between Jersey and Guernsey are often only twice a day. Sark and Alderney are served by small passenger ferries which make the transport of kayaks difficult unless you send them as freight.

Regular flights operate between Jersey and Guernsey, and via Guernsey to Alderney. There is no airport on Sark.

Driving

Speed limits vary between Jersey and Guernsey (40mph and in places much less in Jersey, 35mph or less in Guernsey), and roadside checks are strictly enforced. If you are involved in an accident, you must not move your vehicle until the police – or in Jersey, the Honorary Police – have been called.

Roads are narrow, so it helps to be good at reversing. Allow time to negotiate the labyrinth of single-track lanes and expect to get lost.

Parking at some of the small bays can be tricky, especially at weekends in summer. A kayak trolley is a useful aid to avoid long walks from car parks to the sea. Tides rise very quickly (up to 8cm per minute), and every year the local newspapers feature a couple of cars being submerged on slipways.

Tourist information

The island tourist information offices have a huge range of information and should be your first source of reference when planning to visit the islands.

Jersey: www.jersey.com
Guernsey: www.visitguernsey.com
Alderney: www.visitalderney.com
Sark: www.sark.co.uk
Herm: www.herm.com
Chausey: www.ville-granville.fr

Coastguard

Both Jersey and Guernsey Coastguards are independent entities but work together alongside their French and UK counterparts, and operate in similar ways to the UK Coastguard.

Search And Rescue (SAR) services in the Channel Islands are extensive. Jersey has one all-weather lifeboat and two Atlantic class inshore boats, as well as a smaller fire service inshore rescue boat. Guernsey has one RNLI all-weather boat as well as the St John's Ambulance and Rescue Service marine ambulance, and two inshore rescue boats. Alderney has an all-weather boat and an inshore rescue boat. In addition, the islands can call upon French Coastguard resources, and helicopters from both France and the UK. There is also the Channel Islands Air Search Islander aircraft and radio direction-finding equipment based on Jersey.

It is advisable to let the coastguard know your passage plan, either by marine VHF or mobile phone, especially if you are undertaking an offshore trip. The voluntary CG66 forms used to record details of your craft by the UK Coastguard cannot be accessed by Channel Island Coastguards, so be prepared to supply more information.

In Jersey waters, locally-owned kayaks and other human powered craft must by law have the contact details of the owner displayed on the kayak. It is good practice for visiting kayakers to also have a contact name and number on their kayak. Jersey Coastguard has introduced the Coastguard Safety Identification Scheme (CSIS; www.portofjersey.je/JerseyCoastguard/Safety/Pages/RegisterYourCraft.aspx) to encourage local kayakers and watersports enthusiasts to register their craft for free. Each craft registered receives a sticker and registration number, to help identify and locate the owners and, if necessary, initiate a search and rescue response. Visiting kayakers are exempt from registration, if only staying for a short time.

VHF marine radio coverage is very good throughout the Channel Islands, though beneath cliffs reception may be poor.

Mobile phones

Mobile phone coverage is excellent both around the coastline and offshore in the Channel Islands. Should you need to call for help with a mobile phone dial 112, as this can also be picked up by French emergency services.

Local networks are not the same as those in the UK or France, and some UK network contracts may not work very well in the Channel Islands. You may also be on roaming call and data charges, so it may be worth buying a local pay as you go mobile SIM card, especially if you plan to access web-based weather forecasts.

St Helier to Gorey

| No. 1 | Grade B | 14km (7.5nm) | OS sheet J | 3655, 1137 |

Tidal Port	St Helier
Start	△ Old lifeboat station, St Helier Harbour (649 477)
Finish	○ Gorey Harbour (714 503)
HW/LW	HW St Helier is 4 hours 55 minutes before HW Dover.
Tidal Times	Along the SE coast the E going stream starts 5 hours after HW St Helier, and the W going stream starts about 1 hour before HW St Helier.
	Inshore on the east coast the south going stream ends around 3 hours before high water once the reefs between Seymour Tower and the shore have covered.
	About 1.8km (1NM) south-east of La Rocque Harbour the streams split at about high water. The N going stream heads up the east coast, while a W going stream runs along the south-east coast. Close inshore around St Clements Bay is a weak easterly stream which flows for most of the time.
Max Rate Sp	4 knots.
Coastguard	Jersey, tel. 01534 447705 Channel 82. Routine port traffic St Helier Channel 14.

Introduction

The intertidal zone of the south-east coast is remarkable. Select the right tide and this is literally a paddle on the seabed. Walkers often refer to the area as like a 'moonwalk' but this does not do

149

justice to the fantastic diversity of marine life you encounter. Since the year 2000 the area has been an internationally designated Ramsar wetlands site.

During the third hours the rise and fall is around 7.5cm per minute. Rocks and reefs disappear or seem to rise out of the water as the tide stream sweeps you through the gullies and gutters of this rocky area. Expect to be up to almost 3km offshore if paddling at low tide.

Description

Start at the old lifeboat station in St Helier Harbour; if it is a very low tide expect to wade through some harbour mud. Until 1788 the principal harbour for Jersey was at St Aubin, and most of the land south of St Helier Church is reclaimed. There is little room for large ships to manoeuvre in the harbour approaches, so ensure you observe the Port Control signals and monitor St Helier VTS Channel 14.

On the north side of the Dog's Nest (Le Nic ès Tchians), when it's a low tide below 1m, the wreck of the SS *Diamant* (sunk 1942) is visible. This reef can be exposed to swell along with the Hinguette rocks to the south-east of the Dog's Nest. Both reefs have resulted in many shipwrecks.

Aim 0.5km south of Green Island (3km distant) for La Sambue channel. Initially this may look like a mass of rocks, but you soon notice routes appearing, and your speed will increase as the tide rushes between the reefs. From now on you will be going with the flow as if on a travelator. This is when ferry glides and some river techniques come in handy.

After Green Island you have a choice. Either head offshore to Ic-Ho tower (a coastal defence tower built in 1811), or stay about 0.5km from shore and slip between rocks as the ocean rushes down the gullies. If you end up in a dead-end, wait a bit and the tide will quickly rise over the rocks as you head towards Le Havre de la Rocque (known locally as La Rocque Harbour).

As you cross St Clement's Bay, slipping down gullies like a sea bass going with the flow, observe the seabed and the different types of seaweeds; most are edible (though some don't taste very nice). The deep water Laminaria releases an iodine-like smell; there are records of Laminaria being used as a dressing for wounds during the Nazi occupation. It can also be used as a form of vegetable bouillon, but has a high iodine content. Alternatively, you can stop and search for clams, oysters, scallops, razors and even lobster, as this area is famous for low water fishing.

Approaching La Rocque Harbour aim for La Cônière rock (white), as this sets you up for the gullies running between Seymour Tower and the shore.

The safety beacon (a metal tower 0.75km east of the harbour) is a good target, as the water will be flowing north through dozens of small channels by now. Take care if you climb the tower for the view, as the tide rapidly covers the shingle spit. A detour out to Seymour Tower is worth doing before the tide gets too high to land on the sandy beach beneath the tower.

Seymour Tower was built in 1782 and unlike other Jersey towers it is square. You can stay over a tide on the parapet. The inside of the tower, which is fitted out with bunk beds and cooking facilities, must be booked in advance with Jersey Heritage or Jersey Walk Adventures (www.jerseywalkadventures.co.uk).

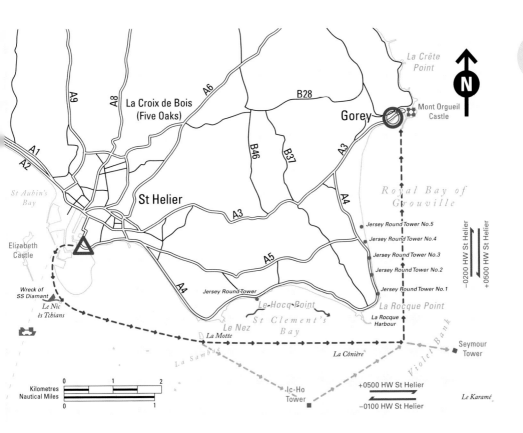

If you have time (or opted for the La Rocque launch) paddle out to Karamé and La Conchiée beacons, where you may spot a seal or a pod of dolphins. This is some 4km offshore and tide streams run fast. With an offshore wind this area can become challenging. The area is also known as the Violet Bank, and it is suggested this name originates from the violet colour of the Lithothamnion algae growing on the rocks.

From Seymour and La Rocque it is a straight run across La Baie du Vieux Château (Grouville Bay) to the busy harbour village of Gorey with plenty of places to eat and enjoy a pint.

Variations

This trip need not involve a car shuttle if you wish to paddle the entire route, or just want to spend more time exploring the Violet Bank and towers. It is possible to catch the bus back to St Helier.

Launching from Green Island, Le Hocq or La Rocque Harbour are excellent options with more time to explore.

At Green Island, head past the boats towards a large lagoon which is the remains of a 19th century oyster farm.

It is a slightly longer walk down the gully at Le Hocq (though it does have a pub nearby).

La Rocque Harbour is also a few hundred metre walk, or trolley, down the gully to get afloat below half tide. This is a good starting point to use, if you plan to spend a day exploring the area. Depart about three hours after high water, and head out to the distant rocks and sand banks which you can explore on foot and by kayak. About two hours after low water you can then begin to drift back inshore. This is best undertaken in good visibility.

Invasion

La Rocque Harbour was the site of the French invasion led by Baron de Rullecourt on the 5th January 1781. The islanders and British garrison wrongly assumed the treacherous reefs of the Violet Bank would stop any landing. What had not been considered was that de Rullecourt had local knowledge from a dodgy character named Pierre Journeaux. At midnight, 26 boats sailed up the main gulley, the nine militiamen on guard had been celebrating Twelfth Night so they were in no fit state to detect the 700 men. The French attack was finally defeated after a brief battle in St Helier, during which de Rullecourt was killed.

A more challenging option is to head 8.5km offshore to the Grande and Petite Anquette reefs which will usually involve a large ferry glide and the ability to navigate with some accuracy. Landing is often tricky on this great offshore experience and about an hour after low tide you may even spot a pod of dolphins.

Tides and weather

You'll need to get your timings right especially on a falling tide, unless you enjoy hauling your kayak half a mile ashore. A trolley is a good backup aid.

The area is best explored if you leave St Helier at low tide; you can leave from other spots a little later. Low tides below 1m are best, but any low tide will give you a remarkable paddle.

The south-east coast is low lying so offshore winds can be a problem. If you opt for Ic-Ho and Seymour Tower you will be 1.8km (1NM) offshore with more exposure to any wind. The inshore gullies give some protection from winds around half tide.

Swell is most likely between the Dog's Nest and Les Marguérittes (near Ic-Ho) from the west-south-west. Closer inshore the outer rocks and reefs break up the swell.

If planning a circular route, leave St Helier about 1.5 hours before high water. Aim to return once you reach Seymour Tower, staying 1.5km offshore.

Additional information

Jersey Walk Adventures, tel. 07797 853033 (www.jerseywalkadventures.co.uk) organises guided walks on the seabed as well as overnight stays in Seymour Tower and edible seaweed, low water fishing and oyster walks. Many paddlers find it a strange experience to walk across spots that only a few hours before were covered by six metres of ocean.

The Seymour Inn, opposite Seymour slip, serves local oysters and mussels from the shellfish farms in the bay.

Gorey to Bonne Nuit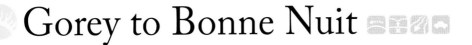

No. 2	**Grade B**	**14km (12NM)**	**OS sheet J**	**3655, 1138**

Tidal Port	St Helier
Start	△ Gorey Harbour (714 503)
Finish	○ Bonne Nuit (641 561)
HW/LW	HW St Helier is 4 hours and 55 minutes before HW Dover.
Tidal Times	From Gorey to St Catherine the N going stream starts 3 hours before HW St Helier, and the SSE going stream starts 5 hours after HW St Helier.
	Along the north coast the inshore E going stream starts about 5 hours after HW St Helier, and the W going stream starts 1 hour before HW St Helier. Offshore streams start a little later.
Max Rate Sp	5-6 knots off headlands. 2-3 knots across bays.
Coastguard	Jersey, tel. 01534 447705 Channel 82. VHF reception may be poor in St Catherine's Bay.

Introduction

The north-east coast changes in geological formation as the low lying coastal area of the south-east disappears behind the higher ground of Mont Orgueil Castle. As you head past St Catherine towards Bonne Nuit expect to encounter a few headlands with faster tides and fewer landing

155

spots. While it is easy to opt to paddle across the bays of Rozel and Bouley, it is worth taking a bit more time to explore the coastline, to go caving, and perhaps see a shipwreck.

Description

Leaving Gorey Harbour there is usually a good north-going stream running between Le Nez du Château rocks just beneath Mont Orgueil castle. If Gorey Harbour is dry, Anneport 1km north is an alternative.

Rather than paddle directly to St Catherine's breakwater, follow the coastline which is best paddled around high tide. L'Archirondel Bay marks the start of the Rozel conglomerate, a product of volcanic eruptions and mudslides millions of years ago.

The harbour that never was

Construction of St Catherine's breakwater in 1847 was a disaster, a product of British panic over French dock improvements along the channel which resulted in a rush of British fortification being constructed between 1844 and 1846. At St Catherine there was not enough water depth to contain the fleet, the Navy was not keen on needing a harbour so near to the French coast, there were huge cost over-runs, and it was badly placed to intercept a southerly attack due to the shallow waters of the nearby Violet Bank. The cost of this governmental failure was an astronomical £234,000 (around £127 million in today's money), before the project was abandoned as worthless.

If you like seal launching your kayak, the beach beside L'Archirondel Tower is ideal. The tower is built upon the second arm of what was to have been a large naval harbour for the British fleet.

Above La Mare slip (100m north of the RNLI inshore rescue boat station) is a small white house. During the construction of the breakwater in 1847 this was used as the hospital.

The slip at St Catherine is a handy take-out, but if there is a southerly wind, or swell, landing can be very awkward, and it may be better to land in Belval to the south of the slip, where there is a small slipway and a car park.

On very low tides Le Grand Fara Beacon (1.5km south-east of the slip) is worth exploring – you might find a few scallops. The reef is covered with the slow-growing and fragile, coral-like fragments of purple Maërl. Many areas of the seabed around Jersey are now off-limits to scallop dredging as a result of the discovery of Maërl.

Unless you are in a rush, explore the usually deserted Fliquet, La Coupe and Scez (or Saie) Bays as you head to Rozel, a small harbour which has long been the departure point for fishermen (and smugglers) heading for Les Écréhous. At low tide a ring of stones is revealed in Scez Bay, and some suggest this may be an ancient fish trap or oyster bed.

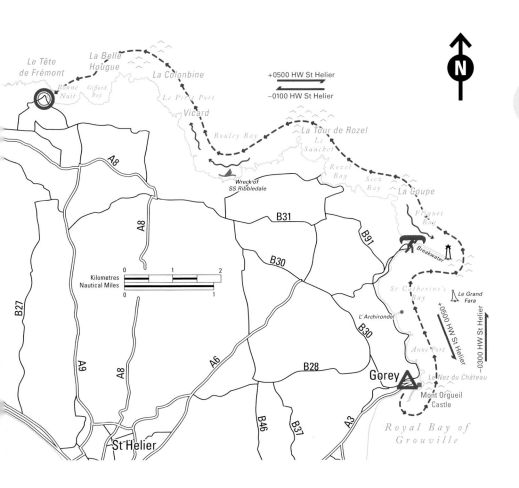

From Rozel to Bouley Bay the inshore route has many tiny coves which are worth exploring. Look out for the table top-like Nazi gun battery at Le Nez du Guet, and a nearby rock that resembles a teddy bear. There are also rock gardens of varying technical levels.

Beneath La Tête des Hougues is the wreck of the SS *Ribbledale* which ran aground during a storm in 1926, and is visible at low tide; all that remains is the engine and boiler. Nearby is a large cave that you can either paddle or walk into depending on the tide. To the right of the cave is a wave-eroded platform from when sea levels were 8m above present levels.

Bouley Bay harbour is worth exploring. There are a couple small caves, a waterfall and blowhole to the east of the beach. An old ship's anchor is visible at low tide about 30m north of the slip.

Le Petit Port, or Égypte, is a tiny cove with an ancient guardhouse that is maintained by the Jersey Canoe Club as bothy-style accommodation. This can be hired by visiting sea kayakers.

Between La Colonbine and La Belle Hougue there is some fascinating geology. A narrow gully running west to east across Les Ruaux can often be paddled. La Belle Hougue Caves 1 and 2 are in the gully below the viewing point, and in very calm conditions it is occasionally possible to land on the rocks to explore the caves. Inside the linked caves is a raised beach 8m above current sea level. Excavations found remains of an insular dwarf race of deer which evolved over 10,000 years as a result of the island's isolation.

Entering Bonne Nuit Bay, Le Chaval Guillaume rocks formed part of the St John's Day celebrations (24th June) when fishermen rowed people around the rocks to bring good luck.

The harbour is the finish point for the annual Sark to Jersey rowing race. The single-seat rowing boats aim to make the 28km (15NM) crossing in around two hours.

Variations

If conditions off the end of St Catherine's breakwater are too challenging, it is only a short portage from the slip over the breakwater into Fliquet Bay.

It is easy to shorten the trip at St Catherine, Rozel or Bouley Bays. All bays have a regular bus service in summer that makes it possible to rejoin a vehicle.

Tides and weather

Tide streams in La Baie du Vieux Château tend to be weak close inshore, and you may encounter an eddy which in part may be caused by the effects of the shallows known as the Middle Bank.

There is a clockwise eddy in St Catherine's Bay throughout the south-going stream.

The end of St Catherine's breakwater has fast water especially during the north-going stream. An easterly stream runs along the south side of the breakwater and meets the north-going stream to create some turbulent water.

In Fliquet Bay there is an anticlockwise eddy, and if heading along the north coast, it is therefore best to stay off-shore and well clear of La Coupe.

La Coupe and Les Brayes rocks produce overfalls. If there is a westerly swell and wind, this headland gives a good indication of how things will be further along the coast and especially off the headlands.

La Tour de Rozel (or White Rock) is a well-known tide race and play spot. The tide stream is best for the kayaker who wants to stop and practise their skills on a rising high tide of about

9-10m from low water to four hours before HW. Larger tide ranges rapidly become difficult to paddle against. The stream is fastest (best for moving water kayaking) on the rising tide (east-going stream). This can be a rough spot when there is wind against tide. Le Sauchet to the east and Le Morté Bay (west) are both out of the main stream, and are good spots to assess conditions before deciding to paddle around the headland.

From La Tour de Rozel to Bonne Nuit the swell is often more pronounced on the rising tide and often starts to decrease about one hour before HW St Helier as the westerly stream develops. As a guide, if it is big at La Tour, it will be even bigger off La Belle Hougue point, and subsequent headlands will be even more exposed.

A clockwise eddy runs around Bouley Bay from Oyster Rocks to Vicard Point for most of the east-going stream.

Expect fast-moving water and overfalls from La Colonbine to La Belle Hougue Point during the third hours of the flood and ebb. Paddling against the stream is difficult unless you are prepared to handrail the coast and use every tiny promontory as a breakout. This is a great place to practise ferry glides, edging and moving water skills, as the stream weakens beyond the headlands.

Additional information

The Jersey Canoe Club boathouse is at St Catherine and the club also maintains the old guard-house at Égypte. It is worth contacting them for advice and paddle trips (www.jcc.org.je).

St Catherine to Les Écréhous ©🔄▨

No. 3 | **Grade C** | **9.2km (5NM)** | **OS sheet J** | **3655**

Tidal Port	St Helier
Start	△ St Catherine (715 531) (49° 13′ 28N 02° 01′ 08W)
Finish	⃝ Marmotière, Les Écréhous (49.283°N, 01.933°W)
HW/LW	HW St Helier is 4 hours 55 minutes before HW Dover.
Tidal Times	A NW going stream begins at 1 hour 40 minutes before HW St Helier. The SE stream starts at 4 hours 50 minutes after HW St Helier.
Max Rate Sp	6 knots.
Coastguard	Jersey, tel. 01534 447705 Channel 82.
	French Coastguard CROSS Jobourg Channel 70 (if heading into French waters).

Introduction

Les Écréhous is a classic destination, and for many visiting paddlers this is the highlight of a visit to the Channel Islands. Local paddlers are drawn back again and again, in some cases over 100

times. Their collections of Les Écréhous pebbles create visual diaries which sit on window sill and desks as reminders of day trips and overnight stays, magically calm days with dolphins and gannets for company, or challenging and difficult paddles through tide races and overfalls.

Perhaps it is the Caribbean-clear waters, the sense of remoteness as you sit on the bench looking towards Jersey, or just the opportunity to reach, by physical effort, a place that has a charm and beauty that is difficult to describe. Les Écréhous is a remarkable and beautiful place which draws people offshore.

Description

Local paddlers may treat this as a regular trip, but probe a little more and you soon discover that the 9.5km (5NM) crossing is not to be treated lightly. Many recount difficult landings, huge ferry glides and even missing Les Écréhous due to the fast tides. This is one route where you need to be confident in your offshore navigation when streams can reach over 5 knots.

Departure points depend on the time and height of the tide (see Variations); St Catherine is a popular starting point at about one hour before high water, with good parking.

Historically fishermen sailed from Rozel to Les Écréhous to fish and quarry the reef. Although the stone was not high quality it had one big advantage; it was free, and many walls around Rozel contain Les Écréhous granite. As a result the islets are in the parish of St Martin, and every year parish officials visit to assess the rates. Just what the hut owners get for their money is debatable as the refuse collection and street lighting is non-existent, but the hut owners can at least call upon the services of the parish honorary police – as they did when French demonstrators landed to protest over fishing rights in 1994.

Expect fast water and overfalls off St Catherine's breakwater (especially at spring tides); for some paddlers this comes as a shock, but it usually calms down after 300m, though you may encounter a beam swell. The beam swell may cause problems and a reduction in speed if paddlers are not used to this. Some may also find it unsettling to be heading on a compass bearing which, having allowed for the tidal stream, seems to be sending you far from the reef; just have patience and trust your navigation and compass (assuming you have got the set and drift right).

Heading offshore there are plenty of good transits along the north coast of Jersey to estimate your drift and position. Avoid aiming too soon towards Marmotière because the tide streams flow strongly north-west towards Grande Rousse as you approach the reef; if you end up at Grande Rousse, you face some big ferry glides and eddy hops to Marmotière.

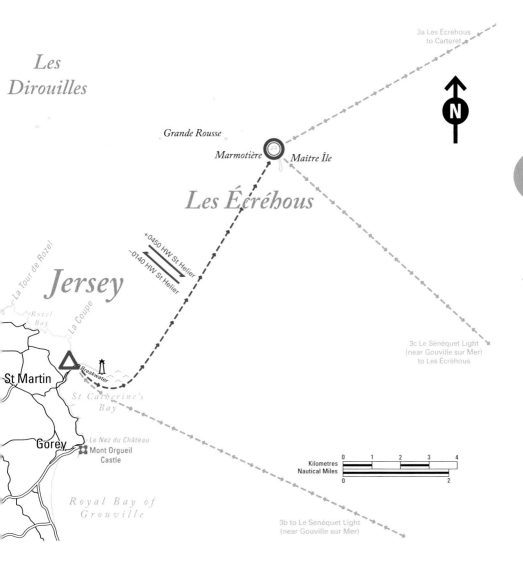

The small jetty at Marmotière is a good landing spot. Tide streams increase in the sound to the north of the islets. River-like conditions occur between the rocks and down the main sound on the ebb tide, and off the south-east point of Marmotière. At high tide La Taille (the steep shingle bank) covers with standing waves, while at low tide a 50 degree slope on the northern side is revealed. This was formed by the fast currents in the sound.

Today Les Écréhous comprises of three islets with 28 former fishermen's cabins and holiday huts built in a higgledy-piggledy fashion on the rocks; their bright colours and small size distort your sense of size and perspective.

Make time to explore the reef either by foot or kayak. The large lagoons have crystal clear water and an abundance of marine life. Seals are often seen in the main lagoon, with the main seal colony near Grande Galère. Try to keep clear of this area as the wildlife needs some space especially on summer weekends when the reef gets very busy.

Variations

On spring tides it may be prudent to depart from Gorey, or even La Rocque, due to the strength of the streams, especially once you near the reefs.

The return trip is usually easier as Jersey is a big target, and many will depart around low water. On spring tides, if you miss St Catherine, you can continue south to Gorey, and then take the inshore eddy back to St Catherine. If crossing during the north-west stream, Rozel or Bouley Bay are options to consider.

History

The Scandinavian origin of the name Les Écréhous is usually explained as deriving from two Scandinavian words sker-holm, meaning 'rocky islets'. A recent interpretation is that it is a derivation of skerjaholm or 'island distinguished by adjacent skerries'. If Les Écréhous was once a single island, it may explain why a Cistercian priory was built sometime in the late 13th century. The first mention of the priory is in 1309, and the ruins can be seen at the southern tip of Maître Île. Between March and July this islet is a very smelly nesting site so landing is not recommended.

Maître Île was leased by the Boot family (of Boots the chemist fame) as a holiday cottage, and their stays were sometimes luxurious. On one trip a Mrs Riley brought her butler to serve meals dressed in whites, with champagne for breakfast. Earlier, the artist Ouless (1884) describes "pipes, grog and songs while sitting around a blazing fire" and breakfasts of "basins of tea and a hot lobster".

In the 17th century the reef was an important smuggling transit point between France and Jersey. Edward Harris, the Lieutenant Governor of Jersey, was so involved he could never be contacted during the day. Later, Philippe Pinel lived on the reef for 40 years with his wife. She eventually left him and fled to Jersey where she accused Pinel of being a drunkard and wife-beater. More recently Alphonse Le Gastelois fled to Les Écréhous where he lived for 14 years; Alphonse was something of an eccentric and a loner on Jersey, and he was therefore a prime target for suspicion when a series of sex crimes occurred. When offered work on Les Écréhous he was happy to accept it to prove it was not him. It was not until 1971 that the perpetrator of the crimes was caught, but by then Alphonse had made Les Écréhous his home, and only returned to live in Jersey in 1975 after being arrested and charged with arson for burning down two huts (he was later acquitted).

On very low tides L'Écrevière Bank is an unusual picnic spot. If the main islets are very busy, the north-western beaches on Les Écréhous are good alternatives, with some remarkable rock formations at low tide.

JERSEY TO NORMANDY

Les Écréhous is a useful stopover for a crossing to Normandy, but you need to consider the French sea kayak regulations. The crossings from Les Écréhous are just within the limits set by the French authorities for offshore kayaking, so you should be okay unless you bump into a very zealous bureaucrat.

3A LES ÉCRÉHOUS TO CARTERET (NORMANDY)

Although a similar distance to the Jersey – Les Écréhous crossing (6NM) this crossing is more difficult in a number of ways. There is little or no assistance from the tides on this section, and it often takes longer than expected. The approach to both Carteret and Les Écréhous has a lot of fast tide streams, so you should not change course too soon.

About halfway between Les Écréhous and Carteret, Basses de Taillepied and Bancs Félés are shallow areas with overfalls and faster tide streams.

While the Jersey to Les Écréhous journey gets a bit of shelter from Jersey, this is lost on the Les Écréhous to Carteret section. If landing at Carteret, the tide goes out a long way and the harbour/marina dries.

3B ANNEPORT (JERSEY) TO LE SÉNÉQUET LIGHT (NEAR GOUVILLE SUR MER, NORMANDY)

This is a very fast route from Jersey to Normandy as the direction of the tidal stream is very favourable.

3C LE SÉNÉQUET LIGHT (NEAR GOUVILLE SUR MER, NORMANDY) TO LES ÉCRÉHOUS

The tidal streams are almost directly behind you on this route, making a good option for a return (via Les Écréhous) to Jersey from the Normandy coast. It is a superb offshore journey in good conditions.

Tides and weather

Tide streams are fast with overfalls about 0.5km off St Catherine and as you near the reef. In poor visibility locating the islets can be tricky as there are no lights on the reef.

At Les Écréhous the south-east stream starts about 1 hour before low water, and the north-west stream 1 hour before HW St Helier, which is not listed on the tidal atlas. On spring tides the breakout at Les Écréhous can be tricky, so it is best to approach close to Maître Île, unless you like big ferry glides.

Jersey provides considerable protection from any westerly swells, and it is only once you are 3.7 km (2NM) offshore that you may become more exposed to the swell.

Additional information

Les Écréhous is a Ramsar wetlands site. Care must be taken during the breeding season (March to July) to avoid disturbing the tern colony at Le Blianque Île; information boards identify the sensitive spots. It is possible to travel over by charter boat and then kayak the reef with Jersey Kayak Adventures (www.jerseykayakadventures.co.uk).

The hut owners value the peace and beauty of the reef so try to keep disturbance to a minimum.

La Grève de Lecq
to Bonne Nuit Bay

No. 4 | **Grade B** | **9km (5NM)** | **OS sheet J** | **3655, 1136**

Tidal Port	St Helier
Start	△ La Grève de Lecq Harbour (583 555)
Finish	○ Bonne Nuit Harbour (641 561)
HW/LW	HW St Helier is 4 hours 55 minutes before HW Dover.
Tidal Times	Along the north coast the E going stream starts about 5 hours after HW St Helier, and the W going stream starts 1 hour before HW St Helier.
Max Rate Sp	5 knots off the larger headlands at Sorel and Ronez Points. Max 2 to 3 knots across bays.
Coastguard	Jersey, tel. 01534 447705 Channel 82.

Introduction

Heading east are some of the best sea caves in Jersey, and 100m cliffs. If there is any swell, look out for blowholes which on a good day can reach over 10m high; just don't get too close.

It is easy to miss some great spots if you head directly to Bonne Nuit. An option is to paddle the entire section, and then do shorter trips focusing on coastal exploration at different states of the tide.

Description

Watch out for dumping surf if launching on the beach by the slipway in the centre of the bay. It is often better to use the harbour slip, or western end of the beach, where there is more shelter.

The harbour is a good example of how they did not always build things to last in the old days. Constructed in 1872, it collapsed within 13 years.

The hilltop on the east side of the bay is a late Iron Age promontory fort. The escarpments are easier to spot from the sea. Beneath the headland is a long, narrow cave that connects with Le Val Roget. This headland is also known for cliff jumping (which on a summer day seems to be Jersey's national sport) and coasteering, and there is a deep rock pool known as the Octopus Pool.

Rounding Rouge Nez you will discover some of the best sea caves in Jersey. Entry to each cave varies depending on the height of tide. Around half tide gives some of the best opportunities to explore caves of up to 100m deep. Between here and Bonne Nuit Bay there are a few small beaches with no easy egress.

Look out for lengths of rope and even ladders leading down to rocky ledges along the coast. They are used to access good fishing spots, making fishing in Jersey an extreme sport.

L'île Agois

L'île Agois is a small tidal stack 200m south-south-east of L'Âne and a stony storm beach situated in a small bay.

Two metal bridges (installed in the late 1990s by an Army engineering team on exercise) are visible on the grassy cliff face, and a steep path runs down the cliff to the beach. The cliff path has deteriorated considerably and is now unsafe.

L'île Agois has a sea arch and a tall, narrow passage running through it which can sometimes be paddled. On spring tides you can circumnavigate the islet, though evidence of recent rockfalls may put you off this idea.

Climbing the islet is not recommended because peregrine falcons sometimes nest here. The top of the islet is an important Iron Age and Medieval occupation site. Excavation has revealed fragments of Iron Age pottery, and the foundations of about 27 circular huts from the 7th and 8th centuries, along with Roman and Dark Ages coins.

Beyond L'île Agois the cave entrance at La Touraille (Devil's Hole) is tricky to find, and lies just below the line of the small valley and before the path swings west. Though facing north-east there is often a swell inside this cave. The name is reputed to come from when a ship's figurehead was washed into the cave in 1851. A statue of a devil was adapted from the figurehead by Captain Jean Giffard, *"stonemason, self-taught stone-carver, prison guardian, master mariner and reputed smuggler"*, and erected above the Devil's Hole as an attraction.

A little to the east is a small waterfall at the end of La Vallée des Mouriers.

Ronez quarry just beyond Sorel Point comes as a bit of a shock, but the coastline improves as you head into St John's Bay; the shingle beach at La Fosse au Ros has a couple small caves. Nearby is La Saline, where salt was produced by the evaporation of sea water; salt was vital in the cod trade to cure fish.

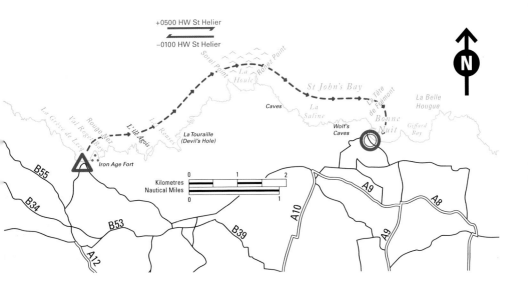

4

Cotil Point, a little to the west of Wolf's Caves, has a mass of different rock formations which look quite different from other sections of this coast.

Close to Le Cormoran Rock is Wolf's Caves. The cliff path descent is very unsafe, but you can land at low tide on the boulders, and enter a tiny entrance on the right at base of the cliff. On calm days (around half tide) it is possible to paddle into the cave system via an entrance between Cotil Point and the boulder beach. A small blowhole sometimes works around half tide. One hundred metres further east is a rock garden known by local paddlers as 'The Toilet', because you get flushed through it.

Variations

This route is a good out and back trip.

The caves and rock gardens between La Grève de Lecq and Sorel Point make great two hour trips. Try to do these at various levels of tide because access to caves and rock gardens will change by the minute. In the space of an hour the sea may rise or fall by up to 3m so it's never the same. The rock gardens are an excellent area to work on paddle skills.

Tides and weather

If you plan to explore the caves and cliffs, it is essential to check the wind direction and swell. La Grève de Lecq is open to swells from the west to north-west. On the flood tide with a westerly wind the swell size can rapidly increase. If swell is breaking on the Paternosters reef, expect swell beyond Rouge Nez Point.

Before entering every cave take time to observe the swell patterns. Even on calm days the swell can vary considerably from one cave to another. This is probably caused by a combination of factors such as the location of submerged reefs, swell direction, swell frequency, and the rising or falling tide. The swell from distant passing ships may also pose a risk. As a rough guide, if you cannot swim out of a cave or rock garden, consider whether it is safe to enter.

At Rouge Nez the east and west streams can be strong, and the strength can come as a surprise to inexperienced paddlers.

From La Touraille (Devil's Hole) to Sorel, offshore boomers (submerged rocks over which only the larger swells break) lie about 0.5km offshore. As you head further east any protection afforded by La Tête de Plémont is gradually lost, and you can encounter some big swell. Once you round Ronez Point and head into St John's Bay the swell usually decreases if you head inshore, though you might still get a 'surprise' if there is any about.

On spring tides, between Le Cormoran Rock and Wolf's Caves, the tide stream can be considerable. Approaching La Tête de Frémont, the swell may again increase as you lose the protection of Ronez Point; although, if you have already come this far from La Grève de Lecq, you'll have paddled bigger swells. Keep clear of the reef that extends out from La Tête de Frémont, as it is easy to cut the corner with the end in sight and get dumped on the reef.

When departing from Bonne Nuit heading westwards, the size of swell at La Tête de Frémont is a good indicator. If it looks big here, it'll be bigger beyond Ronez Point. On an ebb tide and swell from the west, the journey between Ronez Point to La Tête de Plémont can be a big rollercoaster ride. This can be a good introduction to ocean swell, because it allows people to experience the swell with the option to opt out at any stage and head closer inshore. The swell

should decrease as you pick up a bit of protection from La Tête de Plémont. However, if it's a north-west swell, or is being generated by a distant Atlantic depression, it's going to be a big swell in La Grève de Lecq, and you might wish you'd checked the Jersey Coastguard wave height data and shipping forecast.

Additional information

The sea caves along the first 2km are well worth exploring, if conditions allow. Hand torches are often insufficient in the deepest caves, and paddlers have a bad habit of dropping them just when they are in the deepest spots. Communication can also be difficult once in the caves. Try to avoid everyone paddling in together just in case a large swell suddenly arrives …

La Grève de Lecq
to Les Pierres de Lecq ▣▣▣

No. 5 | **Grade C** | **9.5km (5.2NM)** | **OS sheet J** | **3655, 113**

Tidal Port	St Helier
Start/Finish	△○ La Grève de Lecq (583 555)
HW/LW	HW St Helier is 4 hours 55 minutes before HW Dover.
Tidal Times	The E going stream starts about 5 hours 30 minutes before HW St Helier, and the W going stream starts at -1HW St Helier.
Max Rate Sp	5 knots and perhaps more near the reef.
Coastguard	Jersey, tel. 01534 447705 Channel 82.

Introduction

Les Pierres de Lecq, or Paternosters as most locals would refer to it, is an excellent trip to develop offshore paddle skills and navigation, in the knowledge that it is possible to dart back to shore, if it does not seem to be going well.

Description

Departing from La Grève de Lecq, the white tower in the car park is an excellent transit. This Jersey Round Tower was the first to be constructed in 1780, because the bay was considered to be a prime landing spot for any French attack, and barracks (open to the public) were later added.

As you move offshore virtually all the north coast of Jersey is visible. For some paddlers on their first offshore trip, the experience of not having land nearby can be unsettling, and it is common for paddle speeds to slow down.

Near the Paternosters the size of the rocks is apparent, with drying heights of 10m. The reef is a treacherous place due to the set of the tide streams and extensive reefs to the west. In September 1961 the *Heron*, a small coaster carrying tomatoes from Jersey to the UK, sank on the reef, and crates of tomatoes were seen floating on the surface for a few days after the sinking.

The name Paternosters is reputed to come from the Pater Noster ('Our Father' or Lord's prayer). Legend tells of a ship en route to Sark, containing women and children, being wrecked on Les Pierres de Lecq, and their cries being heard during the night; by daybreak all had perished. Passing fishermen used to recite the Lord's prayer in their memory.

In 2005 the reef was given international Ramsar wetland status. The enormous water exchange and strong tidal streams provide ideal conditions to support a wide diversity of marine life, and the water-filled gullies are well worth exploration. The reef is an important bio-geographical boundary zone between the northern and southern parts of the Channel Islands; grey seals and dolphins can sometimes be seen.

Ancient defences

The remains of Le Câtel de Lecq, an Iron Age fort, are on the hill to the east of Grève de Lecq, its defensive banks and ditches being visible from the sea. A theory is that Le Pinacle, Rozel earthworks, Mont Orgueil, and even the prehistoric fortification at Jerbourg on Guernsey, acted as defensive sites overlooking a major prehistoric seaway into France, passing between Jersey and Guernsey.

In addition to the Round Tower at Grève de Lecq, a further 31 towers were subsequently built as coastal defences against attack by the French. The towers were designed to delay the attack and give time for reinforcements to arrive. Many were constructed at the foot of the old roads descending from the hill tops.

Grève de Lecq Barracks are open to the public. When, in 1779, Dumouriez planned to invade Jersey, he arranged that half the force should land at Grève de Lecq; this prompted the hasty construction of a guard house and magazine, followed by the barracks which were in use until 1926.

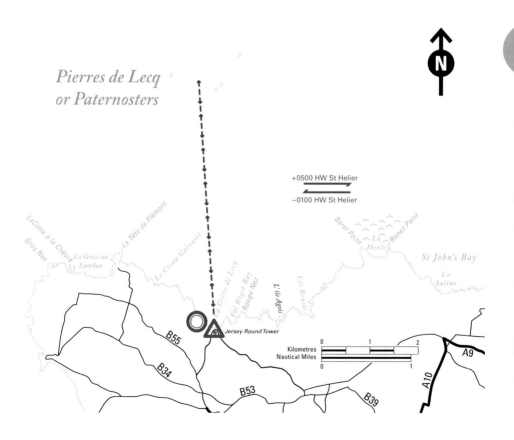

Variations

A longer route is to depart from Bonne Nuit Bay on the last of the west-going stream.

If you enjoy the challenge of offshore paddling, Grève de Lecq to Les Écréhous via the Paternosters and Les Dirouilles is an exciting 24km (13NM) trip. Seven thousand years ago this route would have been a walk along a ridge as Les Écréhous, Les Dirouilles and Paternoster were separated from Jersey by the Le Ruau Channel.

The easterly stream runs from about -0400 to -0100 HW St Helier. If you are running later, it may be necessary to eddy hop and ferry glide into the reef from the Grand Rousse, as there is a fast northerly stream running between Les Dirouilles and Marmotière. This route should only be considered in good conditions.

Tides and weather

This trip requires navigation and chart work skills to allow for the tide streams.

If waves are breaking on the offshore reefs, expect swell as you will be exposed once you lose the protection of La Tête de Plémont. Near the Paternosters swell may make landing difficult or impossible, even on the eastern side of Great Rock. Tide streams are fastest near the reef, so avoid aiming directly towards your landing spot until you are past Flat Rock. The best time to visit the Paternosters is at low tide when there are more landing spots.

La Grève de Lecq to La Corbière

No. 6 | **Grade B** | **24km (13NM)** | **OS sheet J** | **3655, 1136**

Tidal Port	St Helier
Start	△ La Grève de Lecq (583 555)
Finish	◎ Le Petit Port (559 485)
HW/LW	HW St Helier is 4 hours 55 minutes before HW Dover.
Tidal Times	Tide streams split off Gros Nez point. Along the north coast the E going stream starts about 5 hours 30 minutes before HW St Helier and the W going stream starts 3 hours after HW St Helier.
	On the north-west coast the N going stream begins 2 hours 30 minutes before HW St Helier, and the S going stream starts 3 hours 30 minutes after HW St Helier. Inshore the streams seem to turn about 1 hour earlier.
Max Rate Sp	4 to 5 knots and perhaps more off headlands.
Coastguard	Jersey, tel. 01534 447705 Channel 82.

Introduction

The coast between La Tête de Plémont and Le Grand Etacquerel has some of the most spectacular cliffs on Jersey, but is rarely paddled due to the exposed coastline.

Description

The cliffs from La Grève de Lecq to La Tête de Plémont are indented with many small coves. From 1 March until early July there is a 200m voluntary puffin protection zone between Le Douët de la Mer and La Tête de Plémont, though you might be forgiven for thinking that the zone has fallen into disuse as many small lobster potting boats fish below the nests. It is worth staying offshore at Le Douët de la Mer to avoid a rain of shotgun pellets from the clay pigeon range on the hill top. From over 200 puffins in the 1930s, numbers have fallen to less than ten. This is thought to be due to changes in the supply of sand eels, along with an increasing number of rats, wild cats, and possibly the arrival of fulmar who also occupy the cliff ledges.

Le Creux Gabourel is one of the few caves to have a sandy beach. Above the entrance of the cave, wedged into the roof, are rounded boulders from when sea levels were 8m higher.

The small cove of Le Petit Plémont (with evidence of boat moorings on the rocks) is a good spot to assess the tide race and swell off La Tête de Plémont. There can be a huge difference in the size of the swell once you round this headland.

La Grève au Lanchon (Jersey French name for sand eels, and commonly called Plémont Bay) has a few caves. Plémont was a popular tourist spot for our Victorian and Edwardian ancestors, who could even hire a porter to carry them into the caves.

Approaching a stack known as La Vie, there is a sea cave with two entrances which can sometimes be paddled. About 300m west of Plémont beach (and above sea level) is La Cotte à la Chèvre, where some of the earliest Palaeolithic remains of habitation in Jersey were discovered. La Capée is a long gulley with a small waterfall. Beneath the light and Gros Nez Castle the cliffs are much steeper, and there is often some swell about. Little is known about the castle which was constructed around 1430; there is no record of its destruction.

At the base of the cliffs, below the Nazi range control tower, lie the remains of some heavy artillery guns which are visible at low tide. In 1943 approximately 26,800 troops were based in the Channel Islands. The islands were more heavily fortified than any other coastal area held by

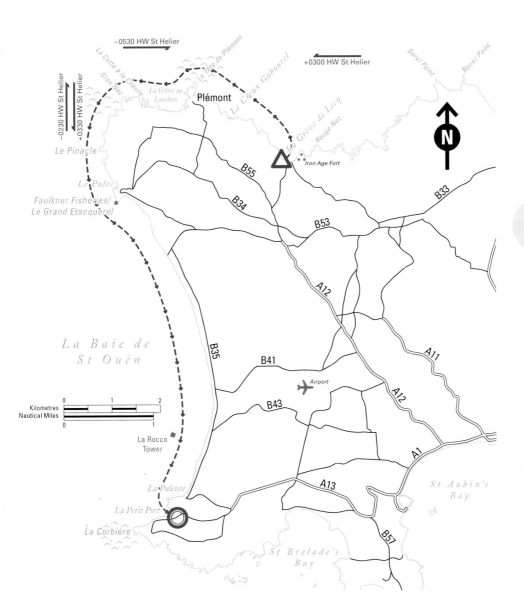

Germany. Nearby there are a few caves running through the cliffs; it is sometimes possible to scramble through these.

Le Pinacle Rock is an important archaeological site with Neolithic, Chalcolithic, Bronze Age, Iron Age and Roman remains. For more than 4,500 years this imposing rock, which resembles a huge Menhir (standing stone), captured the imagination of the inhabitants of Jersey as a very special place. There is evidence of axe production, and a cave runs beneath the headland.

La Baie de St Ouën is an excellent surfing beach on the rising tide, and it is not until you are near La Pulente that you may find a relatively sheltered landing, as the offshore reefs tend to break up the swells. It may be an idea to head inshore towards La Rocco Tower which, like Seymour Tower, is available to hire for overnight stays, and on to La Pulente to get more protection if there is a swell running.

Le Petit Port is only accessible above half tide though there is a vraicing (seaweed gathering) track cut between the rocks heading to sea. The area between La Pulente and La Corbière has many reef breaks, so you'll need to keep a close watch on the wave patterns and keep a good distance apart. I've seen sea kayaks go airborne here as paddlers frantically dash beyond the swells. Landing at the lighthouse can be tricky, as a tide stream runs over the causeway on both the flood and ebb tides. The causeway dries a couple hours either side of low tide. Overfalls occur off the western end of La Corbière, though you can sometimes avoid the worst by handrailing beneath the lighthouse. If you are rounding the lighthouse from the east, you may encounter a considerable change in conditions, especially on a north-going stream at spring tides.

No beer at the lighthouse

The name of La Corbière Lighthouse derives from the word corbîn (crow) and means 'a place where crows gather'. Ignore old stories that the name came about after a lot of beer was washed ashore. Every lighthouse seems to have a claim to fame; La Corbière was the first to be built in concrete in 1874 and is one of the island's most recognised landmarks.

Ashore is a stone sculpture of two hands clasped together to commemorate the rescue of the high speed ferry *Saint Malo* which hit La Frouquie rocks with 307 passengers on board on April 17th 1995, whilst on passage from Jersey to Sark. In spite of it being a spring tide with force 5 winds and moderate to rough seas, all were rescued. Navigating the 200m wide channel required the use of back transits viewed from behind the vessel, and there was little margin for error when travelling at 30 knots. Since the incident, ferry traffic is prohibited from using this inshore route.

Variations

The beach at La Grève au Lanchon covers 2 to 3 hours either side of high tide. Access and egress from the land is difficult, and involves carrying kayaks up many steps to the car park. The beach café has a superb view and the nearby toilets are in the old telegraph cable station.

You can shorten the trip at Le Pulec, though a north-west swell can make the landing/launching tricky due the reef breaks. Le Pulec is better known as Stinky Bay due to the huge quantities of seaweed (vraic in Jersey French) which is washed into the bay, and it was once an important seaweed gathering spot. Vraicing cart tracks are cut through the reefs 50m north of Faulkner Fisheries (a huge Nazi bunker). Faulkner Fisheries is a good place to stop and buy fresh lobster and seafood. If there is any south-westerly swell you can land by using the old vraicing track which lead to a small slipway. The off-lying reefs usually afford some protection. There is also a small slip south of Le Grand Etacquerel with a jetty running down the beach. The car park in front of Faulkner Fisheries is for customers, so you should park a little to the north.

Tides and weather

La Tête de Plémont gives protection from the westerly swells. The tide streams are strong on both the flood and ebb, with overfalls and eddies.

Beyond La Tête de Plémont the cliffs are exposed to any westerly swell and there is little or no slack water.

Shallow reefs extend beyond Le Grand Etacquerel. There are some deep water channels between these reefs which may give a shorter route.

Additional information

The lighthouse and Nazi bunkers at La Corbière are sometimes open to the public. 'What's on Jersey' published by Visit Jersey lists opening times.

Belcroute
to La Corbière

No. 7 | **Grade B** | **20km (11NM)** | **OS sheet J** | **3655, 1137**

Tidal Port	St Helier
Start/Finish	△◯ Belcroute Bay (607 476)
HW/LW	HW St Helier is 4 hours 55 minutes before HW Dover.
Tidal Times	Between La Corbière and Noir Mont the W going stream starts 1 hour before HW St Helier. The E going stream starts 5 hours after HW St Helier.
	From Belcroute to Noir Mont there is an almost perpetual S going stream. This eddy is created by the water in St Aubin Bay circulating in an anticlockwise direction. The S going stream starts about 3 hours before HW St Helier, and runs until 5 hours after HW St Helier.
Max Rate Sp	4 knots.
Coastguard	Jersey, tel. 01534 447705 Channel 82.

Introduction

The south-west coast is full of contrasts, with superb granite cliffs and the potential for some challenging water.

Description

Belcroute Bay can be tricky to find. As you descend the narrow lane it feels like you are about to drive into someone's stately home. It has a small slip and is surrounded by woodland.

About 400m north of Noir Mont there is evidence of raised beaches in the cliffs. Noir Mont Point is an area of fast-moving water; the meeting of the west and south-going streams can create considerable rough water beneath the tower. On the hill top is the Nazi range control tower MP1, part of a chain of inter-island naval artillery control posts. Batterie Lothringen (a naval coastal artillery battery) is worth visiting to give an idea of just how heavily the islands were fortified by the Nazis. The main shipping channel is only 500m wide here, so look out for vessels and their wash.

L'Île Perchie is named after the opening through the rock. A narrow channel between the islet and land can be paddled on spring tides.

A remarkable cavern can be explored at half tide in Le Port d'Île Perchie which probably dates from when the area was quarried.

L'Île au Guerdain in Le Portelet Bay is generally known as Janvrin's tomb. It is named after Philippe Janvrin, captain of the *Esher*, who was quarantined there in 1721 after returning from France while the plague raged. He died and was buried on the islet within sight of his home. The coastal tower usually referred to as Janvin's tomb was built in 1808.

There is a small cave in Rosel Bay, but watch out for the wash of passing motor boats which can increase wave heights.

At Le Fret Point you can either head across the bay towards Le Beau Port or go into St Brelade. The east and west sides of the bay have some good rock gardens. There is a sea stack at Les Jeteuses below Beau Port battery.

Le Beau Port is a jewel. On a sunny day the bay takes on a Mediterranean feel, complete with a few luxury yachts at anchor. The red granite cliffs along this part of the coast have a wonderful, warm feeling. This is the last good landing before La Pulente in St Ouen's Bay.

The cliffs continue from Le Beau Port to La Corbière with many small caves and sea arches that are easily missed, if you stay further offshore. There are a couple of peregrine falcon nests at La Grosse Tête and Trespass Point (La Tête), and lots of birdlife around Les Leaux de Ficquet. It is possible to paddle between La Grosse Tête and the land (approximately 0.5 hour after low water), providing there is not much swell.

Les Caînes reef was the site of the grounding of the SS *Roebuck* in 1911 when, travelling in thick fog at 17 knots, the steamer ran onto the reef in calm conditions.

Just beyond Point La Moye is a large cave. On the cliff top is a huge hole which, some locals recall, once worked like a whale spout in storms. It is very rare that you can paddle into this cave except in calm conditions and even then you need to look out for the swell from passing boats. If you get the chance to enter the cave, look up to see daylight, and the remains of a few old cars that used to be pushed into the hole until the 1960s.

From Point La Moye to La Rosière there are numerous channels and stacks. Nearby is a small, granite tower linked by a rail track which is the water intake for the island's desalination plant. The granite wall at the base of the cliffs in La Rosière was constructed in Victorian times as a tourist path into the caves.

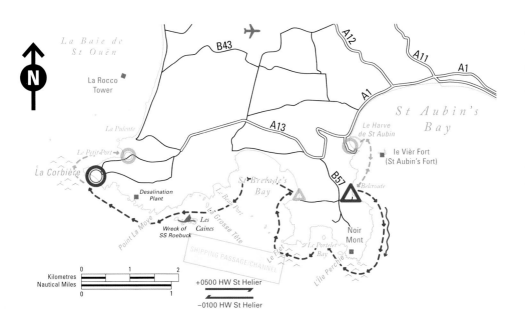

There are fast tide streams over the causeway at La Corbière and the northern side is exposed. West of the lighthouse are overfalls.

Landing at the lighthouse is tricky. If you end the trip at La Corbière, there is a small, sandy beach by the slip on the south side of the causeway. At low tide landing is among the rocks protecting the causeway. Take care if there is a swell.

Most paddlers prefer to return to their start point. The large tidal range makes the return trip very different and worthwhile.

Variations

At high tide it is worth making a short detour into Le Harve de St Aubin. Until 1788 this was the main port for the island. The large quantities of flint on the seabed near St Aubin are a result of the flint being used as ballast in ships sailing unladen to Jersey. Between St Aubin and Belcroute there is evidence of glacial heads and raised beaches. Look out for the Victorian diving platforms and paths cut into the rocks. Le Vièr Fort (St Aubin's Fort) was completed in 1542 to counter French pirate attacks.

St Brelade's Bay and Le Ouaisné are both good put-ins or take-outs. However, at low tide the carry down Le Ouaisné beach can be over 300m, and it is therefore a good idea to use a kayak trolley.

If conditions off Point Le Fret and Noir Mont Point are bad, it is a short drive/walk over the hill to Belcroute. Portelet Bay is an excellent landing spot, but road access is up a long flight of stairs.

There are plenty of shorter options hugging the cliffs, if conditions are poor. Surf landing and launching can be practised at the east of St Brelade's Bay and also in Le Ouaisné around high tide. Observe the beachguard zones.

Le Petit Port (just to the north of La Corbière) is a difficult landing at low tide. At higher tides and a westerly swell the offshore reef breaks make route finding a challenge. La Pulente (1km north) can be a better landing, though you may need to weave your way between reef breaks.

Tides and weather

Wind direction is a major consideration. North-west to north-east winds tend to give the most shelter. Five headlands are prone to overfalls and rough water: Noir Mont, Le Fret, La Grosse Tête, La Tete and La Moye Points.

There is an almost perpetual south-going eddy from Point de But to Noir Mont, which can be up to 3 knots. At Noir Mont the main shipping channel to St Helier is less than 500m wide and can be very busy, so between Noir Mont and Le Fret look out for the wash from shipping. In westerly winds, conditions off Noir Mont can be very different to those in Belcroute Bay.

More paddlers get caught out at Le Fret Point than any other location on Jersey, due to its proximity to the popular kayaking bays of St Brelade and Le Ouaisné. Le Fret Point is exposed to west and south-west swell, and there is an almost constant south-going stream from La Cotte to La Fret. Many a paddler has inadvertently drifted into the tide race while considering what to do next. If in any doubt, stay in line with the Nazi bunker on the cliff while you observe conditions off the headland.

There is often shelter from west to north-east winds if you stay close beneath the cliffs, and any swell about will produce some great paddling.

Westerly swells result in a good reef break at Les Caînes rocks, and if there is swell here, it will be a rollercoaster ride to La Corbière. If this is not for you, then stay in Les Leaux de Ficquet Bay.

La Cotte

La Cotte de St Brelade is one of the most important Palaeolithic sites in Europe. The cave was hollowed out by the sea when it was 20m above today's level; however when sea levels dropped to create a lowland plain stretching nearly 160km westwards, the cave was inhabited by Neanderthal man. Excavations reveal an unbroken record of almost 250,000 years of human activity.

Evidence of hunting behaviour in the form of heaps of mammoth and rhinoceros bones have been found. During this time Neanderthal hunters were responding to massive changes in their local environment, and left a rich record of their hunting and tool use, as well as evidence for the controlled use of fire. La Cotte is of vital importance to our understanding of the Middle Palaeolithic period in northern Europe, and a major evaluation of the site is being undertaken. More information at www.jerseyheritage.org/ice-age-island.

Le Ouaisné to Les Minquiers ▣▣▣

No. 8 | **Grade C** | **22km (12NM)** | **OS sheet J** | **2669, 3656**

Tidal Port	St Helier
Start	△ Le Ouaisné (595 476) (49° 10' 35N 02° 11' 05W)
Finish	◎ La Maîtresse Île, Les Minquiers (48° 58' 3N, 02° 03' 8W)
HW/LW	HW St Helier is 4 hours 55 minutes before HW Dover. HW Les Minquiers is 14 minutes before HW St Helier.
Tidal Times	The E going stream commences at 5 hours 40 minutes before HW St Helier and gradually swings SE until 2 hours 40 minutes before HW St Helier, and then turns E. By HW St Helier a NW going stream is established near La Maîtresse Île. This is not shown on the tide stream atlas. The main W going stream is flowing by 50 minutes after HW St Helier.
Max Rate Sp	4 knots.
Coastguard	Jersey, tel. 01534 447705 Channel 82. Port traffic St Helier Channel 14.

Introduction

There are few islands in the UK which are such a remote paddling destination. Les Minquiers is a wild place compared to the pretty and well-kept huts at Les Écréhous. Step onto Les Minquiers and you feel as if you are at the world's end. Jersey is just a faint line on the horizon. This is a harsh, water-swept terrain, where your eyes are always checking the weather and the seagulls strut about with attitude. You will probably be the only people on the islet. Carry sufficient supplies in case conditions deteriorate.

Description

Most departures leave around low water, and if leaving from Le Ouaisné, expect a long walk down the beach. The advantage of this departure point (apart from The Old Smugglers Inn on return) is that it gives you a little more help from the cross tides and allows you to stay well clear of the main shipping route to St Malo, so you should not need to constantly look out for high-speed craft (apart from crossing the shipping lane into St Helier shortly after your departure).

Paddlers who are unused to offshore trips may paddle a little slower than average because for the first 11km (6NM) you are unlikely to see anything. At low tide this reef dries almost as large as Jersey.

Les Minquiers derives its name from the French word 'minkier' meaning a fish wholesaler and this probably reflects the abundance of fish and seals around the reefs in ancient times. The reef was once important for conger fishing. Today you will see many lobster pot buoys

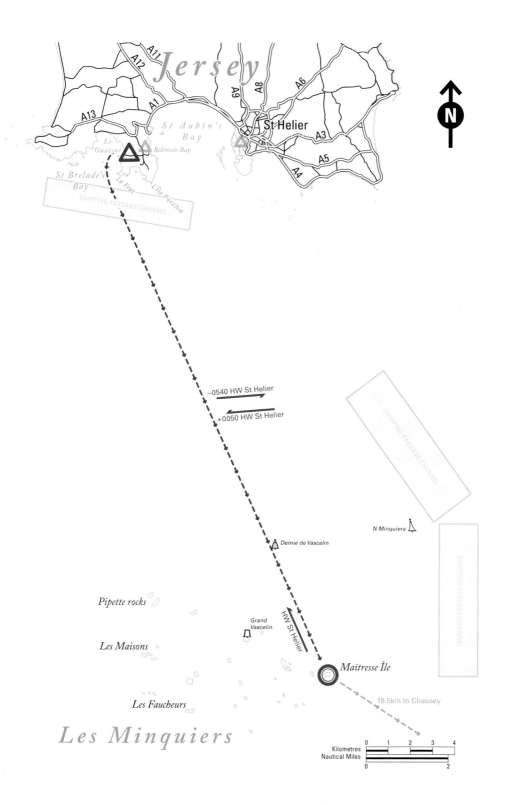

Jersey

A11
A12
A1
A13
A9 A8 A6
St Aubin's Bay
St Helier
A3
Le Ouaisné
Belcroute Bay
A4
A5

St Brelade's Bay
Le Fret
L'île Perchée

SHIPPING PASSAGE/CHANNEL

N

−0540 HW St Helier
+0050 HW St Helier

SHIPPING PASSAGE/CHANNEL

N Minquiers

Demie de Vascelin

SHIPPING PASSAGE/CHANNEL

Pipette rocks

Grand Vascelin

HW St Helier

Les Maisons

Maîtresse Île

Les Faucheurs

18.5km to Chausey

Les Minquiers

Kilometres
Nautical Miles
0 1 2 3 4
0 2

Le Ouaisné to Les Minquiers

which are useful markers to assess the speed and direction of the tide streams. On the biggest equinox tides the reef is a popular low water fishing destination for lobster and ormers (a type of abalone). Approximately 89 out of 440 species of molluscs in the Channel Islands are found at Les Minquiers, so if you get stormbound, you should find something to eat.

Les Maisons rocks can be mistaken for Maîtresse Île, if you are further west than planned, and look as if they have buildings on them.

The Pipette rocks are often one of the first bits of land spotted. An amusing incident is Jersey's version of the film Whisky Galore. In 1953 the coaster Brockley Coombe was wrecked on the reefs. Part of its cargo included a quantity of Bristol Cream Sherry which hut owners from Les Minquiers reputedly rescued before customs officers arrived. Some bottles were never recovered.

The Demie de Vascelin buoy is a good reference point. Aim to pass it to your east otherwise you will have a harder slog to Maîtresse Île. Spotting Maîtresse Île can be difficult, if visibility is less than 9km (5NM). Once within the reef the islet is the last large lump of rock in the east. If you miss Maîtresse Île, your next landfall is Chausey.

Near Maîtresse Île tide streams increase. The flagpole is a good mark as the huts are not easy to spot from the north or north-west. The huts were constructed by quarrymen who were intent upon reducing the islet to nothing in order to build Fort Regent in Jersey. The La Rocque fishermen who sailed (and rowed) down each week to fish and hunt seal became irate at the rapid disappearance of their island base, and resorted to direct action by removing the quarrymen's tools and dropping them into deep water.

The Patagonian invasion

Sovereignty of Les Minquiers and Les Écréhous was disputed by the French and British for many years, and it was only resolved in Britain's favour following a judgement at the International Court of Justice in 1953, though French fishermen were granted rights to fish the reefs. As a result the sovereignty of both reefs is taken very seriously. Hoisting the Union Flag is an almost obligatory requirement for anyone staying on the islets.

Imagine the consternation when in 1984, two years after the Falklands invasion, a fifteen-strong French landing party armed with picnic baskets and a magnum of Bucks Fizz, seized Les Minquiers in the name of the King of Patagonia and hoisted the Patagonian flag. On 30 August 1998 the stunt was again repeated – complete with Bucks Fizz and champagne – at a time when there was still considerable concern over fishing rights in the Channel Islands. Police were sent to the reef, and the stolen Union Flag was eventually handed back to British Embassy staff in Paris.

Landing is at the natural harbour to the east of Maîtresse Île (48º 58' 3N, 02º 03' 8W). Take your kayaks well up the causeway for safety. Years ago fishermen would sink their boats, if bad weather was expected, because they were safer on the seabed than bouncing about at anchor in a storm.

The huts are now used as holiday cabins. The large hut at the north end of the islet was won by Bill Coom in a card game during the occupation, after the owner was unable to pay his gambling debt.

As you explore the islet, look for the carved names and initials written on the granite rocks by the quarrymen. Modern carvings can also be seen, including a concrete kayak at the top of the slip. This was made by some stormbound kayakers who found a sack of cement to keep themselves occupied until conditions improved.

Perhaps the most famous spot on Maîtresse Île is the toilet. This is the most southerly loo in the British Isles and should be used with respect and care. Unlike its counterpart on Les Écréhous, construction of the loo in the 1930s did not create any outrage from the residents or national media attention. When the Les Écréhous loo was constructed by an army engineering team they upset the residents by installing the discharge pipe next to a hut owners front door, and also forgot that it is illegal to discharge raw sewage into the sea.

Variations

Alternative departure points are from Belcroute Bay and St Helier Harbour (by the old lifeboat station), though parking at St Helier is mostly short stay. La Rocque Harbour was once the principal departure point for fishing boats heading to Les Minquiers, but you'd need to leave around +0400HW. When leaving from St Helier you are more likely to be crossing shipping lanes used by high-speed ferries travelling between St Malo and Jersey.

Try to explore the reef at low tide. There are huge 'Caribbean blue' lagoons, channels and enormous sand bars. The east stream starts about 1 hour before low water St Helier.

RETURN

The return trip is similar to the outbound though usually a little quicker. The tower blocks at Les Marais and white apartments above Le Portelet are useful navigational marks.

8A LES MINQUIERS TO CHAUSEY

Les Minquiers is a good stopping off point before heading over to Chausey, a further 18.5km (10NM) because the tide flows are almost directly behind you.

Tides and weather

If you look south-west before leaving Le Ouaisné, you get a good idea of conditions and swell size.

Off Le Fret and Noir Mont Points there may be a tide stream running through at low water; this is unlikely to be much bother.

Once past the Demie de Vascelin buoy, tidal streams are considerably faster than shown on the charts. On spring tides the streams resemble a contra-flow on a motorway, strong eddy currents flowing in completely different directions within a small area. I recall approaching the reef on a 10.5m tide with a fast southerly stream, while 50m away another paddler was slogging against a north-going stream.

Additional information

French charts: SHOM 7161L Des Îles Chausey à Jersey – Plateau des Minquiers. 1:48,500.

Les Minquiers is a Ramsar wetlands site, so take care when visiting during the breeding season. There is no fresh water on the islet. Unless you have arranged use of the Harbours or Impots (Customs) hut expect to camp. There is little soil (and a lot of tree mallow) so you may need to use rocks around the tent.

This is a very remote spot, so it is advisable to carry extra kit in case you are delayed by bad weather. Fortunately, the islet is just within mobile phone range, if you stand by the main flagpole.

Le Ouaisné to Les Minquiers

Jersey to Chausey (Normandy) ▫▫▫

No. 9 | **Grade C** | **42.5km (23NM)** | **OS sheet J** | **2669**

Tidal Ports	St Helier and St Malo
Start	△ Le Ouaisné (595 476) (49° 10′ 35N 02° 11′ 05W) or Belcroute (613 4//) (49° 10′ 35N 02° 10′ 05W)
Finish	○ Îles Chausey (48° 52′ 29N, 01° 49′ 43W)
HW/LW	HW St Helier is 4 hours 55 minutes before HW Dover. St Malo is 5 hours 6 minutes before HW Dover. HW Chausey is 15 minutes before HW St Helier.
Tidal Times	An E going stream which progressively swings SE starts 5 hours 40 minutes before HW St Helier. By 2 hours 40 minutes before HW St Helier the stream is E going again, and then becomes NE. By HW St Helier the flow near Chausey is N going.
	The NW going stream starts 50 minutes after HW St Helier. By 3 hours 50 minutes after HW St Helier this is flowing W.
	Slack water is at +05 hours 40 minutes after HW St Helier.
Max Rate Sp	4 knots.
Coastguard	Jersey, tel. 01534 447705 Channel 82. Port traffic St Helier VTS Channel 14 – useful to monitor ferry traffic. French Coastguard CROSS Jobourg Channel 70.

Introduction

A trip to Chausey combines the colours of Les Écréhous with the ruggedness of Les Minquiers. The maze of tiny islets is surrounded by crystal-clear waters and sandy sea beds, and lies 40.5km (22NM) from Jersey and 18.5km (10NM) from Granville.

Chausey is known as the French Channel Island. Until 1499 it was administered from Jersey and subsequently abandoned to the French. Consisting of 365 islets at low tide, compared to just 52 at high tide the archipelago was a haven for piracy and smuggling.

The island was heavily quarried for the famous Chausey granite in the 19th century. Today, the island is a popular destination for French day-trippers and yachtsmen, with a couple of bars and restaurants and a (usually fully booked) small hotel. Unlike Les Minquiers expect to encounter hoards of people especially at weekends in July and August.

Paddle away from the main island and you quickly slip into a silent world of small islands, sand bars and excellent picnic spots.

Description

There are two potential routes to Chausey. The first, and perhaps easier, is to combine this with a Les Minquiers trip and, having explored the reef, head over to Chausey. An advantage is that you will get help from the east/west tide streams.

Heading east from Les Minquiers the main issue is to look out for high-speed ferries. Their routes vary depending on the height of tide, and it helps to know their times.

The offshore reefs around Chausey are soon in view and it is likely that the lighthouse will already be visible as you depart Maitresse Île. The cardinal marks and numerous lobster pot buoys are useful to assess your speed and drift.

Approaching Chausey, the main sound runs north-west/south-east. Tide streams are fast, especially near the jetties which are often full of yachts.

The best time to explore the archipelago by kayak is + or - 3 HW St Helier. At other times much of the reef dries. If you land on the dropping tide, what was once a couple feet of water rapidly turns into an expanse of sand, and in some spots very deep mud. Between the numerous islets tide streams flow in all directions like rivers. Arrive on a sunny day and the colours are magnificent.

Instead of stopping at the main landing, consider using Port Homard, although like the main sound this dries. The Sound de Chausey dries almost completely except where the yacht moorings

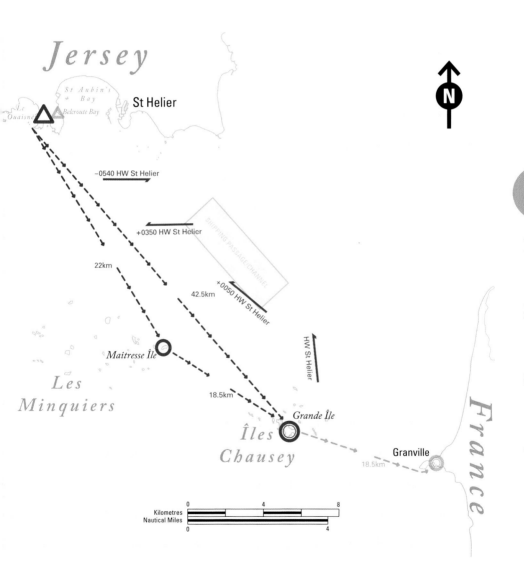

are. Unless you enjoy wading through mud, this is not a good landing spot except at high tide. The popular beach of Port Marie on the south-east of the island is a good landing, with less distance to walk at low tide.

In the little bay to the south of Le Sémaphore are the remains of old fishing boats. I still have photos of when they were recognisable. Today only the rotting keel and engines remain. Nearby are old quarry buildings. Le Sémaphore is an excellent viewpoint.

The south coast of Chausey consists of low cliffs and small sandy coves. Depending on the height of tide it may be possible to paddle close inshore. Look out for lots of quarry workings. Many rocks appear like animals and faces. Some of these 'natural' rock features were 'enhanced' by visiting artists. The Rocher de l'Éléphant, near Grand Grève, is particularly striking.

The island was extensively quarried, with up to 500 quarrymen being employed to extract the blue granodiorite, some of which was used to construct Mont St Michel. It was once a mark of your wealth and prosperity to have a house built, or have a lintel above the fireplace made from Chausey granite. Much of what is called Chausey granite may have been quarried on Les Minquiers, as both islands were once under the control of the Abbot of Mont St Michel.

On the eastern side of the island is Le Fort. Built in 1859 by Napoleon III, 3,000 German and Austrian prisoners of war were imprisoned during the First World War. In 1781 Chausey was the starting point for Baron de Rullecourt's attempt to capture Jersey.

The only permanently inhabited island is Grande Île with a resident population of around 30 but up to 70,000 day trippers visit the island every year. Grand Puceau is frequently inhabited by oyster farmers.

Variations

Paddling straight from Jersey to Chausey is a more direct option with the best tidal assistance if you leave from La Rocque Harbour (49° 09' 54N 02° 01' 53W). However, this will involve a lengthy walk down to the water as you will be leaving after low water. This route means you will be about 16.5km (9NM) offshore. In good weather this can be a superb experience, and has been completed in around 4 hours. A direct return also has favourable tide streams. You will also need to be a reasonably fast paddler to complete this trip before the tide turns.

Kayak trips to Chausey travelling over by charter boat are organised by Jersey Kayak Adventures (www.jerseykayakadventures.co.uk). The canoe club d'Avranches (www.kayakavranches.fr) – dates are usually listed in the "Balades accompagnées" section – also organise trips travelling across by vedette from Granville.

9A CHAUSEY TO GRANVILLE (NORMANDY)

The Chausey to Granville 18.5km (10NM) option is just within the French kayaking regulation limits. Make sure you allow enough time to arrive before dark as night crossings are expressly forbidden.

An alternative return would be to continue down the Normandy coast and on to St Malo (Brittany) where it is possible to catch a ferry back to Jersey or the UK. A trolley to move about the ferry port is useful.

Another alternative return route is to head up along the Normandy coast and cross over to Jersey. From Le Sénéquet to Les Écréhous 31.5km (17NM) the tide streams are directly behind you, and this can make for a very fast crossing. The crossing to Les Écréhous from Port Bail or Carteret 15km (8NM) has more cross tide and can be a bit of a slog.

Tides and weather

Large tides, big crossings and considerable exposure make this an advanced trip which is only possible in settled weather. Unlike Les Minquiers or Les Écréhous, the vedettes to Granville may be able to give you a lift to France, but if you have already paddled this far, you'll probably be keen to head across under your own power. Once within the hundreds of islands that comprise Chausey, kayaking is easy though the tide streams can be quite fast.

Additional information

French charts: SHOM7156L De la Pointe du Grouin à la Pointe d'Agon - Baie du Mont-Saint-Michel - Îles Chausey: 1 : 48 800, SHOM 7134 Îles Chausey: 1 : 15 000.

If using French charts, the standard port is St Malo.

There is no campsite on Chausey, and the small hotel is usually booked months in advance. The former presbytery and school can be rented via the Granville Office de Tourisme (www.ville-granville.fr). They have links to other holiday lets on Chausey. There is only one shop with a limited selection of provisions, though in summer the bar, restaurant and café serve food. The terrace is a great place to enjoy a glass of wine and view the archipelago.

The island is a nature reserve and wild camping is not permitted. Wardens patrol the main island especially in summer. The small islets are off-limits in the breeding season (15th July to 30th September), and many are rat-infested.

Chausey is French territory so as well as carrying passports you must comply with the French regulations governing sea kayaking. In high season you may be stopped and asked how you got to Chausey, and have your equipment and papers inspected. Paddling to or from Granville or Les Minquiers is just within the 6NM limit for kayaking, providing you comply with the French regulations.

Jersey to Sark

No. 10 | **Grade C** | **22km (12NM)** | **OS sheet J** | **2669, 808**

Tidal Port	St Helier
Start	△ Le Pulec (Stinky Bay) (547 549)
Finish	○ Creux Harbour, Sark (521 422) (49° 25' 49N, 02° 20' 37W)
HW/LW	HW St Helier is 4 hours 55 minutes before HW Dover.
Tidal Times	The NE going stream starts at 2 hours before, and runs until 3 hours after, HW St Helier. The SW going stream starts 4 hours after, and ends 4 hours before, HW St Helier.
Max Rate Sp	4 knots. The fastest speed occurs at low and high water. Expect faster streams and eddies near Sark.
Coastguard	Jersey, tel. 01534 447705 Channel 82.

Introduction

This route is an offshore sea kayak trip for the experienced paddler who is comfortable being up to 11km (6NM) offshore. Even in good weather you may encounter swell once clear of the coast. Though longer than the route from Guernsey to Sark there is a little more help from the tide streams.

Description

Ask most locals where Le Pulec is and you will get a blank look and then the reaction "... *you mean Stinky Bay!*" The tiny bay gets its nickname from the huge quantities of vraic (seaweed) washed into the bay. Though vraicing is less common today, you may see people loading vehicles with vraic to fertilise their gardens and fields. There is a regular debate that the famous Jersey Royal Potato tastes better when vraic is spread on the fields. Many of the earliest Jersey Royal cotils (south-facing hillside fields) are at L'Étac. On the left of the narrow channel out of Le Pulec there is sometimes a good reef break, and with really big swells this will close off the channel. An alternative is to launch next to Faulkner Fisheries, an unusual use for a Nazi bunker. There are narrow vraicing cart tracks cut through the rocks to take you to a deep water channel.

The shallow areas north of Le Grand Etacquerel can be a bit bumpy and off-putting when launching, but once in deeper water things often settle down.

The Banc Desormes buoy 7.5km (4NM) north of Gros Nez Point is a handy waypoint to assess your progress. If it's bang on course or to your east, you should hit Sark; if already to your west, there is time to revise your route unless you want to get a view of the north-east coast of Sark, and a harder paddle into shore. From here you cross a shipping route for high-speed and conventional shipping, which often makes course changes near the Desormes buoy. On the return journey their course change can be a good way to spot the buoy.

Near Les Vingt Clos reefs east of L'Étac islet the streams may increase and then drop off near the shore, though you might also notice a south-going eddy running. Avoid changing course for your landing too soon.

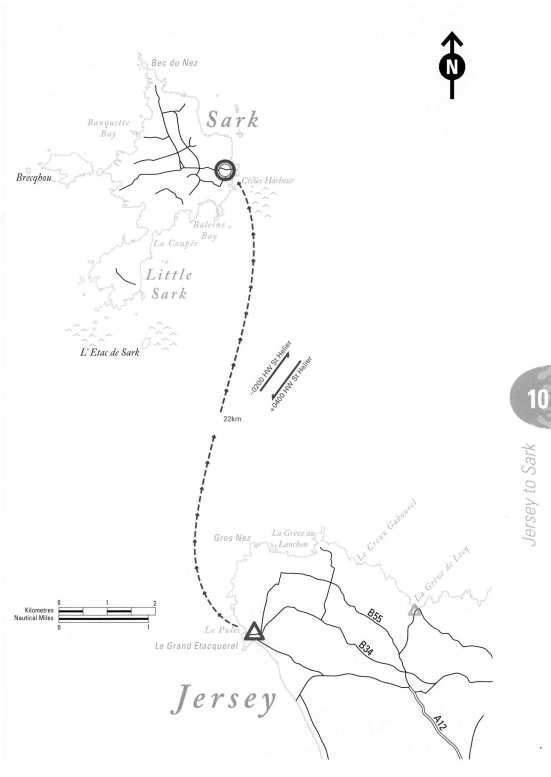

Bec du Nez

Sark

Banquette
Bay

Brecqhou

Créux Harbour

Baleine
Bay
La Coupée

*Little
Sark*

L'Etac de Sark

−0200 HW St Helier
+0400 HW St Helier

22km

N

Gros Nez

La Grève au
Lanchon

Le Creux Gabourel

La Grève de Lecq

B55

B34

Kilometres
Nautical Miles

0   1   2

0   1

Le Pulec
Le Grand Etacquerel

A12

Jersey

10

Vraicing

The gathering of seaweed (vraic) throughout the Channel Islands is an important tradition and was common until the 1950s.

Vraic was harvested from the rocks with a small vraicing sickle and was worth two or three times the value of 'vraic venant' or drift weeds found on the beaches. Both were used as fertilizer on the land, with the summer vraic being regarded as superior to that gathered in the winter.

Vraic was used as fuel for heat and cooking, as well as to burn sea shells, as there was no local source of lime to use in mortar. It was even used as stuffing for a 'lit de fouaile' or 'greenbed' and may have been used in the 16th century to feed sheep when the knitting of woollen stockings was a major industry.

"So eager were the vraic gatherers ... they would sometimes remain on the beach until the carts were floating and the horses swimming; they even carted the precious seaweed on their backs up cliff sides". Customs, Ceremonies and Traditions of the Channel Islands by Raoul Lempriere.

The gathering of this valuable resource was strictly controlled. In Guernsey and Jersey laws limit the vraicing seasons, and nowadays make it difficult for new uses, such as cosmetics and foods, to develop as small scale industries.

Marks were erected in St Ouen's Bay and vraicing commenced once they became visible. Stone slabs were also laid at the bottom of slips to stop carts getting stuck, and cobbles on slips were angled to give horses more grip. Rates were levied to help cover the cost of repairs to the slipways.

Deep water seaweeds such as laminaria absorb large quantities of iodine. Years ago laminaria was used as a dressing, and it is reputed to be good for treating arthritis. On Lihou Island attempts were made to extract iodine commercially in the 19th century, but cheaper South American imports destroyed the business.

Vraicing was hard work but also a time for celebration and fun. In Guernsey, youths and young girls, with garlands of flowers in their hair, wielded 12 to 18ft long vraicing rakes. When the tide turned, and the heaps were safely stacked above the tide line or loaded onto carts, the youngsters went bathing while their elders prepared the food, followed by music and dancing.

Many varieties of seaweed found around the Channel Islands are similar to those used in Japanese cookery. Apparently all seaweeds are edible though some don't taste very nice!

If unsure of your landing spot, the steep cliffs at La Coupée are a good reference point. From there the popular anchorage at Dixcart Bay is easy to spot. Access up the cliffs from Derrible Bay is difficult. Make time to explore any sea caves before landing at Creux Harbour. During the summer a pod of bottlenose dolphins are often spotted along this section of coast.

At Creux Harbour the small shingle beach is a good landing spot, with toilets and showers by the café.

Variations

An alternative departure point is at La Grève de Lecq, but on the outward route you get slightly less assistance from the tides. A weak easterly stream runs along the coast at 0010 before HW St Helier, which gives time to get offshore to catch the remaining north-easterly stream. You may encounter overfalls north of La Tête de Plémont.

From Sark you can continue over to Guernsey and Herm, or even head for Alderney.

For the very experienced and well prepared, in good conditions this trip is an amazing late evening/night paddle. I can recall many July trips where we had almost continuous meteor showers and phosphorescence.

Tides and weather

It is essential to pay close attention to forecasts, if you plan to head on to the other islands, or return to Jersey by kayak. Be prepared to leave earlier than planned, or build in an extra day in case of bad weather. A few paddlers have had tough return trips because they needed to get back to work on a Monday morning, or catch the ferry home.

If heading back to Jersey, the high cliffs surrounding Sark give considerable shelter from any swell and wind originating in the north-west quarter.

We once underestimated the swell and wind when bivvying at Creux Harbour. The forecast, northerly 5, looked okay from the harbour wall; only when we were about 4km (2NM) offshore

did we hit the swell. The trip turned into a fantastic surf ride back to Jersey in about 2.5 hours hitting speeds of up to 10+ knots down waves (I had the GPS on). Fortunately the wind and swell direction was on our stern. I still recall the screams as Helen surfed past us in an Aluet II tandem sea kayak. I'm unsure whether they were screams of fear or excitement!

Additional information

The large car park in front of Faulkner Fisheries is private, but there is car parking on the west side of the access road to Le Pulec slip.

There is no direct freight service from Jersey to Sark. From Sark to Guernsey freight is carried 3 times a week; there is a daily passenger-only service. The seasonal passenger ferry from Jersey to Sark is infrequent, and is prone to cancellation.

Sark

No. 11 | **Grade B** | **16km (8.6NM)** | **OS sheet G** | **808 or 5604.12**

Tidal Port	St Helier
Start	△ Creux Harbour (521 422) (49° 25′ 49N, 02° 20′ 37W)
Finish	○ Creux Harbour (521 422)
HW/LW	HW St Helier is 4 hours 55 minutes before HW Dover.
Tidal Times	From Creux Harbour to Bec du Nez an eddy or slack water occurs during the whole of the NE going stream in the Big Russel (-0200 to +0300 HW St Helier). The strength depends on the height of tide. A bit of handrailing the coast – especially beneath Point Robert – usually works.

On the west coast the NE stream begins 2 hours before HW St Helier. The SW streams starts 4 hours after HW St Helier. The maximum rates are at high and low water. Expect eddies in Banquette Bay.

The Gouliot Passage (50m wide) is very fast flowing. The N going stream starts 2 hours 50 minutes before HW, and the south going stream starts 3 hours 30 minutes after HW St Helier.

In Baleine Bay (see chart 808 or 5604.12) the NE going stream starts 4 hours 45 minutes before HW St Helier. The SW going stream begins at 2 hours 45 minutes after HW St Helier. The streams increase as you approach Derrible Point in the north and in the passage between Breniere rocks and L'Étac rocks to the south.

Max Rate Sp	7 knots in the Gouliot Passage. 5 knots off headlands.
Coastguard	Guernsey, tel. 01481 720672. Passage reports on Channel 20.

Introduction

Sark is a fantastic experience on both the land and sea. The community of 600 inhabitants only changed from a feudal system of government in 2008. This is a place where horses, carts, bicycles and tractors are the main forms of transport, and the daily boat governs many plans.

Sark is surrounded by 75m high cliffs and landing places are limited. The coastline is riddled with caves. To get the most from your visit, aim to spend a couple days exploring.

Description

Dixcart Bay is a good launching spot, but it can be exposed to southerly winds which, if forecast makes Creux Harbour a better option.

Heading towards Point Robert Lighthouse you immediately find caves to explore between Derrible Point and Creux Harbour. Allow plenty time for cave exploration. Almost any cave or gulley is worth exploring. Watch out for swell and the fast rise or fall of the tide inside the caves.

Creux Harbour is a good landing but there is a risk of rock falls by the old tunnel. This was the main landing until Maseline Harbour was completed in 1949. There is a café, toilets and showers Expect fast water between Creux Harbour and Les Burons rocks.

Stay inshore between Maseline Harbour and Bec du Nez. There are small boat landings at La Grève de la Ville and Banquette, with small paths leading up the cliffs.

The Eperquerie landing has a stony beach at low tide. This is where the first settlers landed The name originates from the drying place for conger where all tenants of a fief (ancient feudal

Sark's feudal past

The island is independent with its own laws, but forms part of the Bailiwick of Guernsey. For example, it was not until 2003 that the Chief Pleas (government) voted to vary the long-standing ban on divorce.

Sark is a royal fief. In 1564 Queen Elizabeth I granted a lease to Helier de Carteret, Seigneur of St Ouen in Jersey, to be held by him and his heirs in perpetuity, on the condition that he populated the island with at least 40 men capable of defending Sark from pirates. De Carteret divided the island into forty tenements and let them to the forty families he brought with him from Jersey and Guernsey. Until elections in 2008 the government of Sark was based on these feudal rights.

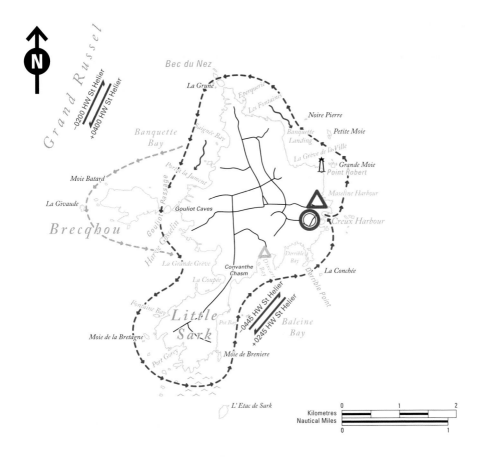

districts under the control of a Seigneur) had to bring their fish, in the same way they had to have their corn ground at the Seigneur's mill.

Bec du Nez has a fast tide stream. You can sneak past by using a channel between La Grune and Sark. Once on the west coast, Brecqhou provides shelter from southerly winds and swell, and makes it possible to explore the caves, sea arches and Les Autelets stacks.

Beneath the Window in the Rock (a cliff opening blasted out to produce a better view of Guernsey) is Port de Moulin, a small shingle beach with a path. This can be a good place to stop and break the trip into a two day exploration, but check the forecasts.

The Gouliot Passage is great for river techniques. If you take a swim on the south-going stream you'll end up in the tiny harbour of Havre Gosselin. This is an excellent landing – if you like carrying your kayak up ladders and steps.

Expect to be tracked by security cameras and staff around Brecqhou. The island is privately owned and landing is not permitted. The owners have made considerable investment on both Brecqhou and Sark to develop the islands' economy. This includes a vineyard and the renovation of many hotels. At Moie Batard and La Givaude islets off Brecqhou there are many shallow reefs where you are exposed to the main tide streams in the Great Russel.

The narrow track at La Coupée connects Sark and Little Sark. It is said that a slightly different dialect of Sercquiais (the ancient language of the islanders) evolved on Little Sark. Each Channel Island has its own language based on Norman French, and it is from Normandy that many of the ancient laws and legal structures originate.

There is a very steep path leading down from La Coupée to the sandy beach at La Grande Grève. The sandy beach covers on most high tides.

The south of Sark is already described in Route 10. At low tide the Adonis rock pool by Moie de la Bretagne and nearby Venus Pool are popular natural swimming pools.

L'Étac rocks are an important breeding site for sea birds, and the tide streams in the channel are fast with overfalls around half tide.

Beyond Moie de Breniere you regain shelter from any westerly swell. If you are not 'caved out' there remain a few more sea caves and arches to explore along this section of coast towards Dixcart Bay.

The east coast of Sark is often a good place to spot bottlenose dolphins. If you are unable to kayak across to Sark, it is possible to join a guided kayak tour with Adventure Sark.

Variations

Make time to explore Sark on foot. There is plenty to discover and lots of really good views.

Tides and weather

Wind direction is a key factor around Sark. The cliffs provide a lot of protection so it can come as a shock when you round a headland and hit the swell.

Expect plenty of tidal anomalies and eddies around the coast.

Additional information

Admiralty chart 5604.12 Sark: 1 : 25 000, which is part of the Admiralty Folio SC5604 – The Channel Islands.

Caving and coasteering on Sark

Sark is riddled with sea caves and arches and many have two entrances. Any cave or narrow gulley is worth exploring as some open into quite large areas. Some caves are large enough for the local charter boat to enter.

The large number of caves and sea arches stems from the amphibolite and granite gneisses, intruded by quartz diorite. The faults have been eroded by the ocean when sea levels were higher.

In 1914 G & L Latrobe explored the coastline and published their guidebook to some nineteen caves, though the enterprising kayaker is likely to find a few that are not listed. There is now an updated version, *Sark Coast and Caves* by John Frederic La Trobe-Bateman. *The Caves and scrambles of Sark* by T Kiernan is a less detailed book. All these guides must be used with caution as routes may have deteriorated since publication due to rock falls and erosion.

Many of the caves can be reached from the land but care is needed. Our forefathers were a hardy bunch, so watch out for La Trobe's comments, "... a rope is usually necessary ..." and "... even for the able bodied it requires care and a certain amount of skill in rock climbing ..." This makes the island a superb coasteering spot, and the La Trobes may well have written the first coasteering guidebook.

Around half tide is usually the best time to paddle into the caves. If you want to explore on foot, spring tides are usually best. Remember the tide range on Sark is 8.6m.

The Gouliot caves are a remarkable tidal cave system which can be explored at low tide by landing on a stony beach on the north side of the Gouliot headland. Sponges, sea squirts, sea anemones, cup corals and rare marine life can be found here, although there are a couple cave systems on Jersey which have many similar creatures. The darkness, huge tide range, and flow of water may all play a part to make the caves a remarkable habitat. The Gouliot caves are a Ramsar site, so take care to avoid brushing against the rock faces which are habitats for rare marine life.

Jersey to Guernsey

No. 12 | Grade C | 30km (16NM) | OS Sheets J and G | 2669, 808, NP264

Tidal Port	St Helier
Start	△ Le Pulec (Stinky Bay) (547 549) or La Grève de Lecq (583 555)
Finish	◎ Havelet Bay Guernsey (385 775)
HW/LW	HW St Helier is 4 hours 55 minutes before HW Dover.
Tidal Times	Between Jersey and Sark the NE stream starts 2 hours before, and runs until 3 hours after, HW St Helier. The SW stream starts 4 hours after, and ends 4 hours before, HW St Helier.
	In the Great Russel the NE going stream runs from 2 hours before, to 3 hours after, HW St Helier. The SW going stream runs from 4 hours after, to 3 hours before, HW St Helier.
	In the Little Russel the NE going streams runs from 2 hours 40 minutes before, to 2 hours 50 minutes after, HW St Helier and quickly builds. By 3 hours 50 minutes after HW St Helier the S going stream is established.
Max Rate Sp	3.1knots. The fastest speed occurs at low and high water. Expect faster streams and eddies off the south of Sark.
Coastguard	Jersey, tel. 01534 447705 Channel 82. VTS Channel 14.
	Guernsey, tel. 01481 720672 Channel 20. St Peter Port VTS Channel 12.

Introduction

The advent of fast single and double sea kayaks make this an exciting challenge for the very experienced paddler in good conditions. However, as there is only about five hours of favourable tidal stream less speedy paddlers should go via Sark (See Variations below).

Description

Leaving Jersey, it may be disconcerting to find yourself on a course which seems to be pointing at the western tip of Guernsey or out into the ocean, but it is essential to allow for the tide streams on this crossing.

If you find yourself near the Banc Desormes buoy (4NM north of Gros Nez Point), you will have been pushed too far east, and you should now modify your plans and head for Sark.

Off the south coast of Sark there is a considerable movement of water. You may encounter large eddies and overfalls near L'Etac. South of Jethou the reefs extend almost 2NM with eddies and overfalls. It may therefore be better to head towards Herm and go through the Percée Passage to Guernsey, or aim further south of Jethou, if you still have time to make this choice.

Variations

An alternative is to go via Sark, and stop at the northern end of the island to await slack water and the start of the south-west stream in the Great and Little Russel channels. This has the advantage of allowing you to break the journey. This route might require some ferry gliding, if you get pushed too far south.

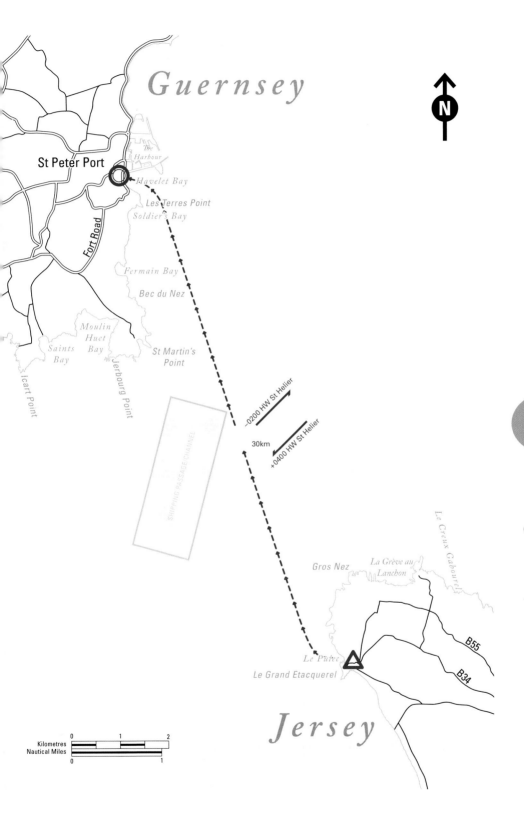

Guernsey

St Peter Port

The Harbour

Havelet Bay

Les Terres Point

Soldier's Bay

Fort Road

Fermain Bay

Bec du Nez

Moulin Huet Bay

Saints Bay

St Martin's Point

Jerbourg Point

Icart Point

SHIPPING PASSAGE CHANNEL

N

~0200 HW St Helier

30km

+0400 HW St Helier

12

Jersey to Guernsey

Le Creux Gabourel

Gros Nez

La Grève au Lanchon

B55

B34

Le Pulec

Le Grand Etacquerel

Jersey

Kilometres
Nautical Miles

0   1   2

0   1

The trip can be a round trip or you can catch the ferry back to Jersey. If you catch the ferry take some kayak trolleys as it can be a long carry at the ferry port. At the time of writing it was advisable to discuss this option with the St Peter Port Condor Ferries office in advance.

If kayaking back to Jersey, it may be more advantageous to paddle via Herm and Bec du Nez on Sark on the last of the north-east going tide (3 hours after HW St Helier), and then catch the south-westerly stream around low water back to Jersey. This will break the journey and makes the north coast of Jersey a larger target to aim for.

Tides and weather

This is an open sea crossing, so your departure time and route will depend upon your average paddling speed and the wind and sea forecast. The largest tidal movements are between Sark and Guernsey. You should therefore be prepared to stop at Sark, if conditions or your timings change. Once in the Great Russel it is still possible to alter your route and head back to Sark or Herm.

Additional information

Landfall on Guernsey is likely to be influenced by where you plan to stay and park the kayaks. Herm is therefore a good destination, as it has a small campsite and it's only a short crossing to St Peter Port to catch the ferry back to Jersey.

It is essential that you are well equipped and carry plenty of fluids.

If you take the direct route to Guernsey, you will be paddling almost parallel to one of the two high-speed ferry routes (the second runs north of the Desormes buoy) so it is advisable to check the timings and listen on the both the coastguard and VTS channels.

Christmas castaway ... so near yet so far

In December 1918 the sailing ketch *Iris* ran aground off Fort Le Marchant on the north coast of Guernsey. The body of a seaman wearing a coat and belt with the name Robert Manning written on them was discovered on Le Galand (Galeu) islet 6 weeks later.

It seems that Manning abandoned the sinking *Iris* with the skipper, Captain Rickard and Jack Collins – whose body was washed ashore in Fontenelle Bay. Had they remained on board it is possible they may have survived. Instead they drifted in a small boat onto Le Galand where the boat was wrecked.

Passing ships with their passengers and crews were probably too busy navigating and looking at Guernsey to spot the shipwrecked sailors, and seamen who fished The Humps were rarely out in December. It is believed that at some point in their ordeal Captain Rickard attempted to swim to Herm and drowned.

On 23rd January, Manning's body was found. A head injury suggested he had fallen. Only later was it learned that it was not Robert but Harry who died. Harry Manning had not been an active seaman for years and had only just arrived in Fowey with his wife and children when he agreed to stand in on the *Iris'* last voyage. Only when his wife read a report in the Guernsey Press that described a tattoo on his chest was Harry correctly identified.

Havelet
to Petit Bôt Bay

No. 14 | **Grade B** | **10km (6NM)** | **OS sheet G** | **808**

Tidal Port	St Helier
Start	△ Havelet Bay (385 775)
Finish	○ Petit Bôt Bay (350 418)
HW/LW	HW St Helier is 4 hours 55 minutes before HW Dover.
Tidal Times	South of St Peter Port to St Martin's Point. A S going eddy starts about 3 hours before the main stream further offshore, which commences around at around 3 hours 50 minutes after HW St Helier. A N going eddy commences 1 hour 45 minutes earlier than the main N going stream around 3 hours 45 minutes before HW St Helier.
	St Martin's Point to Petit Bôt. The W going stream starts at 1 hour 50 minutes after HW and the E going stream starts 5 hours 50 minutes after HW St Helier. There are eddies in the deep bays.
Max Rate Sp	5.2 knots in the Little Russel. 3 knots on the South Coast but more off headlands.
Coastguard	Guernsey, tel. 01481 720672. Passage reports on Channel 20.

Introduction

The south-east and south coast offer perhaps the most dramatic scenery with a wide range o
coastline and sea conditions. Though the landing spots appear near, this section can be quit
challenging, and even a 2km (1NM) paddle can quickly become an epic.

Description

You may find parking spaces near the aquarium. The open air bathing pool is used all year roun
and you may feel very over dressed when launching from here. Rounding Les Terres Point yo
quickly lose sight of St Peter Port, and are faced with a striking coastline of cliffs and sma
coves that are only accessible by kayak or narrow tracks. The Ozanne Steps 0.5km south of Le
Terres were built to allow a family living in a property above to go bathing. Fermain Bay is a
good landing but has very restricted parking and access. The coastal defence tower (often calle
pre-Martello or loophole towers) was influenced by similar constructions in Corsica.

Bec du Nez is a natural harbour and nearby at La Divette is a 14th-century jetty. La Pied d
Mur Bay has a cave with a marble roof accessible by three entrances. The bay marks the easter
extremity of the ramp and ditch defences of the Iron Age promontory fort at Jerbourg. The for
continued to be used into the 13th and 14th century as a refuge against attacks from the French

At St Martin's Point you quickly move into faster tide streams and the more exposed sout
coast. Les Tas de Pois d'Amont (Pea Stacks) is an impressive group of three stacks thrusting ou
of the ocean, one of which appears like a cowled priest. If there is no swell, you can go betwee
them, but watch out on the north side of the gaps for clapotis.

Egress from Le Petit Port with kayaks is difficult. The caves in Moulin Huet show evidence f 8m and 18m raised beaches. Copper veins are visible and as a result small scale mining briefly ccurred. The Dog and Lion stacks are impressive to slip between. Any westerly swell should ecrease as you near Saints Bay.

At Icart Point you again lose any protection from westerlies but you can judge the size of the well by looking east towards Jerbourg Point. Some of the oldest rocks in Western Europe are ound here. The headland has given its name to the Icart gneiss which is 2,700 million years old. Goat Island is barely connected to the mainland by a narrow coupée (a narrow ridge connecting he island to Guernsey). The area was riddled with German mines during the war and the last razing goats had the misfortune of stepping on them.

Le Creux des Chiens (Dog Cave) is nearby. The name may originate from seals living in the ave as there are stories of 'sêirenes' (mermaids) near Petit Bôt. Today you are more likely to see

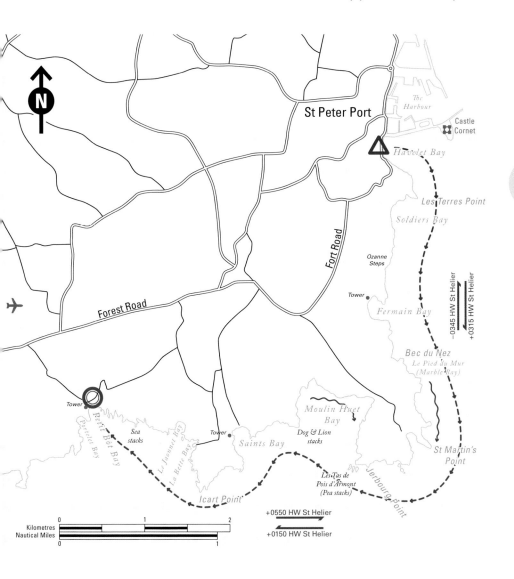

seals around The Humps though I have spotted some off Les Pezeries (near Portelet Harbour
The sandy La Bette and Le Jaonnet Bays are storm beaches; access is tricky via a steep path an
a short bronze ladder.

There are some stacks just before Petit Bôt and fascinating rock formations in the bay. The "pr
Martello tower" is an easy landmark beside the slip. Parking and access is restricted in the bay.

Variations

This trip can be combined with Petit Bôt to Portelet Harbour. However, you will have less tim
to explore close inshore.

Tides and weather

The cliffs along the east coast give considerable shelter from westerly wind and swell. Once yo
round St Martin's Point you will be more exposed.

Commando raids

In 1940 two hastily planned British Commando raids landed at Le Jaonnet Bay and
Icart. Operation Anger involved a Guernsey man, Second Lieutenant Nicolle, landing by
submarine and canoe on a one-man reconnaissance (6th July) in preparation for a second
raid codenamed Ambassador (14th July). Both operations were ambitious and depended
on timing, weather, training and good equipment; all of which were somewhat lacking.
Nicolle landed in a collapsible canoe bought from a London store – so well equipped was
the Navy in 1940. The operation was unsuccessful and Nicolle was lucky to escape being
shot as a spy. Operation Ambassador (14th July) suffered equipment failure, a boat heading
to Herm by accident, and other mishaps, which were largely mitigated by the enthusiasm
and motivation of the Commandos. All provided experience for future Commando raids,
especially emphasising the need for Commandos to be able to swim.

Few, if any, of the Commando raids in the Channel Islands achieved very much. On the
other hand, Operation Basalt, a small scale landing of twelve men at the Hogs back on
Sark (3rd October 1942) had a disproportionate impact. Hitler ordered 1,400 allied prisoners be shackled in retaliation for the German soldiers being tied up. Basalt was partly
responsible for Hitler's notorious Kommandobefehl on 18th October ordering that all
captured Commandos be treated as spies and shot.

Portelet
to Petit Bôt Bay 🏔️🏔️🏔️🏔️

No. 15 | Grade B | 9km (5NM) | OS sheet G | 3654

Tidal Port	St Helier
Start	△ Portelet Harbour (293 427)
Finish	◎ Petit Bôt Bay (350 418)
HW/LW	HW St Helier is 4 hours 55 minutes before HW Dover.
Tidal Times	The E going stream starts 5 hours 50 minutes after HW St Helier. A weaker W going stream starts 10 minutes before HW St Helier.
	Around Pleinmont. The SW going stream starts 10 minutes before HW St Helier but this is an inshore eddy. The main SW going stream starts 2 hours 50 minutes after HW St Helier. Inshore, a weak NE going stream starts 5 hours 50 minutes after HW St Helier.
Max Rate Sp	2.4 knots.
Coastguard	Guernsey, tel. 01481 720672. Passage reports on Channel 20.

Introduction

This trip takes you along the rugged and cave-ridden southern cliffs where there are no decer landings until Petit Bôt.

Description

There is a small car park and toilets at Portelet Harbour. If it is low tide, you can wheel the kaya down the little jetty, otherwise launching is from a sandy beach. The road to Les Pezeries is onl for pedestrian access. Just above the harbour are the former Hanois Lighthouse keepers' cottage

Les Pezeries Bay is a spot where you may occasionally see grey seals. Nearby is a small ston circle known as Table des Pions, and the MP3 range control tower.

Above L'Angle is Batterie Dollman. The 22cm guns had a range of 22km and nearby is th range control tower MP4 which is considered the best example in the Channel Islands. Jus below on the east side of the headland is La Congrelle, a narrow ravine once famous for conge eels. Nineteenth-century guide books often comment on the huge quantities of conger eel caugh in the Channel Islands, and the tasty conger soup. Personally, I consider conger soup to be a acquired taste.

About 250m ahead is a large blowhole known as La Souffleur, though when working at its bes you probably don't want to be anywhere nearby.

In Le Long Avaleux there are a few sea arches, and Le Creux Mahie is reputed to have th island's biggest cave. Access down the cliff path shown on the map is precarious, with what look ke a fire brigade ladder bolted onto the cliffs. The large pipe running down the cliff was used for he discharge of raw sewage until 2010. Today the sewage is pumped to Belle Greve Bay where : is discharged into the sea – unlike Jersey where sewage is UV treated.

The cliff-line continues with plenty of rock gardens, small caves and a large ravine at Le Gouffre.

Pointe de la Moye is a large headland giving a bit of protection once you round it and head >wards Petit Bôt. If you plan to paddle west out of Petit Bôt and want to check conditions, he German range control tower at Le Prevote gives an excellent view of the coast to the west. Jnusually, this tower was built and manned by the German Army.

There is a small landing east of Pointe de la Moye with steep steps and a slipway, where small oats are winched up by hand. Unless you are into British Canoeing 5 star assessment landing spots, : is probably easier to paddle another 1km into Petit Bôt where access is easier and there's a café.

Artillery control towers

This section of coast is marked by the number of Nazi range control towers. Each slot controlled a different artillery battery, the highest slots controlling the long range guns. Almost all the towers and heavy artillery gun batteries on Guernsey were manned by the German Navy. The largest guns at Batterie Mirus near L'Erée consisted of four 30.5cm naval guns with a range of 41km (26 miles), and could shell Jersey and a large area of the channel. They were protected by 2m thick concrete walls.

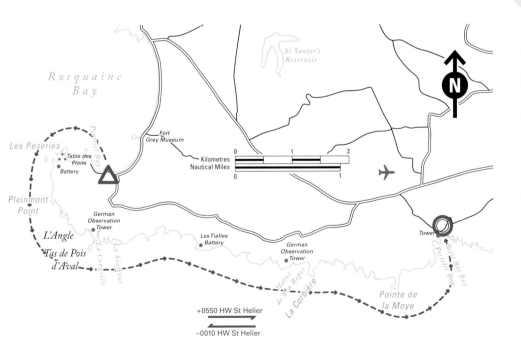

Variations

The Hanois Lighthouse 1.8km (1NM) west of Pleinmont dominates the area. This is an obvious destination provided you are happy being 1NM offshore. The light is reached by following the chain of rocks interspersed by deep water channels and fast tide streams flowing north and south. Expect to encounter a few tide stream anomalies en route. Within 0.5km (0.25NM) of the Hanois the water depth drops to over 50m, so this area is very exposed to ocean swell.

Tides and weather

If exploring the caves, take time to assess the swell frequency. It is prudent to look well ahead for 'future water' in order to anticipate conditions as you near a cave or headland.

The tide streams flow predominantly eastwards. With any swell expect a great rollercoaster ride, just ensure you don't change your mind and want to turn back.

Hanois Lighthouse

Les Hanois Light is one of the island's most notorious landmarks. Many ships have come to grief here, but there was considerable argument and delay over who should fund a lighthouse. The shipwreck of the HMS *Boreas* in 1807 when 127 drowned slightly hastened things, but it was not until Trinity House agreed to fund construction that the project was completed in 1862.

The most significant feature of lighthouse construction in the 19th century is the level of innovation and design that was taking place, with a few key designers revolutionising construction methods around the UK.

The light is 36m tall and built with Cornish granite, and is important in the development of lighthouse engineering. James Douglass suggested that the stones were dovetailed together both laterally and vertically so they could not be separated without destroying the stones. Cement mortar in the joints then bonds the stones.

Before the advent of the channel shipping lanes it was common for ships to sail close to Guernsey. In a storm, problems quickly escalated as ships drifted nearer to Guernsey. Matters were not helped by the ability of some ships crews to mistake Les Hanois light for the Casquets off Alderney.

Portelet
to L'Ancresse Bay ■■○

No. 15 | **Grade B** | **18.5km (10NM)** | **OS sheet G** | **3654**

Tidal Port	St Helier
Start/Finish	△○ Portelet Harbour (293 427)
HW/LW	HW St Helier is 4 hours 55 minutes before HW Dover.
Tidal Times	A weak SW eddy is reported to run inshore from 10 minutes before, until 4 hours 50 minutes after, HW St Helier. A NE stream flows from 5 hours 50 minutes after, until 1 hour 10 minutes before, HW St Helier.
	Off the north of Guernsey an E going stream starts at 5 hours 40 minutes before HW St Helier. By 2 hours 40 minutes before HW this is flowing NE. At 3 hours 50 minutes after HW St Helier the W going stream starts.
Max Rate Sp	1 knot.
Coastguard	Guernsey, tel. 01481 720672. Passage reports on Channel 20.

Introduction

The coastline is low lying with plenty of get-outs in small bays and harbours. Rather than paddle directly up the coast, it is worth exploring the small bays and anchorages, though you should

look out for surf in some bays. The beauty of this route is that the large tidal range allows you to paddle the same route at different heights of tide, with completely different scenery. The extensive inshore reefs mean that at low tide it is easy to lose sight of the land.

Shipwrecked

This coastline was the site of some of Guernsey's worst shipping disasters in the 1970s.

On Christmas Day 1973 the bulk ore carrier *Elwood Mead* ran aground on its maiden voyage carrying 122,954 tons of iron ore. It took two months to refloat. Just days later the *Prosperity* ran aground in force 11-12 winds at La Conchée rocks. All 17 crew drowned and a memorial is at L'Erée headland. In 1978 the *Orion*, a 19,000 ton oil rig on a barge, ran onto Les Grunes reef in a Force 10 storm. This resulted in a dramatic rescue by the RNLI lifeboat coxswain John Petit. The rig, with 10 generators on board, was lit up like a Christmas tree and the lifeboat was seriously damaged during the rescue. One crewman was catapulted into the sea but was saved. The lifeboat's scramble net became entangled in the rig's anchor fluke, and its superstructure was damaged when the lifeboat was squashed against the helicopter landing platform. All the crew were rescued with the aid of the lifeboat and Sea King helicopters from Culdrose in Cornwall. A Guernsey friend was very annoyed by this shipwreck as it grounded on one of his favourite low water fishing spots.

Description

Portelet Harbour is a good starting point, with a car park and slipway access to a sandy beach. The natural harbour is used by small boats for fishing, and was a good vraicing (seaweed gathering) spot. The jetty was used by Trinity House to supply the Hanois Light. On the lowest tides expect to see numerous locals scrambling over the rocks armed with long hooks in search of lobster and ormers (a type of abalone) which, though less common today, may still be found in good quantities – if you know the right spots.

Close by is the Fort Grey Shipwreck Museum which is known locally as the 'cup and saucer'.

Depending on the tides, the passage between Lihou and the coast can be either a mass of fast flowing water, or a 750m walk. If the tide is out, it is a longer detour. Lihou is part of the Ramsar wetlands site at L'Erée. The small rock called Lihoumel is an important nesting site from 1st January to 15th July but it is requested that landing is avoided all year. Since 2006, Lihou has been managed by a charitable trust. The house can be hired to spend a couple days kayaking the

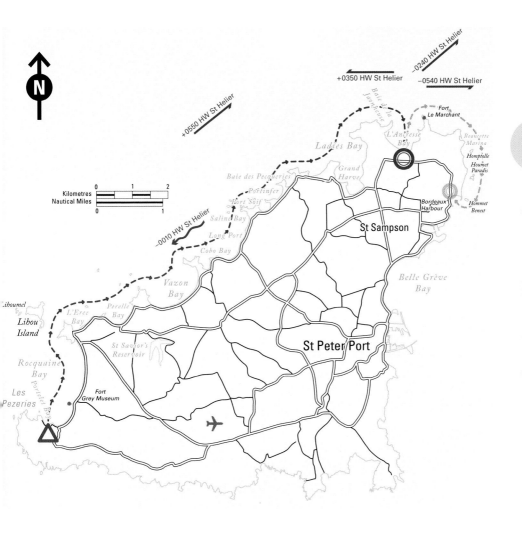

area. Advance booking through the Lihou Trust (www.lihouisland.com) is essential. Lihou is an important archaeological site with ruins of an ancient priory which was supposedly built as a challenge to pagan worship on Guernsey. From 1927 to 1935 a factory extracted iodine on Lihou from seaweed, but was unable to compete against cheaper South American imports.

Inshore, the shingle bank at L'Erée protects the unique habitats in the nature reserve. The tea shop and information centre feels like someone's living room.

La Conchée rocks is a good reef break. Nearby is Vazon Bay which is a popular surf spot and can get very busy with all sorts of water users, so watch out when landing or launching. A pea bed and petrified forest are sometimes revealed at low tides after big storms.

From Vazon Bay it is easy to muddle up the small beaches as they are quite close together. On almost every rocky point British forts and gun batteries grow out of the rocks. The Germans also recognised the strategic value of these locations. What was good for a cannon was also good for a German gun. Nazi maps show the tremendous amount of fortifications all around the west and east coasts of Guernsey. Try to land near a few points to explore and enjoy this coastline from a different angle.

Portinfer comes from the Breton word 'portfa' for harbour. The bay, like all of this coastline, is rich in marine life. If it is low tide, go and explore some of the reefs. These areas are superb spots to observe marine life and even catch a lobster.

There are small harbours at Baie de Port Grat and Grand Havre with old landing jetties. At the north end of Grand Harve are a few old fishing boats decaying into the mud.

Chouet quarry is a landfill site which will soon be filled. Its closure is likely to have a major impact on the seagull population around Guernsey, as it is an important source of food. Seagull numbers throughout the Channel Islands (and Europe) are in decline. Nearby Baie de la Jaonneuse has a stumpy little 'loophole' tower which looks like it is starting to become a Guernsey version of the leaning tower of Pisa. A couple of hundred metres around the headland is L'Ancresse Bay with a massive Nazi seawall and café; the design of the café is clearly influenced by the German defences.

The northern tip of Guernsey, though low-lying, is a fascinating area with a strange ruggedness. At one time the northern parish of Vale was separated from Guernsey by a narrow channel of water which was used as salt pans to dry salt.

Fort Le Marchant is often the first landfall for sea birds coming from England to rest and feed. Could this be the reason it became a shooting range? You may want to check if any red flags are flying. About 1km east is Fort Doyle which is a popular angling spot. To the north you may see Alderney, and across the Little Russel to The Humps, which extend north of Herm and are far more exposed than most realise.

Near Beaucette marina – a former quarry – are two small nature reserves on Homptolle and Houmet Paradis. Access is forbidden from January to August. If the tide is high enough there can be a nice flow between the islets and shore. The high mound of Bordeaux nature reserve (a former quarry and landfill site) is easy to spot beside the car park and landing at Petils Bay. On Hommet Benest ruined buildings dating back over 600 years were discovered. The natural harbour at Bordeaux dries out completely, but was once an important landing place.

Variations

This route can be combined with route 17 or a trip out to the Hanois Light. All of the bays are possible start and finish points and the route is a good return trip.

L'Ancresse Bay is often a good stopping point, especially if you plan to return to Portelet.

Tides and weather

The inshore streams appear as an eddy in the tidal stream atlas. The rates and direction vary depending on how far offshore you are. The streams around Lihou are up to 5 knots.

Offshore reefs tend to break up the swell, but keep an eye offshore as the rise and fall of the tide may quickly cause swell to break over the reefs and reach closer inshore.

In an east to south-east wind the bays are usually sheltered, but as you move away from the beach you will quickly encounter more wind.

Vazon Bay and Cobo Bay are popular surf spots. There are a couple of good reef breaks along this coast. The reef breaks around La Conchée can be large and extend some way out, so it may be easier and safer to do a quick portage over the narrow spit at low tide or stay inshore.

During southerly winds the northern part of this route does allow you to get a little shelter to go afloat. However, any protection from the low-lying land is limited. The tide streams between the islets and shore can be good to develop skills.

Additional information

If you expect to be landing or launching around low tide, a kayak trolley is useful unless you are into long carries over the beach.

In good weather parking can be a problem.

Guernsey to Sark ▢▢▢▢▢

No. 16	**Grade C**	**18.5km (10NM)**	**OS sheet G**	**808**

Tidal Port	St Helier
Start	△ Havelet (385 775) or Fermain Bay (382 429)
Finish	◯ Port de Moulin (503 432) (49° 26′ 06N 02° 22′ 12W), Havre Gosselin or Dixcart Bay.
HW/LW	HW St Helier is 4 hours 55 minutes before HW Dover.
Tidal Times	In the Little Russel the NE going stream runs from 2 hours 40 minutes before, to 2 hours 50 minutes after, HW St Helier and quickly builds. By 3 hours 50 minutes after HW St Helier the S going stream is established.
	In the Great Russel the NE going stream runs from 2 hours before, to 3 hours after, HW St Helier. The SW going stream runs from 4 hours after, to 3 hours before, HW St Helier.
	In Baleine Bay (see chart 808) the NE going stream starts 4 hours 45 minutes before HW St Helier. The SW going stream begins 2 hours 45 minutes after HW St Helier. The streams increase as you approach Derrible Point in the north and in the passage between Moie de Breniere islet and L'Étac to the south.
	On the north-east coast from Creux Harbour to Bec du Nez an eddy or slack water occurs during the whole of the NE going stream in the Great Russel. The strength varies depending on the tides. A bit of handrailing the coast – especially beneath Point Robert – usually works.
Max Rate Sp	5 to 6 knots at springs.
Coastguard	Guernsey, tel. 01481 720672. Passage reports to St Peter Port Radio on Channel 20. Maintain a watch on St Peter Port VTS Channel 12 in the Little Russel.

Introduction

The journey to Sark is both an impressive open sea crossing, and a step back into another world. Until 2008 Sark remained the last Feudal bastion in Europe. A quaint anachronism in a modern world where cars are banned and horses, carts, bicycles and tractors are just some of the differences the paddler notices upon arrival. Time your visit right and you may see the famous Sark sheep racing competition. With no street lighting and little light pollution Sark became the world's first 'Dark Sky Island' in 2010. This is a great place to brush up on your astronavigation.

The 12km (6.5NM) crossing to Sark is a serious undertaking, but unlike Les Écréhous (which is a similar distance) there is an opt out point en route on Herm, if things are not going to plan.

Description

If you opt to leave from Fermain Bay, road access is restricted just after Le Chalet Hotel and the car park is for hotel guests. At Havelet Bay allow time to park. If you leave Guernsey at the latter part of the south-going stream, expect to be pushed south of Jethou. Les Barbées and the nearby marks are a busy route for small craft. The Lower Heads Buoy is a useful guide to assess your drift.

The modern Gothic-style castle on Brecqhou is conspicuous as is the Pilcher Monument above the landing steps at Havre Gosselin. Looking more like a war memorial, the obelisk is in memory of a Mr J Pilcher who, along with four others, died in a storm in 1868 sailing from Sark to Guernsey.

Aim to get in close along the Sark coast to explore the superb cliffs, and also to pick up any eddies, if the north stream has already started. Just before Moie de Port rocks the towers of the old silver mines are visible. Mining commenced in the 1830s and employed up to 80 Sarkese nd many Cornish miners. However, the yield was poor and by 1844 the Seigneur of Sark, rnest le Pelley, mortgaged the island to a local privateer John Allaire. Le Pelley was unable o keep up the payments and faced bankruptcy. In 1849 the Seigneurie of Sark was sold to the eiress of Allaire for £6,000.

If conditions are good, it is possible to use the small landing at Port Gorey which was the oading point for the ore.

Beyond Bretagne Uset you should pick up the north stream to the popular anchorage and each at Dixcart Bay. A path leads up to the Dixcart Hotel and the village.

Variations

Havre Gosselin is a popular anchorage, and was an alternative landing spot for passengers travel-ing from Guernsey when there was swell on the east coast. Be prepared to climb up a ladder if you arrive a couple hours after low water and then have the fun of lifting your kayaks 3m and up a short' flight of about 25 steps onto the harbour wall. Alternatively you can join the many tenders nd moor your kayaks while waiting for the tide to rise.

The island of Brecqhou is privately owned. Landing is not permitted and it is unlikely you will get more than a couple minutes rest before being asked to leave. Free guided visits to the gardens on Brecqhou are possible, if you are staying at one of the Sark Island Hotels belonging

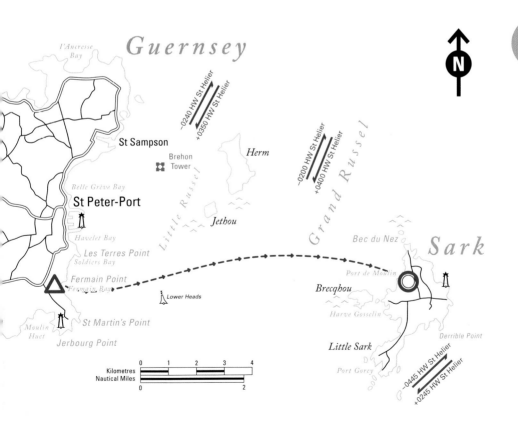

to Brecqhou's owners; otherwise advance booking and payment is required at the Sark Island Hotels office.

If you are running late and the NE stream is increasing, you will lose this stream quite rapidly once you pass inside La Givaude rocks and tuck in along the north coast of Brecqhou. The north-going stream in the Gouliot Passage commences at -0250 HW St Helier, so you will probably be looking at a small shingle/stony beach landing at Port de Moulin lying 1km north of Brecqhou. A steep narrow track leads from the beach onto Sark. The path is not shown to descend to the beach on the latest 1:10,000 map. There are a couple of grassy BBQ areas on the way up past the Window in the Rock. The rocky outcrop of Pegane has a small path which gives a better view of Guernsey and the Gouliot Passage.

Creux Harbour is a good landing and was the main harbour for Sark. Access to the harbour is through the small tunnel next to the café. The larger tunnel was constructed by the Nazis. The evidence of rock falls by the old tunnel may make you think carefully about leaving kayaks close to the cliff. There is a toilet and shower facility opposite the café. It is a 800m walk up the hill (take the small path to the left of the road) or a ride on the tractor bus to the top.

Tides and weather

This is an offshore trip and if you are paddling with people who have not undertaken many offshore trips, paddle speeds are likely to be slower than normal.

Bear in mind that your corrected course to allow for the tidal stream may seem to be heading you offshore and towards Jersey. For some this can be disconcerting.

Once you move into the Great Russel you lose the protection Guernsey may have given from any south-west or westerly swell. If you can see swell hitting the south end of Sark from Guernsey, it may indicate things are going to be 'challenging' in the Great Russel.

On spring tides the streams can reach 5 knots with overfalls which can be large when it is with wind against tide. Remember the maximum rates in the Great and Little Russel occur at high and low water St Helier.

Overfalls are frequent from the Demi Ferrière (south of Jethou) to the Noire Pute rocks. In the middle of the southern part of the Great Russel are the Gropied and Grode overfalls which may extend east towards Brecqhou.

An option is to leave on the last stages of the south going stream which allows landing at Havre Gosselin, but it may be better to head down the south coast and around to landings at Dixcart Bay or Creux Harbour. This will set you up to paddle on to Jersey, if Sark is used as a stop-off point.

On the return to Guernsey the overfalls off Herm and Jethou may come as a bit of a surprise.

Additional information

Allow time to find parking. This is not a trip to be running late.

It is not possible to take kayaks on the regular passenger ferries to Sark that run a couple times each day. There is a three times a week freight service by the Isle of Sark Shipping Company (www.sarkshippingcompany.com) tel. 01481 724059. The very latest they will accept freight is 1 hour before sailing, but it is advisable to arrive earlier.

Onward shipment to Jersey requires that you ship the kayaks back to Guernsey.

There are a few hotels and bed and breakfasts on Sark, plus two campsites, though some ma[y] not be open out of season. If bringing your own camp gear, it is usually possible to get a pitc[h] but in August or during the Sark water carnival and folk festival advance booking is advise[d] (www.sark.co.uk).

Guernsey to Herm and Jethou

No. 17 | Grade C | 11km (6NM) | OS sheet G | 808

Tidal Port	St Helier
Start	△ Havelet Bay (385 775), Salerie Corner (386 459) or Bordeaux Harbour (407 490)
Finish	○ Herm (466 443) (49° 28' 11N 02° 27' 13W) or Jethou (49° 27' 43N 02° 27' 39W)
HW/LW	HW St Helier is 4 hours 55 minutes before HW Dover.
Tidal Times	In the Little Russel the NE going streams runs from 2 hours 40 minutes before, to 2 hours 50 minutes after, HW St Helier and quickly builds. By 3 hours 50 minutes after HW St Helier the S going stream is established.
Max Rate Sp	5.2 knots.
Coastguard	Guernsey, tel. 01481 720672. Passage reports to Guernsey Coastguard on Channel 20. Maintain a watch on St Peter Port VTS Channel 12 in the Little Russel.

Introduction

The usual way to reach Herm and Jethou by kayak is to paddle across from Guernsey. In good conditions this is an excellent paddle, but the tide streams in the Little Russel should be treated

with considerable respect and caution, especially around spring tides, or if there is any risk o
wind against tide.

Description

Where you decide to launch from will be influenced by the direction of the tide streams and
whether you plan to make a round trip.

Havelet Bay has an advantage during the start of the north-bound stream as you can allow
less for the drift onto Herm, although this is a longer crossing. There is a small slip north of th
swimming pool.

The beach and tiny harbour at Salerie Corner is another option, if crossing around the turn o
the tide, though it is important to remember this does not occur at high or low water but at hal
tide. Conger eel was an important export from the 13th to 16th centuries, and the places wher
the fish was salted were known as 'saleries'.

Brehon Tower 2.7km (1.5NM) west of Herm is an excellent mark to assess your speed of drif
and to practise transits. At times it can appear as if the tower is on roller coasters as the stream
build. The tower was completed in 1856 to counter a possible French attack from the recentl
enlarged harbour at Cherbourg.

Brehon Tower and the surrounding beacons and reefs make excellent breakouts from the tid
streams. Remember to lean into the turn as the streams can be like a river in this area. To th
north east of Brehon Tower is Fondu and Grosse Pierre islets. They may be worth a detour, o

erve as eddy hops, if you have been pushed too far north by the stream; miss these breakouts on
 big tide and your short trip to Herm is going to develop into some resistance training!

Variations

This journey is often made as a round trip.

Tides and weather

The Little Russel has fast flowing tide streams and shallow areas. Depths vary from 40m to just
m over The Great Bank. The charted 5.2 knot streams will be exceeded in some locations. On
arge tides good ferry glide skills will be essential as you cross the Little Russel; there are numer-
us transits to use to assess your drift.

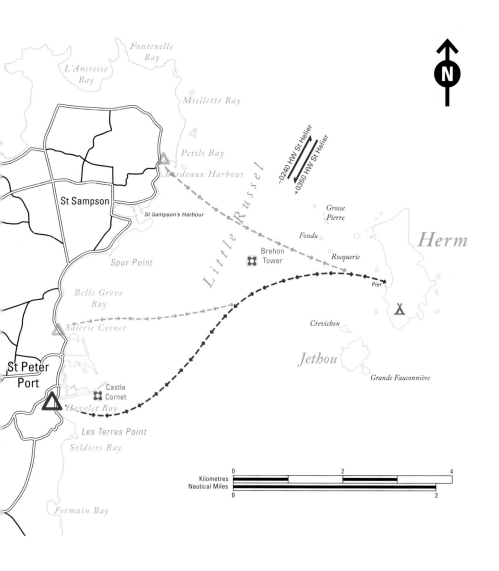

At some point you will be more than 1.8km (1NM) offshore, so any protection provided by the land will be lost, if there is an offshore wind.

Additional information

Allow time to find a parking place. Many a trip has ended up missing the tide because paddlers were late getting on the water due to difficulties trying to park.

The Little Russel is a busy shipping channel used by vessels approaching from both the south and north ends of the passage. Small ferries and pleasure craft heading to Herm and Sark should also be expected. Cruise liners often anchor south-east of St Peter Port with a shuttle of launches moving passengers back and forth. Near Herm and Jethou the inshore passages are narrow and allow little room for vessels to manoeuvre.

Maritime nations

In the 19th century both Guernsey and Jersey punched above their size as maritime nations. This was largely a result of the islands' favourable location and relationship with Britain. Ships could be constructed from oak at a lower cost than in the UK, and both islands also enjoyed favourable tax advantages to import goods into Britain.

Surprisingly, the trading areas of Guernsey and Jersey ships were quite different. In part this stemmed from Jersey being an important stopover point for French ships heading to fish for cod in Canada. Guernsey ships were more likely to be involved in coastal trade, though they did develop a presence shipping fruit from the Iberian Peninsula and the Azores. This resulted in Guernsey ship builders specialising in the construction of fast schooners to bring fresh produce to Britain. Guernsey, Herm and Jethou were extensively quarried as the hard wearing *Guernsey granite* was exported, as an alternative to *Aberdeen granite* used to pave the roads in London.

By 1845 the total tonnage of Guernsey ships engaged in coastal trade was 3,104 tonnes compared to Jersey's 1,293 tonnes. In contrast Jersey played a bigger role in foreign trade with 16,894 tonnes compared to Guernsey's 6,207 tonnes.

By the 1870s the advent of steam, construction of iron ships, and lower costs of these new technologies made Britain an unrivalled shipbuilding nation which the Channel Islands could not compete against. This led to a rapid decline in both shipbuilding and the Jersey and Guernsey fleets.

The recent increase in locally registered ships is a result of both islands setting up registries for 'super yachts'.

Herm ⓒ▨▨▨▨▨

No. 18 | **Grade B** | **6km (3.5NM)** | **OS sheet G** | **3654, 808**

Tidal Port	St Helier
Start/Finish	△○ Herm Harbour (466 443)
HW/LW	HW St Helier is 4 hours 55 minutes before HW Dover.
Tidal Times	In the Percée Passage a strong SF going stream starts at 5 hours 30 minutes before HW St Helier and runs for 9 hours from the harbour to Point Sauzebourge at a max rate springs of 5 knots. The NW going stream is weaker, starts at 3 hours 30 minutes after HW St Helier and runs for 3.5 hours.
	Off the east coast of Herm the streams are similar to the Great Russel. The NE going stream runs from 2 hours before, to 3 hours after, HW St Helier and the SW going from 4 hours after, to 4 hours before, HW St Helier.
	Expect faster streams and eddies amongst The Humps.
Max Rate Sp	5 knots plus.
Coastguard	Guernsey, tel. 01481 720672. Passage reports on Channel 20. Maintain a watch on St Peter Port VTS Channel 12 in the Little Russel.

Introduction

Herm is a remarkable little island and deserves more than a day paddle from Guernsey. Try t stay a couple of days to explore Herm, Jethou and The Humps (see Variations).

Between 1570 and 1737 the island was a playground for the Governors of Guernsey befor being leased to tenants. From 1920 to 1923, the writer and co-founder of the Scottish Nation: Party, Compton MacKenzie, was a tenant. Subsequently the island was leased to Sir Perciv: Perry, chairman of the Ford Motor company.

Herm was the location for a Nazi propaganda film depicting the invasion of the Isle of Wigh during the Second World War. After the war, the States of Guernsey bought Herm from th Crown. The Wood family leased Herm from 1949 to 2008 and transformed the overgrown an abandoned island. In 2008 the Starboard Trust bought the lease vowing to maintain the island a a quiet and beautiful place for visitors to enjoy.

Description

Landing is at Fisherman's Beach beside the tiny harbour. It can be very busy in summer as th Herm ferry and visiting yachts moor here. The Rosière Steps are accessible at low tide, but this also used by the ferry and gets busy.

Heading south-east, the Percée passage is a busy channel used by both yachts and Sark ferrie From Point Sauzebourge the cliffs are worth close exploration. Puffin can be seen during th nesting season (early March to late July). In recent years the maximum count was 24.

If there is a southerly wind or swell you get protection once you pass Selle Roque and Caquorobert rocks. Belvoir Bay is a great spot to rendezvous with non-paddling friends/family and has a South Sea island feel complete with beach café/bar. Nearby is Shell Beach where you will discover hundreds of tiny sea shells which tend to be clustered in bands, especially at the north end of the beach.

The Common is a neolithic burial site, though many tombs were destroyed by quarrying in the 19th century. Around 400 quarrymen worked on Herm to quarry the granite for the military fortifications on Guernsey; some of the stone was also supplied for the construction of London Bridge. A forge, blacksmith, brewery, bakery, and even a prison were built. Quarrying ceased by the end of the century.

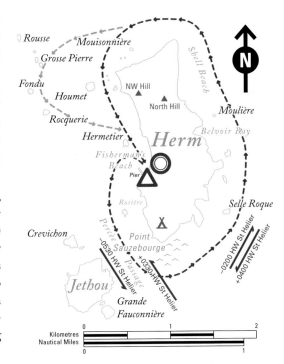

From Shell Beach back to Fisherman's Beach the coast is low and sandy. Expect faster water if you head over to Grosse Pierre and Fondu islets.

Ashore, it is worth taking a walk up to Le Manoir. The neo-Gothic style was commissioned by Prince Blücher von Wahlstatt in the 1890s. St Tugual's Chapel dates back to the early medieval period and the Christianisation of the Pagan sites on Herm by Celtic missionaries. It is believed that in the 6th-century monks from the monastery founded by St Magloire on Sark created the first hermitage on Herm.

Variations

THE HUMPS

Grade C | **16km (8.5NM)**

At La Pointe du Gentilhomme the 3.7km (2NM) paddle to Grande Amfroque and The Humps is a great option in good conditions, but remember you will be up to 3.7km (2NM) offshore. Tide streams run fast between the channels roughly coinciding with the streams in the Great Russel.

Puffins, grey seals, razorbills, guillemots and cormorants may be seen. Avoid landing on the islets during the nesting season which runs until mid July, and check for any nature reserve restrictions. At low tide this is a great place with huge beds of deep water seaweeds and white sands. Heading back to Herm you'll need to keep to the west unless you want to end up in the Great Russel. Expect overfalls and fast tide streams between the islets.

Tides and weather

The south-east stream in the Percée passage produces overfalls. This stream is present from south of the harbour and extends about 1km offshore before you encounter the start of the main stream in the Little Russel.

Overfalls occur throughout the area bounded by Point Sauzebourge, Fourquies, Noire Pute and on up to Grande Amfroque. Close inshore expect eddies on large tides. The Humps to Grande Amfroque is a mass of channels and shallows so expect to use ferry glides. This area can be quite exposed.

Additional information

The campsite is open during the summer season and the hotel from March to October. Self-catering cottages can be booked year round. Advance booking is essential. The Mermaid Tavern is open daily from April to October, with limited opening hours in winter. Contact Herm Island for the current opening times of the hotel and campsite tel. 01481 750000 (email reservations@herm.com).

The transport of kayaks needs to be arranged with Herm Island as the Trident passenger ferries have very limited space.

If staying on Herm, it is best to check where to put your kayaks. Luggage can be transported to the campsite, hotel or cottages by tractor.

There is a small grocery shop, but it is best to bring food for your stay.

Jethou

No. 19 | Grade B | 3.5km (2 NM) | OS sheet G

Tidal Port	St Helier
Start/Finish	Herm Harbour (466 443)
HW/LW	HW St Helier is 4 hours 55 minutes before HW Dover.
Tidal Times	In the Percée Passage a strong SE going stream starts at 5 hours 30 minutes before HW St Helier and runs for 9 hours from the harbour to Point Sauzebourge at a max rate springs of 5 knots. The NW going stream is weaker, starts at 3 hours 30 minutes after HW St Helier and runs for 3.5 hours.
	Between Jethou and Crevichon a NE going stream runs around the times of high water.
	Off the east and south coast the streams are similar to the Great Russel. The NE going stream runs from 2 hours before to 3 hours after HW St Helier, and the SW going from 4 hours after to 4 hours before HW St Helier.
Max Rate Sp	5 knots plus.
Coastguard	Guernsey, tel. 01481 720672. Passage reports on Channel 20. Maintain a watch on St Peter Port VTS Channel 12 in the Little Russel.

Introduction

Jethou is a good add-on to the Herm route, but you'll need to carefully time the crossing of the Percée Passage due to the fast tide streams.

Description

Having crossed the narrow Percée Passage, heading round the island can be tricky due to the fast streams close inshore.

The channel between Crevichon and Jethou dries around half tide.

The demand for granite in the early 19th century was so intense that both Jethou and Crevichon were quarried. It is said that the steps of St Paul's Cathedral are of Crevichon granite.

West of Grande Fauconnière is a rock pool which has been made deeper to allow bathing.

NW of Grande Fauconnière is a small cave called Creux du Diable (Devil's Cave). Above the cave can be seen ancient field terraces. Puffins nest off the south east corner of Jethou.

Variations

If staying on Herm, unless you put in north of Herm harbour you will almost immediately be into the fast streams that run in the Percée Passage.

The southern rocks of Grosse Ferrier and Les Barbées are not as extensive as The Humps at low tide.

Tides and weather

The Percée Passage has a considerable tide stream running. The marked channels are narrow so it essential to keep a look out for other craft.

Expect overfalls in both the Percée Passage and south of Jethou along with some eddies. Shallow areas with overfalls e east of the island between the Fourquies uoy to the Lower Heads buoy.

The reefs to the south of Jethou create ast tide streams which may not correspond vith the charted information. The Tobars Passage runs very close to the island, and s often used by boats en route to Sark and he east coast of Herm.

Additional information

Landing is not permitted on Jethou without permission from the leaseholder, Sir Peter Ogden.

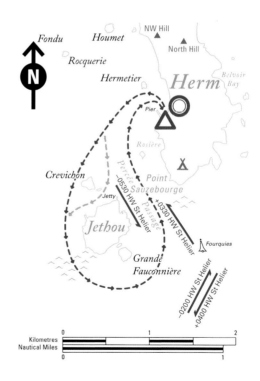

A nefarious past

It is said that in AD 709 a storm washed away a strip of land which connected the island with Herm. However, in 1867 Colonel Montague Fielden, the tenant of both Jethou and Herm, proposed constructing a floating causeway across the fast-flowing Percée Passage. The project was never completed, perhaps because the colonel was too busy smuggling brandy from France to Dorset, using Jethou as a storehouse. This may explain why he employed a team of Bretons and Welshmen to fire on passing fishermen. On the top of the island there is a marker on which pirates were supposedly hanged.

A Robinson Crusoe on Jethou

In 1898 Harry Nilford (pen name E. R. Suffling) wrote *Jethou or Crusoe life in the Channel Islands*, recounting a year on Jethou when he was 21 years old.

Harry wrote about his daily life, which included watching two shipwrecks near Jethou and the subsequent loss of life. Rather than take the body of a drowned seaman to shore he opted for a sea burial to avoid the need to deal with, and attend, the coroner's inquest in Guernsey. This reveals a very different approach to life and death at sea in the 19th century.

Harry had a canoe (perhaps a Rob Roy style canoe judging by the sketches) which we'd now call a kayak. After several narrow escapes kayaking around the coast, Harry adds an outrigger, watertight bulkheads and anchor to go kayak fishing around Jethou and Herm. Sadly his kayak is destroyed when his store is struck by lightning, but not before he has a few adventures around the coast.

The list of fish he catches throws light on how bountiful the sea was in the 19th century. Harry soon discovered that the plentiful ormer (a type of abalone, which is today a rare and expensive Channel Island delicacy) made excellent bait for conger kayak fishing.

Around the Channel Islands conger were plentiful and formed an important part of the local diet. "The sea about these islands", wrote Falle toward the end of the century, "might be called the Kingdom of Congers, so great is the quantity taken at all seasons". In feudal times conger were required to be taken to public drying places known as an 'eperquerie' which enabled the seigneur (a feudal lord) to have the first choice of all conger caught. This subsequently evolved into a feudal tax on fish.

On one kayak fishing trip off Roche Rouge, Harry catches three small conger, several rock fish, and whiting. Deciding to use ormer for bait, Harry hooks a large conger which results in a capsize and a self rescue. Fortunately the line was attached to the kayak and acted as a leash which stopped the kayak (and conger) being lost. Harry calculated the conger weighed 103lbs. Even if you allow for 'fisherman's tales', catching conger from a kayak will have been an experience.

This also demonstrates that kayak fishing is not a new sport! Nor is the use of bulkheads, outriggers, anchoring and leashes anything new in sea kayaking, judging from his book.

Guernsey to Alderney

No. 20 | **Grade C** | **Distance 35km (19NM)** | **OS sheet G** | **3655, 60**

Tidal Port	St Helier
Start	△ L'Ancresse Bay, Guernsey (386 504) (49° 30' 11N 02° 31' 54W)
Finish	⭘ Braye Harbour, Alderney (625 750) (49° 43' 24N 02° 11' 58W)
HW/LW	HW St Helier is 4 hours 55 minutes before HW Dover. HW Alderney is 45 minutes after HW St Helier.
Tidal Times	North of Guernsey a weak E going stream starts at 2 hours 40 minutes before HW St Helier. By 1 hour 40 minutes before HW the NE stream is established with a maximum rate of 3.6 knots. This runs until 3 hours 50 minutes after HW St Helier when it starts to swing west and around the north side of the Casquets while a SW going stream rapidly builds in The Swinge. From 4 hours 50 minutes after HW St Helier a SW going stream develops between Alderney and Guernsey but swings S and then SE until 1 hour 40 minutes before HW St Helier when the NE stream restarts.

In The Swinge, off Sauquet Rock (NE Les Homeaux Florains) a W going stream begins at 5 minutes before HW St Helier and quickly extends along the breakwater at about 4 knots at springs. Further out an E going stream is running at about 4 knots.

Around 45 minutes after HW St Helier the E going stream ceases and a W going stream is established along the north coast from Sauquet Rock to about 1NM north of the breakwater and on down to Corbet Rock.

Around 3 hours after HW St Helier the remaining NE going stream in The Swinge slackens. The W going eddy extends across The Swinge. By 4 hours 30 minutes after HW St Helier the SW going stream is running. By 2 hours 15 minutes before HW St Helier the E going stream is flowing. (In the atlas this is listed as flowing at 2 hours 40 minutes before HW St Helier.)

In the Alderney Race, the fastest streams are on the French side near La Foraine Beacon. The N going stream starts 1 hour 40 minutes before HW St Helier (max rate springs 10 knots). Around 4 hours 50 minutes after HW St Helier a SW going stream is established (max rate springs 7 knots). This swings more S and then SE until 2 hours 40 minutes before HW St Helier.

Max Rate Sp	7-10 knots plus.
Coastguard	Guernsey, tel. 01481 720672. Passage reports on Channel 20. Alderney Harbour Master Coastguard 01481 822620 VHF 16, 67, 74.

Introduction

Alderney is only occasionally visited by sea kayakers. The fast tide streams, eddies, overfalls, and an open crossing exposed to swells make this a paddle in a different league. This is a big offshore trip where 7 knot streams may be expected. The famous Race of Alderney is well known by sailors but it's The Swinge where the action really takes place. Here the water really does flow downhill! Think of Alderney as a rock in a river where the flow changes direction and everything starts to make more sense; the Alderney breakwater makes a great breakout!

Alderney is not a new kayaking destination. In 1830 the Jersey Loyalist newspaper wrote about a Mr Canham from London who had canoed from Cherbourg to Alderney and planned to continue his voyage to Jersey.

Description

A Guernsey departure gives more help from the tide and lets you leave a little earlier (perhaps -0240HW St Helier). At first you get pushed to the east, but you get a bit more time near The Swinge where ideally you want to arrive on the last of the north-east going stream (+0200HW St Helier).

Once clear of Guernsey things speed up. The first time I paddled to Alderney, Steve remarked (after 1.5 hours) that there was still time to turn back. Franco's comment, said with a huge grin, was to the point, *"No, we've passed the point of no return. We're going to Alderney whatever!"*

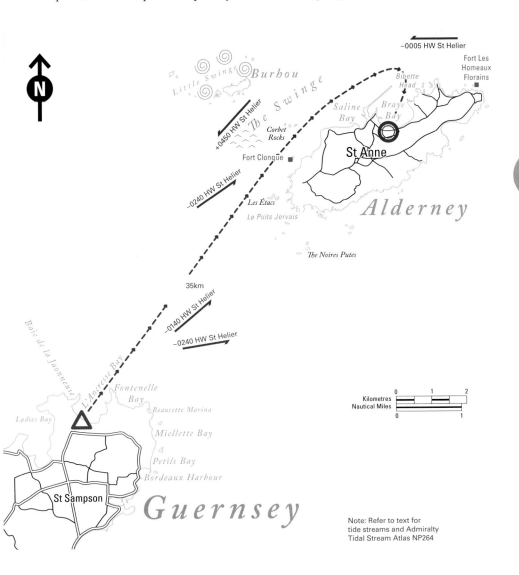

Note: Refer to text for tide streams and Admiralty Tidal Stream Atlas NP264

Nearing Alderney the Gannet Rocks at Les Étacs, and Ortac near Burhou, are easy to spot. If conditions are good, you should be able to move closer inshore to catch a few eddies and get the protection of the off-lying reefs.

Ahead is Fort Clonque, one of the many fortifications constructed by the British to defend the naval base from French attack. The causeway might be a potential landing spot. If the tide is low enough, the Corbet ledges are a strange place with channels filled with coarse sand into which you sink almost to your knees. At around half tide expect some fast-flowing streams between the rocks. The calmest area is said to be close to or even inside of Corbet Rock.

Saline Bay is a steep sloping beach. At the breakwater, look out for the date stones on the wall which mark the year of each section's construction, between 1847 and 1864 as a base for the British Navy. Roughly two thirds of the breakwater structure lies beneath the sea, and repairs are constantly being made. Even after the end of the breakwater was allowed to collapse, the breakwater remains the longest in the United Kingdom.

Braye Harbour has a shop, restaurants, hotel and an essential bar in which to celebrate. The campsite at Saye Bay is behind the dunes with a sandy beach to land on. Bibette Head and reefs can produce some fast water, so it may be best to head to the campsite first before heading off to celebrate.

Variations

Both Sark and Jersey are optional departure or return points. Sark is usually used by Jersey paddlers to break the journey and catch the next tide. Paddlers with high performance sea kayaks

might consider the St Catherine, Jersey to Alderney route via Les Écréhous. Streams are faster east of Les Écréhous and on the French side of the coast, but you only have about 5 hours of northerly stream to cover 61km (33NM).

There is a longer south-bound stream on the direct Alderney to Jersey return 57km (31NM) to La Grève de Lecq. I have paddled this route in around 6 hours using a Nordkapp on a neap tide.

20A ALDERNEY TO BAIE D'ÉCALGRAIN (NORMANDY)

French arrival/departure points of Baie d'Écalgrain and southwards to Diélette are options, but check the CKMer website (www.ckmer.org) for information about the current regulations for sea kayaking in France.

Tides and weather

Crossing to Alderney requires good conditions so be prepared for delays due to bad weather.

The Admiralty Channel Islands and adjacent coast of France tidal stream atlas and the Admiralty Channel Pilot are essential reading.

Large overfalls can develop in The Swinge if there is wind against tide. Slack water in Alderney is of very short duration, if at all.

If you decide conditions are not suitable for The Swinge, or you are running late, your options are limited. By +0430HW St Helier the south-west stream in The Swinge is well established, and from now on the stream will build up. With the tide still dropping it may be possible to handrail the coast south of Fort Clonque which has a causeway connecting to the shore, or even by coming in a little further south at the Les Étacs Gannet Rocks. On the south coast Telegraph Bay covers at half tide, and the path on the Bailiwick of Guernsey map is only usable with great care and a bit of rope to descend the last bit. An option is to head along the coast to Longis Bay but there are complex tide streams and eddies within 1NM of the coast. Once the south-west stream builds, your options are limited to sitting in an eddy behind a large rock until the tide turns, or heading back to Guernsey.

Additional information

If you get stuck on Alderney, Aurigny Airlines operate scheduled flights to Guernsey, Southampton and Jersey via Guernsey. A flight is a great experience, though it feels like sitting in a small car. You will be guaranteed a window seat and a great view. If you end up sitting next to the pilot, don't touch any buttons.

Twice weekly freight only services are operated by:

Alderney Shipping Company (www.alderneyshipping.com) tel. 01481 724810 from Alderney to Guernsey, Jersey and Poole.

Manche Iles Express operates a seasonal passenger only service from Alderney to Diélette in France. Kayaks are not accepted.

Bumble Bee (www.bumblebee.gg) and Lady Maris 2 (www.alderneygiftbox.com) operate scheduled and charter boat services to and from Alderney to Guernsey.

Gannets

If you are paddling more than 1NM offshore around the Channel Islands there is a good chance you will see gannets. Most are believed to be from Alderney where there is a breeding population of 7,500 pairs of northern gannets. Both the gannetries at Ortac and Les Étacs are easy to spot as they appear to be covered in 'white paint'. Gannets are not reported breeding in Alderney in the 19th century and numbers only increased significantly after the Second World War. Research using GPS tracking devices show Alderney gannets make longer trips in search of food than those breeding in UK colonies. One bird was recorded making a 340km round trip and others made two trips to the south coast of England within 72 hours. This data has led to speculation that some gannets seen around Jersey may even be flying 129km (70NM) from Les Sept-îles.

If you approach the Les Étacs to observe the gannets, allow at least 20 minutes or more, since the longer you remain still the more likely the gannets will approach.

Alderney

No. 21 | **Grade C** | **16km (8.5NM)** | **OS sheet G** | **2669, 60**

Tidal Port	St Helier
Start/Finish	△ ◯ Braye Harbour (625 750) (49° 43' 24N 02° 11' 58W)
HW/LW	HW St Helier is 4 hours 55 minutes before HW Dover. HW Alderney is 45 minutes after HW St Helier.
Tidal Times	(see also Route 19)

In the Swinge, off Sauquet Rock (NE Les Homeaux Florains) a W going stream begins at 5 minutes before HW St Helier and quickly extends along the breakwater at about 4 knots at springs. Further out an E going stream is running at about 4 knots.

Around 45 minutes after HW St Helier the E going stream ceases and a W going stream is established along the north coast from Sauquet Rock to about 1NM north of the breakwater and on down to Corbet Rock.

Around 3 hours after HW St Helier the remaining NE going stream in The Swinge slackens. The W going eddy extends across The Swinge. By 4 hours 30 minutes after HW St Helier the SW going stream is running. By 2 hours 15 minutes before HW St Helier the E going stream is flowing. (In the atlas this is listed as flowing at 2 hours 40 minutes before HW St Helier.)

In the Alderney Race the N going stream starts 1 hour 40 minutes before HW St Helier. Around 4 hours 50 minutes after HW a SW stream is established max 7 knots. This swings more S and then SE until 2 hours 40 minutes before HW St Helier.

On the south coast, in theory the E going stream runs for about 9 hours springs and 8 hour neaps. Off the Noires Putes this starts about 4 hours 30 minutes before HW St Helier an the W going stream starts 2 hours 55 minutes after HW St Helier. However, close inshor an E going eddy operates from about 4 hours 50 minutes after HW until 4 hours 40 minute before HW St Helier when the main E going stream is established.

Max Rate Sp   7 knots plus.

Coastguard   Guernsey, tel. 01481 720672. Passage reports on Channel 20. Alderney Harbour Master, Coastguard tel. 01481 822620 VHF 16, 74.

Introduction

Alderney has a population of 2,400 and a surprisingly wide range of cafés, restaurants and bars There is a vibrant and lively night life, especially in the summer. Look out for the 'bunker parties' informal dance music events in abandoned bunkers and more organised events during Alderney Week at the Corporation Quarry ('quarry parties').

Description

The route is described anticlockwise. The clockwise route is a little more awkward as you may hi the west running stream in The Swinge.

Leaving Braye Bay, the numerous gun batteries below Fort Albert demonstrate the level o defences constructed in Alderney. There is rarely a moment when you will not see British and

Nazi gun emplacements on this trip. The area from Saline Bay to Les Étacs rocks is a Ramsar wetlands reserve. At low tide on the shoreward side of Corbet Rocks what at first looks like sand is Maërl (a form of coralline red algae which is perhaps the nearest we get to coral structures) and is worth exploring. In some countries this non-renewable resource is gathered as a fertiliser, but is increasingly being listed as a protected species. Nearby is Fort Clonque, now a Landmark Trust holiday let.

The gannet nests at Les Étacs are easy to spot. Gannets first nested here in 1940 and the Ortac and Les Étacs colonies account for 2% of the world's nesting gannets.

At Les Puits Jervais the SS *Point Law* was wrecked in 1975; this is just one of about 180 shipwrecks around Alderney. Nearby is Telegraph Bay where landing is possible at half tide, but the footpath up is in poor condition. La Nache and Fourquie stacks are great to paddle between.

From Coque Lihou to L'Etac de la Quoire you may encounter strong eddies extending up to Queslingue Rocks. This eddy seems to vary depending on the incoming weather systems and tide heights. The disused Cachalière quarry and pier seem out of place and in poor light this section appears Tolkien-like with the L'Etac rocks looking like something out of a Norse saga.

Blue Stone Beach lives up to its name. There are caves and sea arches around La Tchue Bay.

Longis Bay is a sandy beach with easy access and shelter from westerlies.

Brinchetais Rocks are tricky, if there is a southerly stream but once around them you can tuck in close to the coast. The ruined Fort les Homeaux Florains reminds me of a Venetian fort. Corblets and Saye Bays are sandy beaches before you reach Bibette Head and Braye Bay.

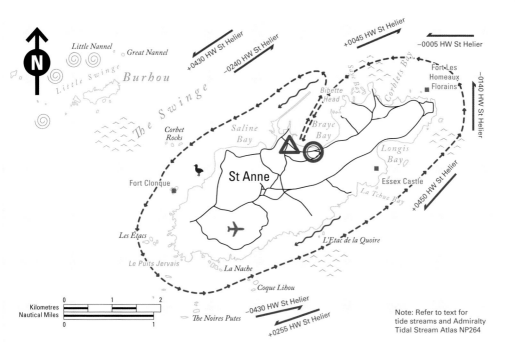

Variations

Burhou is a challenging option, even if the weather is very good and you are confident you have got the timings right. The island is a puffin breeding site and is closed during the breeding season. Alderney Wildlife Trust supply useful advice and have an excellent Puffincam (www. alderneywildlife.org).

The Casquets (49°43.'4"N 2°22.'7"W), 13km (7NM), is an elusive destination. The name is said to originate from the French 'cascade' and alludes to the huge tidal streams pouring around the rocks. The symbols for eddies on the tidal stream atlas are rather worrying; the streams barely pause for a minute before changing direction and it is rare for the water to be calm.

Tides and weather

The tidal difference of Alderney on St Helier is +0040HW. Personally, I still find Alderney tide streams confusing. The main streams are fairly constant but the eddies close in are very changeable.

You'd be forgiven for thinking the tide around Alderney wakes up each morning and decides which way to flow. A more probable explanation is to think of Alderney like a rock in a river. Watch the flow of water around a rock and the volume of water is constantly varying. The river flow is not constant but is influenced by the amount of water moving downstream. The same may be true around Alderney, except that it is approaching weather systems that influence the surges of water.

History

Anyone who is fascinated by military fortifications will be amazed at just how well defended the island has been throughout history. Alderney has been called the 'Key to the Channel'. Archaeological digs at The Nunnery in Longis Bay reveal evidence of a Roman fort, but the biggest impact on the island are the numerous British fortifications built during the 19th century. A consequence of this building frenzy is that the island has something of an English feel.

As the Nazis approached in 1940 the entire population (bar seven) were hastily evacuated to England. Domestic pets were shot and larger valuable items buried or hidden.

The Nazis set about making Alderney an impregnable fortress, riddled with bunkers and gun emplacements built by the Organisation Todt (German non-combatant civilian construction organisation) and forced labour. Four concentration camps were constructed where arbitrary beatings were a daily occurrence and rations were barely enough to support life. Though a war crimes case was prepared against the former commandant of the Norderney and Sylt concentration camps, he never stood trial.

The eddy on the south coast is puzzling. On two occasions I've paddled the same section of coast, at the same time on a spring tide, only to find the tide streams were running completely differently to the previous day. Approaching bad weather from the west may have been the cause of this effect.

There are excellent ferry glides over the ledge between L'Etac de la Quoire and the coast.

Brinchetais Ledges are a good place to practise advanced sea kayak 'river' techniques. From about low water St Helier the south-west stream flows downhill between the ledges. There is a big eddy pool from Raz Island to the ledges to pick up the pieces.

At low water St Helier in The Swinge near Corbet Rocks, the stream runs at its fastest. Look out for overfalls, eddies and boils as the stream thunders by.

Additional information

The Alderney tourist board is an excellent source of information and publishes the *Yachtsmen Guide to Alderney* booklet (www.visitalderney.com).

There are shower facilities for visiting yachtsmen at Braye Harbour and the Alderney Sailing Club usually has weather forecasts on display.

Camping is at Saye Bay – info@sayebeachcamping.co.uk – www.sayebeachcamping.co.uk – tel. 01481 822556.

A kayak trolley is useful in case you need to move to another spot around the coast or get your kayak shipped out as freight.

An impregnable fortress

During the Nazi occupation the Channel Islands were more heavily fortified than any other coastal region, and this far outweighs the strategic importance of the islands to the Nazis. Around 10% of the entire Atlantic wall defences were constructed in the Channel Islands. By 1944 an incredible 244,000 cubic metres had been excavated compared to 2,550,000 cubic metres for the entire Atlantic wall in Europe. The Führer greatly prized the islands, in part because he had captured the oldest possessions of the British Crown, and in occupying British territory German soldiers had begun the breakup of the British Empire. Hitler ordered that all plans for the islands must be sent to him personally for approval. Both Hitler and his officials paid more attention to their defence than was necessary. By 1943, 42,800 Germans were based in the Channel Islands – equivalent to two thirds of the civilian population.

Sea Kayaking in France

If you are completing a tour of the Channel Islands by crossing via the French coast, it is feasible to complete the circuit by heading along the Normandy coastline and back to your start point to pick up your car. A number of possible routes are outlined in this guide (see routes 3a, 3b, 3c, 8a, 9a, 20a).

The western coastline of Normandy consists of mostly low-lying land and lots of sand dunes. Many villages are set back inland with numerous holiday homes, so shopping for supplies may be limited. There are however plenty of restaurants (seasonal opening) and you should be able to dine well on local oysters!

Tidal streams are quite fast and flow north/south. Most beaches are flat and you may find you are faced with a long walk at low tide.

Near Cap de Flamanville is a nuclear power station. Security is tight and paddlers report being shadowed by French security boats when crossing in the vicinity.

French sea kayaking regulations

Unlike in the UK, French law controls the use of sea kayaks around the coast. Visiting kayakers should be aware of the regulations to avoid falling foul of the authorities, and also to respect the considerable amount of work undertaken by French sea kayak organisations who worked to get the law changed. Few sea kayakers paddling to France from Jersey have ever been stopped by the French authorities, and this may reflect the level of experience and safety kit carried by the paddlers involved.

Some may baulk at these rules. If this is the case, there is a simple solution – don't sea kayak into French waters.

First tour de Bretagne by sea kayak

Until 1980 sea kayaking was very strictly controlled, and a sea kayaker could not venture more than 300m from shore. In 1980 Loïck Bourdon obtained dispensation to complete the first officially recognised tour of Brittany with three other Breton paddlers and Jerseyman Franco Ferrero. As a result inroads were made to relax the regulations. Anyone old enough to remember the BCU Sea Proficiency award may notice that the equipment carried bears a resemblance to the requirements for this old award.

Since then the regulations have evolved thanks to the effort of French sea kayak organisations such as CKMer (www.ckmer.org) and Pagayeurs Marins (www.pagayeursmarins.org)

The following outline of the regulations is based on Colin Appleby's http://brittany-kayaking.com/paddling-in-french-waters/ explanation of the regulations.

Outline of French sea kayaking regulations

Regulations exist in France for all leisure craft navigating on the sea.

The first category covers just about everything that floats, and is defined as 'beach leisure craft'. Any home-built craft, i.e. skin on frame, is likely to come within this category (unless construction and floatability meets the required standard).

Any French craft that is not registered with the 'Affaires Maritime' will by default fall into the 'beach leisure craft' category. This limits you to staying within 300m of the shore. Follow the registration guidance below and you should be able to paddle further offshore and keep the officials happy!

There are three aspects of the regulations that affect sea kayakers:

1. Registration
2. Construction and fitness for purpose
3. Zones of navigation and required equipment

Registration of sea kayaks

To paddle further offshore French residents need to have their kayaks registered with the French authorities. Craft that are registered will have paperwork proving ownership, construction and floatability, and will be issued with a registration number and registration card.

There is no requirement to register a kayak under UK law. However, you may wish to voluntarily register your kayak on the MCA *Small Ships Register* (a fee is charged). This gives you an SSR number that must be displayed on the kayak, and a registration card from the MCA which proves the kayak is from the UK.

PROOF OF OWNERSHIP

If you decide not to register on the SSR, then a document to prove ownership should be carried. The original bill is fine, but if you have no original document, a formal 'self certificate' (Attestation sur l'honneur – Attestation de propriété) detailing your ownership will 'probably' be acceptable. A template can be found at http://brittany-kayaking.com/paddling-in-french-waters/

A Red Ensign should be displayed prominently on the kayak (if you are British).

Construction and fitness for purpose

This is established in the registration process usually with certificates issued by the manufacturer. There is a 'floatability' test which involves flooding the cockpit with a 50kg weight on the seat; the cockpit combing should remain 2cms above the water.

Commercially-built UK sea kayaks will conform with this requirement, but it may be handy to carry a 'self certificate' known as an 'Attestation sur l'honneur – Déclaration de conformité d'un navaire de plaisance non immatriculé en France' (Declaration of conformity of a non-registered pleasure vessel in France). A template can be found at http://brittany-kayaking.com/paddling-in-french-waters/

Zones of navigation

Once registered, or you complete the 'Attestation sur l'honneur' for registration and construction, and display a Red Ensign, two limits of navigation are imposed. This is based on the type of equipment carried.

TWO NAUTICAL MILES

The first limit is up to two nautical miles from *'a safe landing place' (an arbri in French)*

1) PFD minimum 50N

2) Torch

3) A means of getting back on board. Some French carry paddle floats, but full deck-lines satisfy this requirement

4) If the boat is not self emptying (i.e. a sit-on-top kayak), a pump must be carried; sit inside kayaks must have spraydeck

5) A tow rope, and a permanently fixed tow point (small stainless eyebolt or eyestrap) must be fitted on the kayak

6) Owner's name, address written on a fixed name plate on the kayak

7) Most French kayakers also name their kayak with this visible at the bow

8) A loud whistle (some French paddlers carry 'air horns')

TWO TO SIX NAUTICAL MILES FROM A SAFE LANDING

In addition to the above you must carry:

9) Three red hand flares

10) Signal mirror

11) Magnetic compass

12) Nautical chart for the area you are paddling in

13) A sticker showing IALA 'A' buoyage system and kayak safety signals

NOTE

Crossings such as Carteret – Les Écréhous, Granville – Chausey, Chausey – Les Minquiers, Coburg/Baie d' Écalgrain – Alderney just fall within the limits of the 6NM category.

Night paddling by kayak in French waters is prohibited.

Kayaks fitted with sails

These 'hybrids' are precisely defined under French law and if you use a sail, you can enjoy reading up on the definition of whether your kayak is a sail craft or kayak here: "kayaks équipés d'une voile" at www.pagayeursmarins.org. In simple terms it depends on how large the sail is, but I'll leave the reader to study the formula and calculations!

To summarise

Carry proof of ownership, have your contact details visible on the kayak, declare your kayak i seaworthy, and be in possession of the right kit for the zone you are in.

Wild camping in France

If you plan to camp on a beach, it is vital to consider both the environmental impact and adopt leave no trace principles. Fire pits take a very long time to disappear and human waste builds up quickly in popular places. Do not be surprised if you are bothered, or asked to move on, if you select a popular or easily accessible beach to camp on.

Carefully choose a suitable spot, preferably on the foreshore below the highest astronomical tide line.

Erecting your shelter can only happen between sunset and sunrise (between 2000 and at the latest 0900).

Shelters can only be erected for one night and must be dismantled each morning.

Shelters can be for a maximum of six people and can consist of a bivouac bag, canopy or small tent in which you cannot stand.

Refer to the CKMer (www.ckmer.org) website for detailed information on shoreline sea kayak camping rights in France, as this is subject to change with the increase in marine protected areas and nature reserves.

In practice, if you select a quiet and discreet spot, you are unlikely to be disturbed.

Index of Place Names

Index of Place Names

Index of Place Names